SCHOOL AND SOCIETY IN VICTORIAN BRITAIN

Joseph Payne and the New World of Education

Richard Aldrich

GARLAND PUBLISHING, Inc.
New York & London / 1995

Library of Congress Cataloging-in-Publication Data

Aldrich, Richard.
    School and society in Victorian Britain : Joseph
Payne and the new world of education / Richard
Aldrich.
        p.   cm. — (Garland reference library of social
science ; vol. 935. Studies in the history of education
vol. 1)
    Includes bibliographical references.
    ISBN 0–8153–1558–9
    1. Payne, Joseph, 1808–1876.   2. Educators—Great
Britain—Biography.   3. Education—Social aspects—
Great Britain—History—19th century.   4. Great Bri-
tain—History—Victoria, 1837–1901.   5. Education—
Great Britain—Philosophy.   I. Title.   II. Series:
Garland reference library of social science ; v. 935.
III. Series: Garland reference library of social science.
Studies in the history of education ; vol. 1.
LB675.P32A43   1995
370.19'0941'09034—dc20   94–17106
                                                    CIP

Printed on acid-free, 250-year-life paper
Manufactured in the United States of America

STUDIES IN THE HISTORY OF EDUCATION
VOL. 1

SCHOOL AND
SOCIETY IN
VICTORIAN BRITAIN

GARLAND REFERENCE LIBRARY
OF SOCIAL SCIENCE
VOL. 935

STUDIES IN THE HISTORY OF EDUCATION

EDWARD R. BEAUCHAMP
Series Editor

**SCHOOL AND SOCIETY
IN VICTORIAN BRITAIN**
*Joseph Payne and the New World
of Education*
by Richard Aldrich

Contents

Illustrations
(Following p. 283)

1. Joseph Payne: A carte-de-visite photograph, Richard Aldrich Collection.
2. Joseph Payne: A photograph in the family album of John Waite.
3. Joseph Payne: Professor of Education, aged 65. A portrait etched by W. Sherborn from a photograph by Messrs Sawyer and Bird. From the first volume of the collected works.
4. Eliza Payne: A photograph in the family album of John Waite.
5. Joseph Frank Payne: A portrait by John Singer Sargent in the Royal College of Physicians of London.
6. Denmark Hill Grammar School about 1870: A drawing in the Southwark Local Studies Library.
7. The Mansion Grammar School, Leatherhead: A photograph of the rear dated 1859, Richard Aldrich Collection.
8. The Mansion Grammar School, Leatherhead: An engraving of the rear upon writing paper in the possession of G. D. Powell.
9. Rodney House Academy today.
10. Grove Hill House today.

Acknowledgments

I am happy to express sincere appreciation to Garland Publishing for their belief in this book, and particularly to Edward Beauchamp, Marie Ellen Larcada, Jennifer Sorenson, and Chuck Bartelt. My gratitude is also due to all who have afforded me access to the special collections in their care: Tim Wheatley and the Council of the College of Preceptors who allowed me to rescue and retain manuscript and other materials; John Henderson of Christ Church, Leatherhead; Peter Waters of the Girls' Public Day School Trust; Joan Clanchy of the North London Collegiate School; Susan Mills of Regent's Park College; P.S. Morrish of the Leeds University Library; W.G. Simpson of the University of London Library; Doris Jones of the West London Institute of Higher Education; and all staff of archive centres, record offices, and libraries in which the research for this book has taken place. Particular mention must be made of William Reese of Indiana University for his assistance in locating American editions of Payne's works. Linda Heath and her colleagues of the Leatherhead and District Local History Society gave considerable support, and they and Tony Wilson of the Camberwell Society allowed me to include short articles on Payne in their respective journals for the purpose of soliciting local help.

With respect to the illustrations, John Waite most kindly brought to my attention the photographs of Joseph and Eliza Payne in his family album and allowed me to take copies. Sir Christopher Booth, Harveian Librarian of the Royal College of Physicians of London, graciously granted permission for the reproduction of the portrait of Joseph Frank Payne. G. D. Powell supplied me with copies of the Mansion Grammar School writing paper. Preparation of these and other illustrations owes much to the photographic skills of Robert Lawrence.

Others who have responded generously to my requests for assistance include James Albisetti, Eamon Blake, Bradley Borum, Gordon Brewer, Julian Browning, Margaret Bryant, J. Vincent Chapman, Gillian Collins, J.R. Clube, Geoffrey Davenport, Dennis Dean, Marc Depaepe, Charles Farrow, Peter Gordon, Roger Hayden, Mary Haynes, John Hobson, Michael Humby, Valerie Hunt, Eileen Lawrence, Doreen Lee, Sue Lickfold, Leo McCartie, Frank Mullan, Stephen Pickles, Anthony Quick, John Roach, Wendy Robinson, Bryan Seagrove, John and Margaret Shackell, Jana Sims, Richard Smart, Nicola Smith, Thomas Stanley, Chris Stray, Jack Stuttard, and Patricia Thomas. I thank them all.

My greatest debt, however, as always, is to Averil Aldrich, who has been fully involved throughout the writing of this book, from the earliest searches at Bury St. Edmunds to the completion of the final manuscript.

Series Preface

Garland's Studies in the History of Education series includes not only volumes on the history of American and Western education, but also on the history of the development of education in non-Western societies. A major goal of this series is to provide new interpretations of educational history that are based on the best recent scholarship; each volume will provide an original analysis and interpretation of the topic under consideration. A wide variety of methodological approaches from the traditional to the innovative are used. In addition, this series especially welcomes studies that focus not only on schools but also on education as defined by Harvard historian Bernard Bailyn: "the transmission of culture across generations."

The major criteria for inclusion are (a) a manuscript of the highest quality, and (b) a topic of importance to understanding the field. The editor is open to readers' suggestions and looks forward to a long-term dialogue with them on the future direction of the series.

Introduction

In 1988 Sheldon Rothblatt began a substantial and incisive essay review with a series of major criticisms of "much of the historiography of English (and European) education," which he characterized as:

> future-oriented, even whiggish, as historians flirt with policymaking. The historiography is pointed toward the development of centralized state systems of education, with governments as the principal suppliers of schools, colleges, and universities. It is often concerned with the builders of such systems, the proto-bureaucrats of the great period of change in the mid-nineteenth century; and it just as often assumes that state provision for mass education, with particular regard to the improvement of life chances for working-class groups, is far and away the most important of all themes in the history of education. Private or independent sectors of education are generally viewed with suspicion or dislike as obstacles to political democracy and wider social opportunity, and the historiography implicitly favors their removal or curtailment by a vigilant state bureaucracy empowered with the necessary parliamentary authority. . . .

> Historians must also take into direct consideration the play of market forces in the history of education, for it is precisely in the market that so much of real educational interest occurred. Experiment, innovation, and change took place in accord with new trends and ideas, including ideas that a number of historians would regard as "progressive."[1]

The main purpose of this book is to provide a series of insights into school and society in Victorian Britain through an examination of the life and work of Joseph Payne. This would be a worthwhile activity in its own right but, given Rothblatt's criticisms, it may also serve the larger purpose of helping to redress some of the perceived imbalances in the historiography of British education. Such redress may achieve not only some modification of current interpretations of school and society in Victorian Britain, but also (given that historical study can never be concerned solely with the past) of current and future educational policymaking. For no assumptions are made in the following pages as to the superiority, or otherwise, of centralized (or indeed localized) state educational systems. This study is concerned neither with systems nor with systems builders. It does not focus upon mass education for working-class groups. Its principal subject is a private schoolteacher who was struggling daily with market forces, supply and demand, and who was strongly committed to wider social opportunity and political democracy. After years of toil and hardship, however, he achieved some recognition both as a scholar and a gentleman. In educational terms he was always a "progressive."

This introduction is divided into two parts. The first provides a brief context: the nature of society in Victorian Britain; a survey of existing interpretations of the relationship between school and society. The second is concerned with the construction and shape of the book.

Context

Queen Victoria came to the throne in 1837. Her reign, the longest in British history, lasted until 1901. She ruled not only over a United Kingdom of Great Britain and Ireland, but also over the largest empire the world had ever seen. In 1876, the year of Payne's death, she assumed the further title of Empress of India. In 1851 British commercial and industrial supremacy was confirmed by the Great Exhibition held in the Crystal Palace in London's Hyde Park, but thereafter that supremacy was strongly challenged, principally by Germany and the United States of America. Commercial and industrial development was accompanied by population explosion. In 1841 the population of

Britain stood at some 18.5 million and that of Ireland at 8 million. By 1901, while the population of Britain had doubled to 37.5 million, Ireland's population had fallen to 4.5 million. Given the small size of Britain, such a population explosion led to increased urbanization. By 1851 one-half and by 1901 three-quarters of the population lived in towns.

A variety of factors, both internal (railways, cheap postal services and national newspapers) and external (imperialism and foreign wars) helped to forge modern British society and the British state, but substantial divisions and inequalities remained, and in some cases were increased. These were based not only on the separate "nationality" and culture of the Scots and Welsh (in spite of the Act of Union of 1800 the Irish were never absorbed into the "British" nation), but also upon differences of sex, class and religion. For example, although Britain was ruled by a queen, throughout the nineteenth century women were not allowed to vote or to stand as candidates in parliamentary elections. Girls were excluded from the most prestigious schools, and not until the 1870s did women begin to make modest inroads into the ancient universities of Oxford and Cambridge. Though the male franchise was gradually broadened, both Houses of Parliament, Lords and Commons, remained aristocratic in composition and in temper. There were no revolutions, as in other European countries, and members of Parliament received no salary, so that only a few working men could gain admittance. One indication of differences in wealth and the several gradations of social class were the hordes of servants. Service, indeed, constituted by far the largest single category of paid employment for female workers. Their numbers showed the continuing economic ability of the few to employ the many for personal, rather than productive, functions.

Religion was another distinctive and divisive feature of Victorian society. In 1851 a Religious Census conducted by Horace Mann in conjunction with the General Census of that year indicated that there were no fewer than 35 different religious sects in Britain. Although the Census figures must be treated with considerable caution, it would appear that on Census Sunday, 30 March 1851, the combined total of those who attended Protestant Dissenting or Roman Catholic places of worship was greater than the number who attended services of the established Anglican Church. Nevertheless, in spite of the fact that its adherents might be in a minority, both among those who attended places of religious worship and more significantly in respect of the population as a whole, the Anglican Church remained, indeed remains to this day, the state church. Queen Victoria was not only head of the state, but also head of the Anglican Church. Archbishops and bishops were nominated by the government, often on political grounds. These prelates sat in the House of Lords and changes in Church liturgy and law had to secure the approval of Parliament. Not until 1828 were Protestant Dissenters (for example Baptists, Congregationalists or Independents, Methodists and Presbyterians) and from 1829 Roman Catholics, allowed to enter Parliament and to hold other public offices. Numerous other grievances remained. For example in 1833 Protestant Dissenters were still required to register births in the parish church; to be married in the parish church, to be buried in the parish churchyard, and to contribute to the upkeep of the parish church. It was not until 1868 with the abolition of compulsory Church rates that the last of these grievances was removed.

In Victorian Britain education was seen first and foremost as being the responsibility of churches and of parents, rather than of the state. Anglican control of the country's principal educational institutions, which had been reestablished in the 1660s at the time of the restoration of the Stuart monarchy, remained strong. It was not until 1860 that endowed grammar schools were formally opened to the children of Dissenters and not until 1871 were posts at Oxford and Cambridge, except for the Regius professorships in divinity, opened to non-Anglicans. Even when government grants in aid of elementary schools were introduced in 1833, some 80 percent of the money was given to Anglican schools. Such predominance resulted partly from the fact that between 1843 and 1867 some Protestant Dissenters, mainly Congregationalists and Baptists who were known as Voluntaryists, refused government money for their schools for fear of state control.

Many of the facts of schooling in Victorian Britain, for example those connected with Acts of Parliament and Royal

Commissions, with numbers of schools and prescribed syllabuses, with the establishment in 1839 of a Committee of the Privy Council to oversee education, and the legislation of the 1870s to introduce local boards for elementary schools, which enabled such schooling to become both compulsory and free by the end of the century, are well known. There is no intention to repeat them here, although background information is supplied, as necessary, at appropriate points in the book. But if the facts of schooling and society of Britain in the nineteenth century have been broadly known and agreed upon, nevertheless, there have been many differing interpretations and emphases in respect of those facts, five of which are outlined here.

In a book first published in 1960, but subsequently retitled and reissued in 1974, Brian Simon employed a Marxist analysis of British schooling and society to question the general belief in progress in matters educational from the 1830s. The first volume in his history of education in Britain from 1780 to 1990, *The Two Nations and the Educational Structure, 1780–1870*, emphasized the extent to which nineteenth-century schooling was firmly organized along lines of social class. Simon argued that by the 1850s, the descendants of the educational reformers of the later eighteenth century, the Enlightenment figures of Birmingham and Manchester, of Edinburgh and Glasgow, had lost their humanism and breadth of interests and emerged

> as a class whose characteristics had changed, whose purposes were narrower, and who were engaged in a sharp struggle on two main fronts—against the landed aristocracy on the one hand, and against the emerging proletariat on the other.[2]

Simon concluded this volume with the judgement that

> in the period 1850–70 a conscious effort was made to establish a closed system of schools; so to divide and differentiate the education given to different social classes that privilege could for ever withstand the pressure of the working masses.[3]

Though Marxist interpretations have naturally focused upon changes in production—the advent of industrialization and urbanization and its economic and social consequences—in

Schools for the Shires: The Reform of Middle-Class Education in Mid-Victorian England, David Allsobrook argued that schools for the children of the middle classes, as reformed in the 1860s and 1870s, were not cast as might have been expected in an urban and industrial mould, but rather in that of traditional rural Classicism. He concluded that as a result, "a gentlemanly, liberal tradition in secondary schooling long eclipsed the claims of practical and useful forms of secondary education."[4] This interpretation was consistent with that of Martin Wiener, in his wide-ranging book, *English Culture and the Decline of the Industrial Spirit, 1850–1980.* Wiener began his study with the statement: "The leading problem of modern British history is the explanation of economic decline."[5] He rejected Marxist explanations based on the inherent weaknesses of capitalism, and the conclusions of those economic historians who argued that there was no real decline in the second half of the nineteenth century but simply a natural change in the balance of economic power with the emergence of larger and more powerful states in Germany and the United States. Instead, Wiener posited a cultural explanation. He attributed Britain's economic decline to the continued commitment of the ruling classes to the ideal of a "green and pleasant land," and to the concept of a Victorian gentleman. A gentleman was, by definition, one who did not have to work for a living. Were he to do so he would not sully his hands in the common business of manufactures. A gentleman's wealth might be based upon land or dealings in the financial world, even employment in public service or the professions, but not in industrial occupations. Wiener, in common with Allsobrook, argued that the reformed boys' public and grammar schools of the second half of the nineteenth century, together with the ancient universities of Oxford and Cambridge, were key elements in socializing the sons of the middle and upper classes into Classical, aristocratic and rural values, as opposed to a culture of modernity, democracy, urbanization and industrialization.

Neil Smelser, another transatlantic observer of the British educational scene, concentrated not upon the education of the élite but of the poor. His recent book, *Social Paralysis and Social Change: British Working-Class Education in the Nineteenth Century,* published in 1991, was distinguished by three particular features. The first was his analysis of the similarities and differences between educational provision in the separate parts of the United Kingdom of that time: England, Ireland, Scotland, and Wales. This was an important set of distinctions, and it must be acknowledged that, on occasion, the use of the terms "Britain" and "British" in the pages of this volume masks considerable variations in educational provision and practice. For example, at the beginning of the nineteenth century there were more universities in Scotland than in England, and none at all in Wales. The second feature was Smelser's identification of "certain starting and ending points in historical sequences (labelled *moments of change* to signify their transient character and *truce points* to underscore that they are usually established as the result of a political process)."[6] Such analysis led Smelser to identify five arenas of social change which shaped the evolution of working-class education in Britain in the nineteenth century. These were class hierarchy, consciousness and conflict; economic forces affecting parents and children; religious contests, particularly between the established Anglican Church and Protestant Dissenting; the political scene of governments, Parliament and administrators; and the internal politics of the educational system—including pupils, pupil teachers, teachers, inspectors, and managers.

Although Smelser's book incorporated both a modest comparative dimension (a brief consideration of education in New York) and a survey of theories of nineteenth-century schooling—for example as an accompaniment to an industrializing society and the production of a disciplined factory work force, or as an element in the building of a nation— the most substantial recent comparative treatment of these issues is contained in Andy Green's book, *Education and State Formation: The Rise of Education Systems in England, France and the USA*. In spite of the Scottish Enlightenment of the late eighteenth and early nineteenth centuries, Britain's success in the first industrial revolution seems to have taken place in a country many of whose formal educational institutions, for example its grammar schools and universities, were in a comparatively moribund state. It is possible that this situation, coupled with the exclusion of non-Anglicans from educational and civil rights, was instrumental in diverting many of the best brains and talents from scholarly and political into economic activity. Such success was widely attributed, both by contemporaries and some later observers, to natural ingenuity, a lack of government intervention, and to the doctrine of free trade.

Other commentators, for example such promoters of popular education as Matthew Arnold, Henry Brougham and James Kay Shuttleworth, warned, however, that in spite of Britain's successes, a state-directed system of national education was urgently required. Green supported this interpretation and showed that other countries, notably France and Prussia, created national educational systems in advance of Britain

> to provide the state with trained administrators, engineers and military personnel; to spread dominant cultures and inculcate popular ideologies of nationhood; and so to forge the political and cultural unity of burgeoning nation states and cement the ideological hegemony of their dominant classes.[7]

Such efficient national educational systems which might, as in the United States, actually be organized at the local level, were better fitted to cope with the demands of the second and subsequent industrial revolutions. Green accordingly welcomed recent measures introduced in Britain, principally under the aegis of the 1988 Education Reform Act, to establish some form of national curriculum and national testing, although he rejected the market element in these reforms. His conclusion was:

> If the past has any lessons at all it is that the mechanisms of the market and the ideology of *laissez-faire* serve education very ill indeed. It would be a sad irony if the country which was last to create a national education system, and which never quite completed the job, should be the first to dismantle it.[8]

The final interpretation to be noted here is that of E. G. West, an interpretation which in many senses has underpinned the educational philosophy of Conservative governments in Britain since 1979. West argued that the Elementary Education Act of 1870, which introduced the first local school boards into

England and Wales, should be seen as an extension of bureaucracy and producer control, rather than as a true extension of education. Its chief function was not, as was stated, to "fill up the gaps" in school provision, but rather to displace the private working-class school for which parents had readily paid school fees, and to bring schooling under unnecessary, and ultimately retrogressive, bureaucratic control.[9] Supporters of this interpretation, rather than deploring the market element in recent government reforms, argue for more consumer, and less central and local government control in educational matters, not least in the hotly debated area of the national curriculum.

Each of these five interpretations—Marxist, Classical-rural, truce points, state formation and free market—is of interest in its own right and contributes important insights into schooling and society in Victorian Britain and more widely. But, valuable though they are, none of these interpretations and none of these books, whether by Simon, Allsobrook, Wiener, Smelser, Green or West, provides any strong sense of education as such, whether with respect of individuals or of groups. Of course numerous references are made to individuals and to schools and other educational institutions, but the purpose of such references is invariably to substantiate the general patterns of such themes as educational policy and administration, social organization and culture. In sharp contrast this book provides an entry into the actual educational world of Victorian Britain, its teachers and pupils, through the experiences of a quite remarkable, but hitherto-unremarked learner and teacher.[10]

Construction

Some would argue that there is such a thing as history; others that there are only histories. I incline towards the former position, while acknowledging the force of the latter. Such acknowledgment requires some explanation of the construction of this particular piece of history. Historical writing involves at least three processes: the identification of a subject, collection of evidence, and the ordering, analysis and presentation of that evidence in written or other form. These processes require an interaction between the past and the present. At each stage the historian must make choices. The purpose of this section is to make explicit some of the choices involved in the construction of this book.

As yet, Joseph Payne is an unknown figure in respect of British histories of education. He has little or no place in general accounts of nineteenth-century education. Indeed, apart from references in Chapman's study of the College of Preceptors,[11] it would appear that the only substantial study of Payne was a lengthy article, written by Miriam Fitch and "Contributed by the College of Preceptors," which appeared over five issues, from February to June 1934, in the pages of the *Journal of Education*.[12] That article was prompted by the 1933 inauguration, 60 years after Payne began his duties as professor, of the Joseph Payne Memorial Lectures. The series was initiated by the College of Preceptors to mark the change in status of the London Day Training College into the Institute of Education of the University of London. The lectures were held in the Institute's building in Southampton Row, London, just a few yards from the College's own premises in Bloomsbury Square.

My choice of Joseph Payne was dictated by a number of factors, many of which were pure coincidences. Payne's first school post was in Southwark, in south London, the home of my parents and grandparents. Indeed, a block of flats named after my maternal grandfather, Albert Barnes, stands on the other side of the New Kent Road from the Rodney House Academy where Payne taught. For several years I lived in Leatherhead in the county of Surrey, and there regularly used the local library without realising that it was the very building, The Mansion, in which for some 19 years Payne had lived and carried on his final schooling. Like Payne I began working for the College of Preceptors in connection with examinations for teachers. Like Payne I became involved with the historical study of education and with the promotion of an enhanced professional status for teachers. A growing sense of identity with the subject, therefore, was the prime reason for my choosing to study Joseph Payne. Clearly such identification brings dangers: biography may all too easily slip into autobiography.

The survival of evidence in respect of Payne has also involved strong elements of chance and choice. Some has been destroyed on purpose. Some has been saved from destruction. Some has survived through foresight and the normal processes of conservation. Other material may yet come to light. The greatest tragedy was when Evelyn Murphy, in October 1964, upon depositing four diaries of John Dyers, Joseph Payne's father-in-law, in the Angus Library of Regent's Park College, Oxford, informed its principal, Ernest Payne,[13] that although she had kept these four as an example of Dyer's minuscule handwriting, other family papers in her possession, including other diaries, had been deliberately destroyed. Evelyn Murphy, then a 79-year-old widow living in Headington, Oxfordshire, was the granddaughter of Joseph and Eliza Payne, one of the four children of their second son, Joseph Frank. Although she had two daughters, her reason for the destruction was that there were no grandchildren to whom she could pass on these family archives. She acknowledged this action as "an unaccountable lapse of judgement."[14]

On the other hand, in the summer of 1991, much historical material relating to the College of Preceptors was rescued from the loft of its premises in Theydon Bois, where it had long been subject to the depredations of birds and assorted rodents.[15] In addition, in 1993 a collection of manuscript material which included three of Payne's journals, a commonplace book, and more than 50 letters, was offered for sale and purchased by the author. As a consequence, the first section of the book draws upon previously unknown manuscript sources, while the second is based upon a wide range of unused and underused materials, both manuscript and printed. As to the third section, which is concerned with Payne's educational ideas, evidence comes principally from his lectures and writings. The greater part of these were collected and edited by Joseph Frank Payne and published in two volumes after his father's death.[16]

In seeking to impose shape upon evidence, the historian must choose between the demands of chronology and themes. This book is organized into three thematic sections, of which the first two are broadly chronological in treatment. The first employs a brief survey of Joseph Payne's life in education as a means to explore some unfamiliar aspects of school and society in Victorian Britain. Attention is focused upon his role in the foundation of two private schools. References to other members of his family, particularly the relatively well-documented lives of his father-in-law and two eldest sons, provide glimpses of the varied worlds of Dissenting missions, literary life, and the professions of public school teaching and medicine. The second section is concerned with Payne's interaction with the educational establishment of his day. He was a fierce critic of educational inefficiency and privilege, whether in the ancient boys' public schools or in the new state-supported elementary school system. But he also proposed solutions, for example the extension of educational opportunities and rights to girls as well as to boys, and the establishment of a trained and certificated teaching profession. He was prominent in such groups as the Women's Education Union and the Social Science Association, but the main body through which Payne pursued his reform campaign was the College of Preceptors. He was present at its foundation in 1846; in 1873 he became its first professor of education, and the first such professor in British history. The third section examines Payne's educational ideas. He was a true pioneer in the science and art of education and provided his own analysis of fundamental educational issues. In so doing, he drew not only upon his long experience as a practising teacher, but also upon a deep understanding of the historical and comparative dimensions of education, with particular reference to continental Europe and to the United States of America. Payne's analysis of educational issues, many of which are as central today as they were a century and more ago, has a timeless quality. The final chapter draws together some conclusions and considers the enduring value of Payne's work for a new and better world of education. Thus the book presents three frames of reference in which the overall topic of school and society in Victorian Britain may be considered. The first is personal, the second institutional, and the third intellectual.

NOTES

1. Sheldon Rothblatt, "Supply and Demand: The 'Two Histories' of English Education," *History of Education Quarterly* 28, 4 (Winter 1988), pp. 627–8. For a collection of other comments on British history of education see Peter Gordon and Richard Szreter (eds.), *History of Education: The Making of a Discipline* (London, 1989).

2. Brian Simon, *The Two Nations and the Educational Structure, 1780–1870* (London, 1974), p. 70.

3. *Ibid.*, p. 366.

4. David Ian Allsobrook, *Schools for the Shires: The Reform of Middle-Class Education in Mid-Victorian England* (Manchester, 1986), p. 264.

5. Martin J. Wiener, *English Culture and the Decline of the Industrial Spirit, 1850–1980* (Cambridge, 1981), p. 3.

6. Neil J. Smelser, *Social Paralysis and Social Change: British Working-Class Education in the Nineteenth Century* (Berkeley, 1991), p. 347.

7. Andy Green, *Education and State Formation: The Rise of Education Systems in England, France and the USA* (London, 1990), p. 309. For an introduction to Marxist and feminist perspectives upon the role of the state see Pavla Miller, "Education and the State: The Uses of Marxist and Feminist Approaches in the Writing of Histories of Schooling," *Historical Studies in Education/Revue d'Histoire de l'Éducation* 1, 2 (Fall 1989).

8. Green, *Education and State Formation*, p. 316.

9. E. G. West, *Education and the Industrial Revolution* (London, 1975). For the private working-class school see Phil Gardner, *The Lost Elementary Schools of Victorian England: The People's Education* (London, 1984).

10. But see Leonore Davidoff and Catherine Hall, *Family Fortunes: Men and Women of the English Middle Class, 1780–1850* (London, 1987) for an excellent introduction to families in the contexts of religion, ideology, gender and economic opportunity; and, with specific reference to education, Barbara Finkelstein, "Redoing Urban Educational History," in *The City and Education in Four Nations*, eds. Ronald K. Goodenow and William E. Marsden (Cambridge and New York, 1992), pp. 172–92.

11. J. Vincent Chapman, *Professional Roots: The College of Preceptors in British Society* (Epping, 1985).

12. Miriam G. Fitch, "Joseph Payne, First Professor of Education in England," *Journal of Education* 66, 774–9 (January-June 1934). Fitch drew upon her University of London M.A. thesis of 1931, entitled "The History of the Training of Teachers for Secondary Schools in England."

13. For Ernest Alexander Payne, 1902–80, see W. M. S. West, *To Be a Pilgrim: A Memoir of Ernest A. Payne* (Guildford, 1983).

14. Evelyn Murphy to Ernest Payne, 2 October 1964. See also Murphy to Payne, 27 September 1964, and Payne to Murphy, 28 September 1964. Angus Library, Regent's Park College, Oxford.

15. I am most grateful to my coworkers in this enterprise—Averil Aldrich, Mary Haynes, and the indefatigable Sue Lickfold.

16. Joseph Frank Payne (ed.), *Lectures on the Science and Art of Education, with Other Lectures and Essays, by the late Joseph Payne* (London, 1880); Joseph Frank Payne (ed.), *Lectures on the History of Education, with A Visit to German Schools, by the late Joseph Payne* (London, 1892). Hereafter referred to as Payne, *Works*, I, and Payne, *Works*, II.

School and
Society in
Victorian Britain

From Bury St. Edmunds to Grove Hill House

Bury St. Edmunds

Joseph Payne was born on 2 March 1808 at Bury St. Edmunds in Suffolk. His beginnings were humble; his origins obscure. His entry in the *Dictionary of National Biography,* for which information was supplied by his second son, Joseph Frank Payne, simply stated that he was "born of poor parents." Diligent searches in the parish records of Bury St. Edmunds and those of the surrounding areas, and in the local newspaper (the *Bury and Norwich Post),* have failed to reveal any conclusive information either in respect of his baptism or of the marriage of his parents. All surviving records of the churches of other denominations in the neighbourhood have also been searched without success. Both of Payne's parents, however, appear to have been alive in the 1820s, when he recorded correspondence with them and visits to the family home. In 1837 on the occasion of his own marriage Payne gave his father's name as Joseph and his father's trade as that of "Builder." One piece of evidence may give some clue to the character of Joseph senior and serve as a reminder of some of the cruel elements of the society into which the young Joseph was born. At the rear of a commonplace book used by Joseph Payne there is an entry dated 28 November 1801 which refers to three reports of bull baiting, including one particularly horrific instance where the bull's hoofs were cut off and he had to fight the dogs perched on his mangled stumps. The signature below the account deploring this barbarous practice, is that of "Joseph Payne, Bromley, Middlesex."[1] The only other entry at the end of this book, and in a different hand, concerns the purification of casks, a procedure taken from the *Monthly Magazine* of 30 May 1803.

Similarly few details have been discovered of Joseph Payne's early education. In 1833, when Payne's name was placed on the books of St. John's College, Cambridge, he was described as having been "privately educated."[2] That might have meant that he was educated at home or self-educated, or at one or more elementary or private schools. In the first half of the nineteenth century there were many private schools both for the children of the working classes as well as for those of the wealthier portions of society. Unfortunately very few records of such schools have survived, in contrast to those of the public elementary, endowed grammar and public schools. Although the compiler of the *Biographical List of Boys educated at King Edward VI Free Grammar School, Bury St. Edmunds from 1550 to 1900* suggested that a "Payne" listed in the second form in 1822 as a "Royalist" (a boy living at home in Bury) might have been Joseph Payne, no other evidence has been found to support this hypothesis.[3]

The fullest information hitherto known about Payne's schooling was given in 1876 in Charles Mason's obituary of Payne, which stated:

> His early education, was very incomplete and it was not till he was about fourteen years old that, at a school kept by a Mr Freeman, he came under the instruction of a really competent teacher. This advantage, however, he did not enjoy very long. At a comparatively early age he was under the necessity of getting his own living, which he did partly by teaching, partly by writing for the press. His life at this stage was laborious and not altogether free from privations. He found time, however, for diligent study, and numerous extract and common-place books testify to the wide range of his reading in the ancient classics and in English literature.[4]

Though as yet it has not been possible to identify with certainty the "Mr. Freeman" referred to above, Payne's recently discovered journals provide other details of his youthful years. Thus a journal of 1824,[5] when Payne was a mere 16 years old, indicates that he was then furthering his own education, and possibly acting as an assistant, at a boys' school at Olney in Buckinghamshire. At that time Olney was particularly associated with the name of the eighteenth-century poet, William Cowper, who had lived there for much of his adult life. Payne took great delight in walking in the surrounding countryside and in visiting Cowper's own favourite haunts.

The major theme of this journal, however, was Payne's ferocious devotion to duty. He rose early, on one occasion at 4.30 in the morning to write a letter home, read on his own account a variety of authors in Greek and Latin, French and Hebrew, ploughed through works on English grammar and syntax, attended prayer meetings on weekday evenings and devoured three sermons each Sunday. Nevertheless there were some lighter moments. On 19 August he "read a book through called *Adelaide or the Intrepid Daughter*," and on 27 August he "took the boys for a short walk—In the afternoon all had a holiday and went to the National School in Olney where there was a sale of Fancy Articles for the benefit of Olney School and I bought a puzzle and Whitlock gave me an article which he bought with lavender in it." Not all was sweetness and light, however. The young Joseph suffered regularly from toothache and was also subject to boils, at one time having four on his face, "one of which was as big as an egg." There were also occasional differences with a member of staff, and it appears that Payne's parents took the decision that he should leave Olney at the end of 1824.

In the late eighteenth and early nineteenth centuries it was quite common for people as young as 16 to be engaged in teaching. For example, Joseph Lancaster, pioneer of the monitorial or "mutual" system of instruction, himself taught in schools from the age of 14 and, six years later in 1798, set up his own school in Southwark in Borough Road. When, in 1846, the government devised a system for assisting the provision of teachers in elementary schools, the foundations of that system (the "sinews" as Matthew Arnold called them) were the pupil teachers. Pupil teachers began their five-year apprenticeship at the tender age of 13. They taught in the school during the day and received instruction from the master or mistress after school hours.

The New Kent Road

By 1827 Payne was teaching in London. In that year he was employed as an assistant master at a boys' private school, Rodney House Academy, at 3, Rodney Buildings in the New Kent Road. Payne, no doubt, lodged in the school itself, although the family home was in the vicinity. On Sunday, 4 March, after morning attendance at church, he walked there in the afternoon, pondering as he went his debt to his parents:

> those dearly beloved friends—whose affection *ad mortem* is undoubted. . . . Time can never witness the dissolution of the ties which bind them to our hearts. . . . In the gay scenes of childhood and in the thoughtless levity which these scenes inspire we are not sufficiently grateful to the kind friends who watch over us with such unwearied attention. Selfishness prevails generally over every other passion and we receive all acts of kindness as if they were richly merited and as if it would be unjust to deprive us of them. . . . I found all at home tolerably well, at least not worse than usual, Amelia looked very languid and M appeared weak and infirm.[6]

The school at which Payne taught was run by John Gowring, who was also resident at 3, Rodney Buildings, a school which Payne later described as "A private school—a small boarding and large day school," attended principally by "the sons of the tradesmen of the neighbourhood."[7] The only question at issue is whether it was originally at 3, Dover Place and then moved to Rodney Buildings, was carried on simultaneously at both addresses, or whether some error or change in the designation of the buildings had occurred.[8]

Fortunately the house, in contrast to many others in the New Kent Road at that time, has survived. It is a substantial property on some four floors with a subbasement. A coping stone to a new brick pillar which stands at the entrance to the property still bears the legend "Rodney House Academy."

Though the house remains in private occupancy, as do many of the surviving properties of what was then Dover Place, others of Rodney Buildings have made way for commercial premises. For example, part of the original number one is still, as it was in Payne's day, the Crown and Anchor public house, but the rest of the ground floor has been transmuted into the Five Star Fish Bar!

Around 1830 Rodney Buildings and Dover Place constituted a continuous line of some 30 properties which occupied the south side of the New Kent Road, from Garmouth Row and Rodney Place in the west to Paragon Place in the east. Rodney Buildings was to the west of Dover Place. Both fell within the parish of St. Mary, Newington, but Paragon Place and the turnpike which stood at the east end of the New Kent Road, where it joined the Old Kent Road and Bermondsey New Road, were in the parish of St. George. At the back of the long gardens of the houses in Dover Place and the even larger plots of the more substantial houses in Rodney Buildings, was the rapidly disappearing open space of Lock's Fields. Just beyond the eastern edge of the Fields, between Townsend and Mason Streets and fronting on to the Old Kent Road, was the substantial building and extensive grounds of the Deaf and Dumb Asylum. Lancaster's Borough Road School, which by 1830 had become the training institution for the British and Foreign School Society, was a short walk away to the northwest.

The inhabitants of Rodney Buildings were engaged in a variety of callings. In addition to Gowring's academy, the Crown and Anchor public house stood at number one and, at the time of the 1841 Census, other occupants included a solicitor, a clerk, a merchant, a tobacco manufacturer, a tea dealer and a street merchant. Pigot's *Directory* for 1838 recorded that by then John Robinson was master of the day and boarding academy at 3, Rodney Buildings. The 1841 Census shows that in addition to the 45–year-old Robinson, his wife Augusta, who was born in Greenwich, and their four children, the establishment included two teachers—John Laxton, a Classics master, aged 35; and a young assistant, William Crook, aged 17—and two lodgers—George Boyce aged 20 and employed at the Ordnance Office; and an 18–year-old medical student Richard Warren. There were 20 resident pupils (all boys): four aged 14, one of 13, seven aged 12, one of 11, four aged 10, two of 9 and one aged 8, supplemented no doubt by day scholars.[9]

On 2 March 1827, his nineteenth birthday, Payne commenced a new journal with a reflection upon his former and current states.[10] In 1822, after "an almost uncultivated boyhood," he had known of the existence of the ancient and modern languages, but had never expected that he should ever learn them. At that time he been "accustomed to look on learned men with a kind of religious veneration as persons moving in a superior rank of life to all others and to receive their sayings as oracular decisions." Now, a mere five years later as a teacher at Gowring's school, he could take pride in the development of his "rational faculties" and "intellectual perceptions" and was also keenly aware of having "arrived at what has been called the ambiguous state of life, when the passions not being controlled by the dictates of prudence and of experience, exert a more powerful influence." At this stage in his life he was an avid reader of romantic poetry and prose and a great admirer of the "genius" of Lord Byron and the "beauties" and "power" of Sir Walter Scott. He was also clearly fond of Gowring's daughter, who died on 5 March 1827 after a brief illness. Payne's journal entry for that day recorded:

> I feel deeply this stroke. I sympathize with the father and I deplore the premature removal of one who was certainly the ornament of the family. I cannot forget that I have spent many pleasant hours in her society—that she has walked many times with me supported by my arm, that I have conversed with her on many subjects on which her opinions coincided with my own, that but a month back she was all life and gaiety and vivacity, that now she will never return.

Not surprisingly Payne was "too gloomy" in the following days to apply himself to study and, while sympathizing with Gowring's loss, recorded grudgingly in his journal, "Attended the Ladies' School for Mr G.—troublesome work."

Nevertheless, the main feature of the journal of 1827, as was that of 1824, was Payne's remarkable quest for learning. On 2 March, between breakfast and morning school, he read an account of the Greek Revolution of 1825, and at lunch time composed a poem in celebration of his birthday. In the evening when school had finished, he read the latest copy of the *Edinburgh Review*, and went to hear a lecture on combustion. He also wrote up the day's events in great detail, but concluded upon rereading the entries that "I find I must restrict myself to shorter notices and more original remarks in future."

Later that month after voracious reading of Scott's poetry and novels, he penned a paragraph of advice to himself under the heading "Seductive influence of works of imagination on the mind," and resolved to "break the spell in which I am bound and endeavour first to lay in a stock of solid information." Another awesome personal reading list, which in addition to periodical publications included works in English and French, Latin and Greek, was duly drawn up.

Did Payne begin his teaching career in the New Kent Road? Many years later in 1865, when he gave evidence to the Taunton Commission, Payne stated that he had taught "In the first instance as an assistant master; secondly, as joint-principal of a large school; and, thirdly, in a school of my own." In answer to Lord Taunton's question "In the first place, where were you assistant schoolmaster?" Payne replied, "At a school in the New Kent Road, London."[11] It is possible that Payne had some earlier experiences of teaching of a less formal kind to which he did not refer, for example at Olney, and it would appear that in the later 1820s he was producing short articles for publication. An alternative interpretation might be that Mason's statement that Payne supported himself "partly by teaching and partly by writing for the press," referred essentially to his teaching at Gowring's school and to the pamphlet which he wrote in 1830 about the work of Jacotot.

Jacotot

Payne might have pursued a lifelong career as a worthy but humble schoolmaster had he not, in 1830, at the tender age of 22, written a 56–page pamphlet entitled, *A compendious exposition of the principles and practice of Professor Jacotot's System of Education.* This pamphlet attracted immediate and widespread attention and was well reviewed in such journals as the *Athenaeum, British Magazine*, and *Teachers' Magazine*.

Jean Joseph Jacotot was born on 4 March 1770 in Dijon, the eldest of 11 children of a butcher. He died in Paris on 2 August 1840. As a boy Jacotot attended the college at Dijon where he gained the reputation of being somewhat objectionable, a reputation which stemmed from a lack of deference towards his teachers and of interest in their lessons. He preferred to study independently. Payne noted that "Even as a child nearly everything he knew he had taught himself."[12] Jacotot left school at 14 and was persuaded by his cousin, a professor of physics and chemistry, to add studies in the areas of mathematics and physical sciences to those in humanities and the law. He thus came to hold qualifications in letters, in science and the law.

As an instinctive rebel and questioner of authority Jacotot was a firm supporter of the French Revolution. In 1791 he became a soldier and soon attained the rank of captain of artillery. He saw foreign service in Belgium under Dumoriez, but in 1793 returned to Paris with responsibility for the supervision of the manufacture of gunpowder. In 1795, with the formation of the Écoles Centrales, he was appointed to a scientific chair in the École at Dijon. The breadth of Jacotot's learning, coupled with great energy and powers of organization, meant that he was much in demand when new chairs were founded, and he subsequently held posts both in Classics and in law. In 1815, on the return of Napoleon from Elba, he was unwillingly elected to the Chamber of Representatives and thus became involved in the brief and unsuccessful attempt to restore the Empire. Napoleon's defeat meant that Jacotot's life was in some danger (he had already been taken as a hostage by the Austrians in 1814) and accordingly he fled from France and eked out a precarious living in Brussels by giving private tuition. Even there he might, perhaps, have still felt it advisable to glance frequently over his shoulder, for in 1816 he suffered from torticollis or wry neck. This gave his head a permanent twist which necessitated the use of a heavy bandage to keep it straight. In 1818 Jacotot was appointed Professor of the French Language at the University of Louvain. There he developed and expounded his system of "universal instruction." Twelve years later the 1830 Revolution and the accession of Louis-Philippe made it possible for him to return to France where he continued his work of teaching, both in Paris and Valenciennes. He died in Paris in 1840.

At Jacotot's funeral some 500 mourners followed the cortège through the streets of Paris to the cemetery of Père la Chaise. His disciples erected a monument to his memory, on the four sides of which were inscribed the following principles:

> I believe that God has created the human mind capable of instructing itself alone, and without a master to explain.
>
> An enlightened father may teach his son all that he is ignorant of.
>
> We must learn some one thing and refer everything else to it; according to this principle, all men are equal in understanding.
>
> He who does not believe himself capable of teaching that of which he is ignorant, does not yet understand me.[13]

It is not clear how Payne first came to know of Jacotot and of his educational theories. He himself simply said that while he was teaching at Gowring's school he "became acquainted accidentally with Jacotot's system of teaching."[14] On another occasion he implied that he was introduced to it by a friend who "spoke of the remarkable results of the system, both in regard to the economy of time and actual attainments—results which had been verified on the spot by enquirers every way competent and impartial."[15] Certainly in the 1820s there was widespread interest in Jacotot's methods, both in his adopted country and in his homeland. Deputations from the governments of France and the Netherlands visited Louvain, as did a variety of educationists and eminent personages. These included the Marquis de Lafayette, soldier and hero fêted on both sides of the Atlantic, and the French statesman, Casimir Périer. Schools modelled on the Jacotot system, which was proclaimed as being equally applicable to the children of the poor as to those of the rich, and to students of all ages, spread rapidly in France and the Netherlands.

In February 1830 the *Foreign Quarterly Review* published an article on Jacotot's system which, while acknowledging this continental interest, claimed to be "the first, or all but the first periodical that has broached the subject on the neighbouring shores of Great Britain."[16] At the head of the article were 11 titles in French, with the eighth edition of Jacotot's own *Enseignement Universel*, published in Louvain in 1827, first in this list. Of the other ten all but one dated from 1829. Six had been published in Paris and three in Louvain. There is no doubt that Payne read this account avidly and was moved to further action himself,[17] although if Payne's interest in Jacotot was prompted or heightened by this article then he must have worked quickly in order to have his own pamphlet published in 1830.[18] Another possibility is that Payne actually saw Jacotot's system in operation. In its review of his pamphlet in 1831 the *Quarterly Journal of Education* stated that it would "Give some account of the method, as it is explained by an Englishman, (who, it is believed, went to Louvain and saw it in operation)."[19] There is no other evidence to support this belief.

Payne put one of Jacotot's maxims—"learn something thoroughly, and refer everything else to it"—into practice with one of his own pupils. A boy of 11 had been learning the Greek grammar and was about to start upon simple translations. Payne, who had just become acquainted with Jacotot's methods, took away the grammar book and gave him instead a copy of Homer's *Iliad* with an interlinear translation into English. The boy was set to learn six lines a day, until a total of one hundred lines were impressed upon his memory, both in Greek and in the English translation. Payne's pamphlet concluded with a near-verbatim account of his questioning of the boy and of his answers. From this experiment Payne concluded that after little more than 12 hours of lessons, the boy had the ability to cope with the rest of the *Iliad* on his own.

Payne's pamphlet was widely and substantially reviewed. For example the organ of the Society for the Diffusion of Useful Knowledge, the *Quarterly Journal of Education*, devoted no less than 13 pages to a favourable review headed by Payne's pamphlet alone.[20] Such reviews gave Payne a reputation which it would have been difficult to acquire by any other means and brought him into contact with some of the leading educational reformers of the day. For his part, although he soon became critical of some of Jacotot's educational theory and practice (there was a basic inconsistency between pupils learning large amounts of text by heart in order to promote the basic aim of learning with interest), Payne always referred to Jacotot as his master. No doubt he felt some identification with Jacotot. Both were boys from relatively humble circumstances, both were of an inquiring turn of mind, and both were largely self-educated, destined to make their ways in the world as theorists and practitioners of education: the similarities were clear.

The Jacotot pamphlet was the means by which Payne made an almost instant transition from humble assistant in an unfashionable private school to an instant youthful celebrity, though his subsequent account of this process probably lost little in the telling.

> I became deeply interested in the method, made experiments with it; studied Jacotot's works; rushed into print myself; sent my pamphlet to all the leading men of the day interested in education; gave courses of lectures upon the system to crowded audiences; corresponded with Jacotot; and became generally recognised as an authority on the pretensions of "Universal Instruction. . . . " I received and answered hundreds of letters on the subjects, and furnished explanations, directions, arguments, illustrations, by the thousand, to all sorts of enquirers, doubters, sneerers, and enthusiasts—to those resolved to be, and to those resolved not to be, convinced.[21]

A copy of a letter from Jacotot in Paris, dated 15 March 1831, and addressed "*Au Disciple* Joseph Payne," which urged him to continue his efforts in the cause and asked for news of the results of his teaching, was included in the two-volume edition of Payne's works published by his son.[22]

In spite of his newly found fame Joseph Payne was never one to rest upon his laurels. The next logical step was to write books of his own that would enable English-speaking pupils to learn speedily both the Classical and modern languages according to the Jacotot method. Latin, the principal language of boys' grammar and private schools alike, was his first target, and in 1831 he produced *Epitome Historiae Sacrae*, which gave a shortened version of the sacred history in verse, from the

Creation to the time of Herod, originally compiled by Professor L'Homond of the University of Paris. The book was 128 pages long, with the Latin text printed on the left hand pages and the English translation on the right. There is no indication that the book was a great success and no more were produced in the projected series, though in 1831 the *Monthly Repository* published an article on Jacotot which referred both to Payne's original pamphlet and to the *Epitome* in very flattering terms.[23] It warned, however, against learning languages at too high a cost, and in 1865, when giving evidence to the Taunton Commission, Payne reported that the excessive memorization and repetition, which strict adherence to Jacotot's system required, was counter productive. Nevertheless, the key principle for which Payne became well known—that classrooms should be places of "learning not lecturing"—he attributed in part to his early contact with Jacotot's writings. In a more specific sense many nineteenth- and twentieth-century pupils studied Latin and Greek authors with the aid of English translations.

The best-known element in the Jacotot story was that as Professor of French Language and Literature at Louvain, he was faced with classes of students the majority of whom spoke Flemish (a language he did not know himself) and not French. To some extent, therefore, his maxims about the ability to teach what one does not know and the insistence on repetition and self-instruction were born out of necessity. It is interesting that one of Payne's most positive statements about Jacotot as a teacher did not quote the Louvain experience but referred back to his earlier period as Professor of the Method of Sciences at Dijon during the revolutionary and Napoleonic era.

> His method of teaching was looked upon as very original. Instead of pouring forth a flood of information on the subject under attention from his own ample stores— explaining everything, and thus too frequently superseding in a great degree, the pupil's own investigation of it—Jacotot, after a simple statement of the subject, with its leading divisions, boldly started it as a quarry for the class to hunt down, and invited every member to take part in the chase. All were free—as free as he was himself—to worry and bait the question . . . the teacher confined himself to asking questions, to suggesting

a fresh scent now and then . . . but of teaching in the old and favourite sense of the term—i.e., of communicating out of the fullness of the teacher in condescension to the intellectual feebleness and ignorance of the pupil—there was none. The Professor used to close the debate by a careful *resumé* of the arguments that had been adduced and the facts arrived at.[24]

Payne did not believe that all pupils were equally intelligent, nor did he think that ignorance of a subject was a necessary qualification for teaching it, and that the teacher's role was merely that of knowing a method and supplying a superior will. But he did believe that children had a much greater capacity for learning than was commonly supposed, and that one of the main reasons for the failure to achieve such learning was that educational institutions were too concerned with teaching and not enough with learning. In seeking out the essence of Jacotot's method, as he interpreted it, Payne was not averse to putting words into Jacotot's mouth. "'I am,' he would have said, 'to be the guide and friend, not the *bearer*, of my pupil. The journey we are to make together he must make on his own legs, not mine.'"[25]

In the conclusion to his 1830 pamphlet, the 22–year-old Payne stated that the main advantage of Jacotot's system was that "It calls into action the mental faculties of the pupil himself."[26] Upon that principle he determined to base his subsequent career as a teacher.

David and Elizabeth Fletcher

It is not clear exactly how far and how quickly Payne's reputation was spreading in the early 1830s, but it certainly reached the neighbouring area of Camberwell which at that time was a fashionable residential location. David and Elizabeth Fletcher, then resident in Vicarage Place, Camberwell, were among many who were impressed by the enterprising and determined young scholar and teacher. David Fletcher, who was 40 in 1831, had been born at Henley-on-Thames in Oxfordshire; his wife Elizabeth, came from Ottery St. Mary in Devon. It appears that it was she, rather than her husband, who approached Payne to become tutor to their own three young children and to two others from a neighbouring family. The *Dictionary of National Biography* stated, "Impressed by his account of Jacotot's system, Mrs David Fletcher, a Camberwell lady, invited him to teach a small class consisting of three children of her family and two others." Payne's own account, given some 30 years after the event, was as follows:

> The consequence was that I was applied to by a lady at Camberwell, having no school at that time, but educating her own family, consisting of three members, together with, I think, two children of a friend of hers. She was interested in what I had written upon the subject, and asked me to superintend this little family class. I was induced, therefore, ultimately to leave the engagement I had, and to take the entire charge of it.[27]

Exactly which of the Fletcher children were in Payne's charge is not entirely clear. Discrepancies between the 1841 and 1851 Census Enumerators' Returns were frequent, not the least in respect of ages. Thus while the Census of 1841 showed David Fletcher as 50 and his wife as 40, by 1851 Fletcher was recorded as 60 but Elizabeth as 53.

As to the Fletcher children, the Census of 1841 indicated that there were four: William aged 20, Sarah 15, Alfred 14 and Emily 12. The more explicit Census of 1851 recorded two daughters and two sons: Sarah (now listed as 30) and Emily aged 22, Loughton aged 28 and Alfred aged 24.[28] Sarah and Loughton were entered as having been born in Henley, Alfred in Middlesex and Emily in Camberwell. In 1851 both girls were teaching in the junior school attached to Denmark Hill Grammar School. Loughton was an engineer, Alfred a student at University College, London. It is not clear whether one or even two of the Fletcher children placed in Payne's charge was a girl, nor, if that were so, is it certain that this was his first major experience of teaching girls. The invitation, however, was to lead indirectly to the establishment of two substantial private schools: the Denmark Hill Grammar School for boys, and the Grove Hill House School for girls.

Though the invitation to Camberwell was obviously welcomed by Payne, at this time he appears also to have been considering an alternative career as a writer and lecturer. This perhaps explains his move from Beaumont House in Camberwell, where he was living in 1831, to an address in central London at 61, Pall Mall. One correspondent who wrote to him there, on 26 January 1832, was the Socialist and educational reformer, Robert Owen.[29] Another possibility was to return to East Anglia and study there, perhaps even take a degree at the University of Cambridge. There is clear evidence of this intention for on 5 July 1833 Payne's name was placed upon the books of St. John's College, Cambridge, as a sizar. Sizars were poor students who paid lower fees and worked their way through college by acting as servants and performing menial tasks. His certificate of suitability (which has not survived) was signed, according to the College Admission Book, by L. Stephenson MA of St. John's. This no doubt was Lawrence Stephenson, a native of Beverley in Yorkshire, who spent most of his long life as rector of Souldern in Oxfordshire (he died in 1889 aged 87) but who was a Fellow of St. John's and Sadlerian Lecturer between 1826 and 1835.[30] In 1833 Payne's address in the register of John Hymers, the College tutor, was once again given as Beaumont House. Nothing came of the Cambridge venture. Payne did not take up residence and on 28 October 1833 his name was removed from the College books.[31] The young Joseph, still only 25, thus turned his back on furthering his scholastic career by study in a traditional and public academic environment and continued instead in the private world. Payne's tutorial class grew in size as other parents (to quote Payne himself) "wished to avail themselves of the same opportunity."[32]

Poor rate books of the early 1830s confirm that the Fletchers were still living in Vicarage Place, Camberwell; indeed a commercial directory of 1834 listed David Fletcher, Vicarage Row, Camberwell under "Academies."[33] The Camberwell poor rate book for 1834, however, indicated a decision to move to larger premises, for although David Fletcher still occupied his house in Vicarage Place, his name also stood against a house and land on Grove Hill. The rate book of 1835 shows that by that date he had moved his family, and the school, to Grove Hill.[34]

At the end of 1837 two events occurred which were to shape the rest of Payne's life. The first was professional. On Christmas Day 1837 David Fletcher entered into an agreement with Henry and Frederick Perkins to rent for 21 years for the sum of £210 per annum, a substantial house and six acres at the foot of Denmark Hill.[35] The new school was listed in Pigot's *Directory* for 1838, "Fletcher and Payne (grammar) Denmark hill."[36] No longer was Joseph Payne a mere assistant or tutor; he was now a partner and headmaster in what was to become one of the most famous and successful of nineteenth-century private schools. The second event, which also involved a new partnership, was of a more personal nature. On 28 December, at the parish church of St. Giles, Camberwell, the 29–year-old Joseph was married to Eliza Dyer, daughter of the well-known Baptist minister, John Dyer. The marriage was witnessed by John Dyer and David Fletcher. With the Fletchers now established at Denmark Hill, the Paynes took up residence at Grove Hill House where Eliza, herself an accomplished schoolmistress, continued to keep a school for girls.

John Dyer

No direct evidence has yet been found about the relationship between Joseph Payne and his father-in-law but there is a substantial amount of material about the life (and death) of John Dyer, and a smaller amount about his relationship with his daughter. Such evidence is interesting in its own right, but is also important in providing insights into the intellectual, educational and religious worlds with which Payne came into contact as a result of his marriage into a prominent Baptist family, which was subsequently to influence his attitudes towards education. There are two major sets of sources for John Dyer. The first are those public documents and writings connected with a man who was the first full-time secretary of the Baptist Missionary Society, a post he held for some 24 years. The second are the four Dyer diaries for the years 1823, 1827, 1836 and 1837.[37]

John Dyer was born in Devizes in Wiltshire on 3 January 1784, the son of James Dyer who, after working as an excise man, became a Baptist minister, first at Whitchurch in Hampshire and then at Devizes. John received his early education at the hands of the Presbyterian minister of Devizes and subsequently from the Rev. Henry Gauntlett, an Anglican clergyman, both of whom were impressed by his scholarly aptitude. He thus acquired a knowledge of the Classical languages and some acquaintance with Hebrew. But James Dyer died when his son was only 13, and John moved to live with an aunt at Broughton where he came under the influence of a young pastor, William Steadman, who subsequently moved to a new ministry in Plymouth. Steadman took John Dyer with him, helped him to secure employment, baptized him and, on 21 March 1803, performed the ceremony when John Dyer married his partner's daughter, Agnes Burnell, born on 14 July 1783. In 1810 John Dyer himself became a Baptist minister, first at the chapel in Howe's Lane, Plymouth, and then at Hosier's Lane, Reading. In 1817 he gave up this charge when he was asked to become full-time secretary of the Baptist Missionary Society, a post he occupied until his tragic death in 1841.[38]

The Particular Baptist Missionary Society for Propagating the Gospel among the Heathen had been founded in 1792, and its first secretary was Andrew Fuller, who combined this post with a ministry at Kettering.[39] Steadman, who was a personal friend of Fuller and other leading lights in the Society, seems to have encouraged Dyer's interest in missionary activity and Dyer, while still at Plymouth, joined the committee of the Society at a meeting held in Kettering on 29 September 1812.[40] Another who joined on that day was Mark Wilks of Norwich. From Fuller's death in 1815 the secretaryship was held jointly by John Ryland, president of the Baptist College in Bristol and minister of Broadmead; and James Hinton, minister at New Road, Oxford, who also kept a school. When Hinton resigned in 1817 the Society determined to appoint Dyer as full-time secretary and to move its centre of operations to London, although Ryland, then 64, continued his part-time role until 1825. One of John Dyer's major tasks was to effect the move to London. The first headquarters were in Wood Street, the second in Wardrobe

Place, Doctor's Commons. Finally, the Society became tenants of the Particular Baptist Fund at 6, Fen Court, Fenchurch Street, a "gloomy abode,"[41] and not very convenient for Dyer who was living to the south side of the Thames.

Dyer's role as secretary involved him in much correspondence, in many meetings, and (before the days of railways) in frequent and strenuous journeys to make known the work of the Society and to raise funds. For example, in 1823 he made a tour of Devon and Cornwall which lasted 37 days and covered some 700 miles.[42] In 1818 the Society's committee even resolved to send him to India, but the decision, made in June of that year, was rescinded in August. Nevertheless he had many personal connections with those who worked overseas; for example, in 1814 his wife's sister, Eliza, married Thomas Trowt and accompanied him on his mission to Java in the East Indies.

Although during Dyer's secretaryship the Baptist Missionary Society increased its area of operations—there were new missions in West Africa and Jamaica—India, however, remained at the centre of interest and provided the great controversy of Dyer's period of office. This controversy sprang from the work of three Baptist missionaries, William Carey, Joshua Marshman and William Ward, who founded and developed the Serampore Mission. The three, who received no regular salary from the Society, had made the most of their talents. Carey became Professor of Indian Languages at the East India Company College in Calcutta; Marshman and his wife Hannah established a boarding school for European children; and Ward made a profitable venture of the Mission Press. The men and their families lived frugally and devoted the resources which flowed from their various labours to the work of the Mission. Their success was plain for all to see. Stations were established in many parts of India and beyond, including that at Java.

Carey, Marshman and Ward had been accustomed to acting independently. Indeed, while Fuller was secretary, they had been encouraged to do so. The arrival of Dyer coincided with the committee's attempt to exercise a greater control over their activities and, in particular, to receive accounts of the Mission's finances. Carey found it difficult to communicate with

Dyer and he turned instead to Ryland. "I cannot write to Mr. Dyer: all his communications are like those of a Secretary of State, and not, as was formerly the case with dear brother Fuller, those of a Christian friend."[43] Both Marshman and Ward returned to Britain to justify their actions, but in vain. On 23 March 1827, a formal deed of separation between the Society and the Mission was signed at Fen Court, by John Dyer and Joshua Marshman. Unfortunately the matter did not rest there. The Society and the Mission found themselves in direct competition for supporters and funds. A Society in Aid of the Serampore Mission was created, with its own treasurer and secretary. A bitter pamphlet war ensued as each side tried to justify its actions and to secure missionary funds. For some ten years the Particular Baptists were divided. In 1830 John Clark Marshman, son of Joshua, wrote a lengthy pamphlet which provided detailed criticisms of Dyer and of his role in the controversy.[44] Not until 1837, by which time both Carey and Ward were in their graves, was the controversy laid to rest.

By that date other issues had come to the fore, principally that of the abolition of slavery, in which William Knibb, a Kettering man who at the age of 21 had gone to Jamaica in the service of the Society, was to play a leading role. It was Knibb who, back in Britain in 1832, in a series of fiery speeches which dismayed the cautious Dyer convinced the Baptists that slavery must be ended forthwith, because Baptist converts were being flogged by their owners whenever they were caught praying. In 1833 the British Parliament agreed to abolish slavery within its dominions; midnight of 31 July 1838 saw the final liberation of the slaves.

There can be little doubt that Dyer found the Serampore controversy to be a great strain, particularly since in 1826 he was devastated by the death of his wife, upon whom he relied greatly for the management of his household, family and finances. Some indication of Agnes Dyer's workload comes from a letter written by her husband on 13 May 1819 from Reading to his old friend, Reverend John Saffery of Salisbury. John Dyer stated that his wife, who had just delivered her tenth child:

> was favoured with a very merciful degree of strength, so
> that at the end of 9 days she was able to resume attention

to her classes in the School as usual. . . . Indeed I have
much reason to be thankful for a partner so able to relieve
me from the care of superintendence of my family.
Otherwise it would not be duty to be so constantly leaving
home.[45]

Eventually, and not surprisingly, she succumbed to the strain.
Agnes and John Dyer had no fewer than 14 children, of whom
ten were alive in 1826 when their mother died on 31 January in
giving birth to a stillborn boy. The previous casualties were
James, the first-born on 19 February 1804, who died at birth;
Mary, the sixth, born on 10 August 1811, who died on 19
February 1812; and Sarah, the eighth child who, born on 15
January 1816, died on 28 January 1826, a mere three days before
the death of her mother.[46] The remaining ten (with their dates of
birth) were:

James	3 October 1805
Eliza	17 December 1806
William	30 May 1808
John	15 November 1809
Mary	21 March 1813
Samuel	13 July 1817
Joseph	10 April 1819
George	16 November 1820
Henry	16 August 1822
Agnes	26 August 1824

John Dyer now not only had to provide for his children, but to
take care for them as well. Though his mother was still alive, she
was of advanced years and died in 1833 at the age of 87.[47] No
doubt considerable responsibility fell upon Eliza, the eldest
daughter, who was 19 at the time of her mother's death. John
Dyer's annual salary from the Baptist Missionary Society was a
not inconsiderable £300, but his outgoings, with ten children to
house, feed and clothe, dictated a continuous struggle to make
ends meet.

Eliza

It would appear that from an early age Eliza was destined to receive the type of education that would enable her to assist her mother in running the school. Evidence on this point, and on the nature of the Dyer school, comes in a long letter of January 1822 from Agnes to Mrs Saffery, who had inquired about sending Mary, one of her daughters, to Mrs Dyer's school.[48] Clearly the Safferys, who were frequently in dire financial straits themselves, and who in 1821 were also running a school, a school which John Dyer had urged them to give up and to move to a smaller house,[49] were hoping that their daughter might both be employed as a teacher and receive further education in the Dyer household. In response to the Safferys, Agnes stated that "the variety of objects pursued and the constant routine of duties to be performed in such an establishment as mine precludes the possibility of carrying on intellectual education with advantage." She continued that arrangements were such that Miss Saffery could only be employed in "superintending the practice of Music and teaching a junior class in French." As for Eliza, Agnes stated that:

> if my circumstances would bear such expense, I should place her in a select school in this country under the personal superintendence of an intellectual, accomplished and vigilant woman, but I feel it a duty to qualify her as speedily as possible to occupy a useful station in my own school, and this it appears will be best accomplished by sending her to France.[50]

So it was that Eliza was sent to France where she lodged for some time in Paris, in the house of Mark Wilks, and returned to England with a considerable knowledge of both French language and literature.

John Dyer's diary references to his eldest daughter were invariably fond: "my dear Eliza." Unfortunately, the cryptic nature of the entries—there was only one page per month with about a quarter of an inch for each day—provide few extended comments. In 1823 the Dyers were living at Devonshire House in Battersea, and John Dyer had to travel to Fen Court by public coach, or by pony chaise. Sometimes, when there was no cheap transport available, he had to walk home, a journey which was made more difficult by his frequent colds and attacks of gout. Agnes was not always on hand to greet him and on 6 August, when John Dyer returned home after his long tour in the southwest, he recorded that he was "received by my dear eldest daughter."

It would appear that in 1827 the Dyer children were dispersed and that their father spent much time in his "solitary chambers" at Fen Court. In February Eliza was supplied with new clothes and other sundries and sent off to Woolwich, probably to teach in a school. There she remained throughout the rest of that year, although she and her father exchanged letters at frequent intervals and there were individual meetings and family gatherings. One such occurred on Christmas Day, an occasion which prompted the sober John Dyer to record "More levity than was agreeable to me."[51] The most interesting and tantalising entry for 1827, however, was that for Thursday, 23 August. On that day John Dyer confided in his diary, "Walked in afternoon to New Kent Road but returned without accomplishing my purpose." Did he go there to have words with the young Joseph Payne?

Whether Joseph and Eliza met during one of her journeys via the New Kent Road to Woolwich is not clear. What is certain is that by 1833 circumstances were conspiring to bring them together as near-neighbours in Camberwell. The 1833 and 1834 poor rate books for St. Giles, Camberwell, show that John Dyer had a house at Chatham Place, on the west side of Camberwell Grove. That for 1835 gave his address as Park Place, which lay across the road on the east side of the Grove, and this is confirmed by the entry in John Dyer's diary for 1836 which showed his address as 8, Park Place, Camberwell Grove.

In the early months of that year Eliza was frequently ill. Her father, as always, was very busy. In addition to his normal duties as secretary, his preaching engagements and prayer meetings, there was a west country tour in April, and much calling at the Colonial Office to see Sir George Grey. On 22 July 1836 Eliza returned from a visit to Ramsgate, and on Thursday, 28 July John Dyer and his daughter had a discussion about

Joseph Payne. The following entries gave some indication of John Dyer's concern.

> 28 July: Talked with my daughter about Payne. Wrote many letters. P. called in evening. Greatly perplexed.
>
> 29 July: Called on Mrs Fletcher. Afterwards to town.
>
> 8 September: Saw Mr Payne.
>
> 10 September: Payne in evening.
>
> 14 September: Mr and Mrs Fletcher called after Lectures. Source of inquietude.
>
> 28 September: Payne here.
>
> 3 December: P. here in evening.
>
> 20 December: Eliza to Maidstone.
>
> 22 December: Home to my solitary dwelling.
>
> 29 December: Eliza from Maidstone.[52]

The new year brought old problems. Eliza, who was living at Park Place, was often ill, her father was in dire financial straits. On the last day of January, John Dyer recorded that he was "disconcerted and grieved in different ways."[53]

Nevertheless, romance was in the air. Eliza was no doubt as surprised as anyone to learn that her father intended to marry again. John Dyer began courting a 46–year-old spinster, Mary Jackson, who lived in Dorking. There was much exchange of correspondence, many visits and walks. In Dyer's diary "M. J." became "dearest Mary." His letters to his first wife were burned and on 22 August 1837 John Dyer and Mary Jackson were married at the Camberwell Register Office. Eliza was the official witness for the Dyer family.[54] John Dyer was obviously pleased by the occasion, "All was pleasant and orderly." The wedding night was spent at the Crown at Sevenoaks in Kent. On the next day the couple set off for Hastings on the Sussex coast, where the bridegroom was happy to find that they were lodged in a "quiet, respectable house."[55] With her father safely out of the way Eliza and Joseph could get on with preparations for their own wedding, and for the substantial reorganizations which would result from the Fletchers' move to Denmark Hill and their own occupancy of Grove Hill House.

On Thursday, 28 December, Eliza was married to Joseph Payne in the parish church of St. Giles, Camberwell, "according to the rites and ceremonies of the Established Church."[56] Eliza's address was simply entered as "Grove." Though later she was to be described as "a stimulating and capable teacher, of great energy and character,"[57] there was no entry for her under "Rank or Profession." Joseph's profession was given as "School Master," his residence as Grove Hill, his father's name as Joseph Payne and his father's profession as "Builder." John Dyer acted as witness on behalf of Eliza, David Fletcher on behalf of Joseph Payne.

It is difficult in the absence of personal documentation to know precisely what attracted Joseph and Eliza to each other. Certainly they appeared to have much in common: of a similar age, though Eliza was some 14 months older than her husband; both were teachers; both had a profound interest in French language and literature. Herbert Quick, indeed, wrote that it was an alliance characterized by "the sympathy of the intellect as well as of the heart."[58] As to their compatibility in religious matters there can be little doubt that John Dyer, who had so recently himself exercised the register office option and had been married according to the rites of his own church, was disappointed that his daughter's union should take place in an Anglican church. His diary entry for that day was as follows: "Marriage of my dear Eliza with Mr Payne—at Church, through necessity, all very orderly and pleasant. They left at 3."[59] It is possible that Joseph and Eliza continued to worship at different churches before their move to Leatherhead in 1845, where they both attended the Congregational church. Certainly the young Joseph had an inquiring attitude towards the several manifestations of Christianity. He was open to different denominational influences when at Olney, and while teaching at Gowring's school was prompted by the comments of a Roman Catholic pupil on the state of limbo "to endeavour to obtain more information on this and other tenets of the Catholics."[60] After her marriage Eliza continued to work as a school teacher, but now at Grove Hill House. The imposing eighteenth-century house still stands. Currently in private ownership its interior has been elegantly and tastefully restored.

Grove Hill House

The major source for the school at Grove Hill House which Payne and Fletcher developed from 1834 is a Journal of Business Transactions kept by Payne which covers the period from June 1834 until November 1835.[61] Prospectuses and cards for the new establishment were sent out in July of 1834, and advertisements placed in various newspapers and journals, including *The Times* and the *Evangelical Magazine*, informing friends and the general public of the removal of the school from Beaumont House to Grove Hill. The new premises in which the school opened on 29 July were extolled as offering "extensive and most eligible accommodations," with "every advantage of salubrity, exclusion and facility of access." The first batch of 250 prospectuses was exhausted by October when a new edition of a further 250 was produced. The school year was divided into two halves, rather than three terms, and the first half lasted until 18 December when Payne despatched the boarders to their homes, commenting thankfully, since there had been a severe outbreak of scarlet fever, that "nearly every boy went home quite well." The new half commenced on 22 January 1835, and two days earlier an advertisement in *The Times* for "Grove Hill House, Camberwell" stated that:

> Messrs Fletcher and Payne beg to announce that the young gentlemen of the above named Establishment will recommence their studies on Thursday the 22nd Inst.
>
> The constant inculcation of religious principles, the energetic employment of the most improved methods of instruction and unremitting attention to health and comfort, form the grounds on which the confidence of their friends has hitherto rested and on which they now venture to solicit the support of the candid and intelligent.

Though it is difficult to be precise about pupil numbers it would appear that in the second half of 1835, from Midsummer to Michaelmas, the school had some 27 boarders and 15 day boys and "day boarders," while a further seven boys had left during this period.

Many boys were accepted at a tender age, some as young as four or five. At the other end of the spectrum there was an inquiry on behalf of an adult American pupil, for whom Payne quoted a fee of between £80 and £100 per annum, "with any advantage requiring peculiar attention and care £120." Although fees were set out in the prospectus, Payne often entered into negotiations with parents for special terms. These might be simple reductions, as in the case of Crisp, the son of a missionary, or package deals for brothers, as for example in the case of the three sons of a Mrs Coombs. Parental stipulations concerning amenities and curricula also produced variations in fees, and indicated the extent to which the private schools were responsive to consumer demand. One parent wanted separate bedrooms for his 14- and 15-year-old sons, sound Latin and French and an emphasis upon commerce, but no Greek. Another wanted no Classics whatsoever, but rather French and German and plenty of "useful knowledge." On the other hand young Master Freeman, a boarder from Milbank Street, Westminster, was not to study French, but was to have a single bed and learn "Military Exercises."

Versatile as Payne was, he clearly could not cope with teaching all of these subjects himself. Visiting masters were engaged for such accomplishments as dancing, drawing, music and drill, in addition to full-time assistants for core areas. In July 1834 a Mr Bragg was appointed at the sum of £25 per annum (together with board and lodging but not including washing). In addition to teaching he was to undertake playground duties, to prepare in the evenings for his classes of the next day, but to have two evenings free during the week, together with Sunday evenings to attend a Dissenting chapel. In spite of his strong recommendation and reference, however, Mr Bragg departed at the end of September. Payne noted, "paid him £7.10 for salary—parted amicably." Early in August 1835 in response to an advertisement in *The Times* which called for "a thoroughly competent assistant—of decidedly Evangelical sentiments —" a Mr Hunter commenced work at a salary of 35 guineas per annum. His principal duties were to teach English, junior Latin and French. Another consequence of this varied curriculum was that Payne had to order considerable supplies of books and other equipment. For those boys who succeeded in the annual examinations, there were prizes and presents. Not surprisingly, William Fletcher was a prizewinner and on 14 October 1835 Payne noted his departure from the school for the purpose of further study at the University of London. Not all pupils were so successful, however. Another William, William Newnham, was (according to his father) handicapped by an hereditary weakness in the subjects of Geography and History, to which the son had added "an almost unconquerable indisposition to study." Letters of 1834 and 1835 from the father to Payne expressed pleasure at young William's progress in Greek, but regretted his lack of general knowledge.[62] Later that year the boy was withdrawn from the school.

Overall, however, the school must have flourished, so that in 1838 the boys were transferred to the new premises of the Denmark Hill Grammar School, while Grove Hill House became home to Joseph and Eliza Payne and to a school of a different kind. The Census of 1841 shows that by that date Grove Hill House was a flourishing girls' school.[63] Eliza was listed as the schoolmistress, and there were five resident female teachers. Four of these were aged between 20 and 30; the age of the fifth, Eleanor Evans, was given as 15. The school also housed 27 female pupils, aged from six to 20, although the vast majority, some 20, were aged between 12 and 15. Given the number of teachers per resident pupils, it is most probable that there were also several other girls who attended as day scholars. The household was completed by five female servants, not one above 30 years of age. At that date Payne, apart from his two-year-old son John Burnell, appears to have been the only male amongst the 40 occupants of the house.

Not all was work, however. Prior to her marriage Eliza had acted as hostess for her father,[64] and both she and Joseph had a considerable circle of acquaintances with philanthropic and literary backgrounds. For example, notable guests at this time were the Irish writers Anna Maria Hall and her husband, Samuel Carter Hall. The Halls were heavily involved in journal editorship and it appears that it was in this capacity that Joseph Payne first made their acquaintance in 1829.[65] Anna Maria's outstanding novel, *Marian, or a Young Maid's Fortunes*, was published in 1840, the same year as their jointly authored *Ireland, its Scenery, Characters etc.*, which provided an excellent record of conditions prior to the horrendous famine of 1845–1846. Anna Maria Hall was also a noted philanthropist, for example she was involved in the foundation of the Governesses' Institute, the Home for Decayed Gentlewomen and the Nightingale Fund. Other visitors and friends of longstanding, renowned for their literary and philanthropic achievements, included members of the Gurney family. The Gurneys were resident at Denmark Hill and prominent in the Baptist cause, and no doubt Eliza first made Joseph Gurney's acquaintance through his connections with her father. Though Joseph Gurney, like his father before him, held the post of shorthand writer to the Houses of Parliament, he also managed to serve for more than 50 years on the committee of the Religious Tract Society, to be treasurer of the Baptist College in Regent's Park, and to write several popular commentaries on the Bible. He was the father of the educational reformer Mary Gurney who, after Payne's death, helped to edit at least one of his works, while Mary's great aunt, Maria Gurney, author of the popular *Rhymes for my children. By a mother*, published in 1835, was recorded as a guest at Grove Hill House in 1841.[66]

NOTES

1. Joseph Payne, Commonplace Book, Author's Collection.

2. Admission Book, 5 July 1833, St. John's College, Cambridge. There was no mention of Payne's parentage. He never resided in the College and his name was removed from the Residence Book on 28 October 1833. I owe this reference to Charles Farrow.

3. S. H. A. Hervey, *Biographical List of Boys educated at King Edward VI Free Grammar School, Bury St. Edmunds from 1550 to 1900* (Bury St. Edmunds, 1908), p. 291. From 1808 to 1829 the headmaster was Benjamin Heath Malkin.

4. Originally published in the *Educational Times* XXIX, 182 (June 1876), p. 57, and reprinted in Payne, *Works*, I, p. 8.

5. Joseph Payne, Journal July-November 1824, Author's Collection.

6. Joseph Payne, Journal March 1827, Author's Collection. The school address was given in Payne's preface to his pamphlet of 1830 on Jacotot, Payne, *Works*, I, p. 339.

7. Parliamentary Papers, 1867–8, XXVIII, *Report of the Royal Commissioners on Schools not comprised within Her Majesty's two recent Commissions on Popular Education and Public Schools*, iv, p. 663. Hereafter cited as *Taunton Report*.

8. Pigot's, *London and Provincial New Commercial Directory 1826–7*, p. 167 gives Gowring as master of a boys' day and boarding academy at 3, Dover Place, as does that for 1828–9. The same directory for 1832–3–4, however, p. 218, situates Gowring and his school at 3, Rodney Buildings. The St. Mary, Newington Poor Rate Books from 1828 to 1832, held in the Southwark Local Studies Library, show that throughout this period John Gowring lived at 3, Rodney Buildings. Another resident of 3, Rodney Buildings was a John Freeman, though there was no indication that he was a teacher.

9. Census Enumerators' Returns, 1841.

10. Joseph Payne, Journal March 1827, Author's Collection.

11. *Taunton Report*, iv, p. 663.

12. Payne, *Works*, II, p. 137.

13. *Educational Times* I, 5 (February 1848), p. 103. For a recent interpretation of Jacotot see Jacques Rancière, *The Ignorant Schoolmaster: Five Lessons in Intellectual Emancipation*, ed. Kristin Ross (Stanford, 1991).

14. *Taunton Report*, iv, p. 663.

15. Payne, *Works*, II, p. 135.

16. *Foreign Quarterly Review* V (1830), p. 656.

17. Payne, *Works*, II, p. 136.

18. Nevertheless, one of the titles at the head of the article in the *Foreign Quarterly Review*, written by a member of the *Académie Française*, M. le Duc de Levis, had itself been published in Paris only in 1830.

19. *Quarterly Journal of Education* I, 2 (1831), p. 349.

20. *Ibid.*, pp. 349–62.

21. Payne, *Works*, II, p. 136. One correspondent was Henry Brougham, the leading Whig educational reformer, who wrote in complimentary terms to Payne on 4 June 1830, Payne, *Works*, II, p. 295.

Not all the replies were so prompt. Robert Owen, the factory owner, Socialist and infant school pioneer, then fully engaged in a variety of schemes, appears to have been a reluctant respondent. Owen to Payne, 26 January 1832, Author's Collection.

22. Payne, *Works*, II, p. 159.

23. Joseph Payne, *Epitome Historiae Sacrae, adapted by a literal translation to Jacotot's method* (London, 1831); *Monthly Repository and Review of Theology and General Literature* V (1831), pp. 256–67.

24. Payne, *Works*, II, p. 138.

25. *Ibid.*, p. 141.

26. Payne, *Works*, I, p. 386.

27. *Taunton Report*, iv, p. 663.

28. Census Enumerators' Returns, 1841 and 1851. It is possible that William and Loughton were one and the same, and that Sarah's age was confused.

29. Owen to Payne, 26 January 1832, Author's Collection.

30. J. A. Venn, *Alumni Cantabrigienses, 1752–1900*, (Cambridge, 6 vols. 1940–7), VI, p. 30.

31. *Ibid.*, V, p. 53.

32. *Taunton Report*, iv, p. 663.

33. Pigot's, *National, London and Provincial Commercial Directory for 1832–3–4*, p. 218.

34. St. Giles, Camberwell Poor Rate Books, 1832, 1833, 1834, 1835, 1836, 1837, 1838, Southwark Local Studies Library. The Tithe Commissioners Camberwell Schedule for 1837 gives Joseph Payne as the occupier of Grove Hill House. The tithe payment for the house and grounds of some one and a half acres was £1. 2s. 6d. At the same date the tithe on the Denmark Hill School, which stood in the names of both Fletcher and Payne, was £2. 13s. 6d. Tithe Commissioners Schedules, Southwark Local Studies Library.

35. William Harnett Blanch, *The Parish of Camberwell* (London, 1875), p. 310.

36. Pigot's, *London Directory for 1838*, p. 428.

37. The Dyer diaries and other papers deposited by Evelyn Murphy are in the Angus Library, Regent's Park College, Oxford. The four diaries for 1823, 1827, 1836 and 1837 are catalogued as 1/4/1, 1/4/1A, 1/4/1B and 1/4/1C respectively. For other information on Dyer see Ernest A. Payne, "The Diaries of John Dyer," *Baptist Quarterly* XIII (1949–50), pp. 253–9; Ernest A. Payne, *The First Generation: Early Leaders*

of the Baptist Missionary Society in England and India (London, 1936), pp. 120–6.

38. Edward Steane, *A Sermon occasioned by the death of The Rev. John Dyer. To which is annexed the oration at the grave, by F. A. Cox* (London, 1841), p. 20.

39. The General Baptist Missionary Society was founded in 1816, A. C. Underwood, *A History of the English Baptists* (London, 1947), p. 154.

40. F. A. Cox, *History of the Baptist Missionary Society, from 1792 to 1842* (London, 2 vols. 1842), I, p. 221. See also, *The Centenary Volume of the Baptist Missionary Society, 1792–1892* (London, 1892); F. Townley Lord, *Achievement: A Short History of the Baptist Missionary Society, 1792–1942* (London, 1942); Ernest A. Payne, *The Great Succession: Leaders of the Baptist Missionary Society during the Nineteenth Century* (London, 1938); Brian Stanley, *The History of the Baptist Missionary Society, 1792–1992* (Edinburgh, 1992).

41. Lord, *Achievement*, p. 114.

42. John Dyer's diary, 6 August 1823, 1/4/1, Angus Library, Regent's Park College, Oxford.

43. Carey to Ryland, 14 June 1821, W. Carey, *Letters, official and private, from the Rev. Dr Carey relative to certain statements contained in three pamphlets lately published by the Rev. John Dyer. . . .*(London, 3rd edition 1828), p. 23.

44. John Clark Marshman, *Review of two pamphlets, by the Rev. John Dyer, and the Rev. E. Carey and W. Yates. . . .*(London, 1830).

45. Dyer to Saffery, 13 May 1819, R/16/6, Angus Library, Regent's Park College, Oxford.

46. This list is in the back of John Dyer's diary for 1827, 1/4/1A, Angus Library, Regent's Park College, Oxford. A single sheet, headed "1780 6 August John Burnell and Agnes Lavers married," which lists the dates of birth of their nine children gives Agnes Dyer's death as 30 January 1826, Author's Collection.

47. Ernest A. Payne, *First Generation*, p. 125.

48. Agnes Dyer to Mrs Saffery, 5 January 1822, R/16/12, Angus Library, Regent's Park College, Oxford. Agnes Dyer was too busy to finish this letter and John Dyer had to do so on her behalf.

49. Dyer to Saffery, 18 July 1821, R/16/9, Angus Library, Regent's Park College, Oxford.

50. Agnes Dyer to Mrs Saffery, 5 January 1822, R/16/12, Angus Library, Regent's Park College, Oxford.

51. John Dyer's diary, 25 December 1827, 1/4/1A, Angus Library, Regent's Park College, Oxford.

52. John Dyer's diary, July-December 1836, 1/4/1B, Angus Library, Regent's Park College, Oxford.

53. John Dyer's diary, 31 January 1837, 1/4/1C, Angus Library, Regent's Park College, Oxford.

54. Marriage Certificate, John Dyer and Mary Jackson, Camberwell Register Office, 22 August 1837.

55. John Dyer's diary, 23 August 1837, 1/4/1C, Angus Library, Regent's Park College, Oxford.

56. Marriage Certificate, Joseph Payne and Eliza Dyer, St. Giles Church, Camberwell, 28 December 1837.

57. *Dictionary of National Biography*.

58. "Introduction by the Rev. R. H. Quick" to Payne, *Works*, I, p. 3.

59. John Dyer's diary, 28 December 1837, 1/4/1C, Angus Library, Regent's Park College, Oxford.

60. Joseph Payne, Journal March 1827, Author's Collection.

61. Joseph Payne, Journal of Business Transactions 1834–5, Author's Collection. Subsequent quotations are from this source.

62. Newnham to Payne, 30 July 1834 and 22 January 1835, Author's Collection.

63. Census Enumerators' Returns, 1841.

64. John Sheppard to Eliza Dyer, 8 November 1836, Author's Collection.

65. A letter from Samuel Carter Hall, dated only 24 May (probably 1829) referred to Payne's journal articles, while one from Anna Maria Hall of 30 October 1829 invited Payne to tea at the Halls' residence at 59 Upper Charlotte Street, Fitzroy Square, London, Author's Collection.

66. A letter dated only 30 January (1841?) from L. H. Sigourney to Payne, thanked him for the loan of a copy of Elizabeth Barrett's poems and expressed a wish to meet the author. Another letter from Sigourney to Eliza Payne, dated 26 February 1841, accepted her invitation to an evening function at Grove Hill House at which the Halls would be present, asked if she could bring Maria Gurney, and thanked Joseph Payne for the loan of a copy of one of Anna Maria Hall's books, Author's Collection. The connection continued after the Paynes and Gurneys had moved from the Denmark Hill area, William Brodie Gurney (father of Joseph Gurney) to Payne, 29 November 1850, Author's Collection.

CHAPTER TWO

The Denmark Hill Grammar School

Camberwell

In the 1830s Camberwell, including Denmark Hill, still bore many of the characteristics of a rural idyll:

> Leaving London, you came on a stage coach, along the white road, sometimes between "hedgerows, elms and hillocks green," past a certain windmill, and up to this retreat, where, amid cedars, oaks, and blossoming thorns, charming nests of wealth and elegance were being made for merchants to retire into, with no prospect of anything coming to disturb its serene hush.[1]

To journey from Gowring's school in Rodney Buildings to the Denmark Hill Grammar School would be to join the Walworth Road at the Elephant and Castle at its junction with the New Kent Road and to continue southwards along the same route. Just north of the junction with Albany Road the Walworth Road became Camberwell Road, which ran as far as Camberwell Green. From Camberwell Green, Denmark Hill climbed southwards, with Grove Hill and The Grove running in parallel fashion up the hill a short distance to the east. From the crossroads at the Green, Camberwell New Road proceeded northwestward to Kennington, while Camberwell Church Street, with St. Giles Church and Wilson's Grammar School on the southern side and the Vicarage on the north, led eastward into the Peckham Road.

In the nineteenth century, Camberwell, as defined by the ancient parish of St. Giles, comprised some 4,450 acres. Its northern boundary was situated one-and-a-half miles due south of the River Thames, with its ancient crossing into the City at London Bridge. The southernmost tip lay a further four-and-a-half miles away. Its broadest point from east to west was about two-and-a-half miles.[2] In the late-eighteenth and early-nineteenth centuries, therefore, Camberwell was a healthy and reasonably wealthy rural retreat, at but a short distance from the City of London. In 1779 it received a particular stamp of approval when the leading medical practitioner of the day, John Lettsom (who in 1800 described Camberwell as having "Few poor inhabitants and not many overgrown fortunes")[3] took up residence on Grove Hill.[4]

The popularity of residence south of the River Thames was transformed by three factors: bridges, roads and railways. Improved access to the major centres of the metropolis was provided by the completion of bridges at Lambeth in 1750, Blackfriars in 1769 and Vauxhall in 1816.[5] Road developments which extended the benefits of these new river crossings included the several turnpikes which radiated out from St. George's Circus, which lay to the south of Blackfriars Bridge. The road from Newington to Camberwell was turnpiked in 1782, while Vauxhall Bridge led to the construction of the Camberwell New Road, completed in 1818, which ran directly from Kennington to Camberwell Green.[6] Along such roads travelled coaches—by 1834 some 17 were plying between Camberwell and the City—and omnibuses, which by 1852 were leaving Camberwell at ten-minute intervals.[7] Even these services were insufficient to cope with the ever-increasing demand, but for those who for one reason or another missed the bus, as John Dyer sometimes did, it was always possible to walk.

Not until the 1860s did the third element, the railways, play any significant part in bringing the inhabitants of Camberwell to the centre of London. The South London Line, which linked Victoria and London Bridge, was begun in 1862; a station was opened at Denmark Hill in 1866; the whole was completed in the following year.[8] The coming of the railways with their cheap "workmen's" tickets for early-morning travellers, and the trams, at first horse-drawn but later electrified, marked the end of Camberwell and Denmark Hill as the Dyers, Fletchers and Paynes had known it. By 1900 the population of Camberwell had reached nearly 260,000. As H.J. Dyos, the historian of the suburbanization of Camberwell has noted, "Over the nineteenth century as a whole, it could be said that in multiplying her population over sixty-five times Camberwell grew more in relation to its original size than any other district of London."[9] House building reached a peak in the 1870s, and at the beginning of that decade Denmark Hill Grammar School, the foundation of Fletcher and Payne, which would be continued with even greater success by Charles Mason, fell victim to the apparently insatiable demand for building land.

Private Schools

There were many types of schools in Britain in 1837, the year in which Queen Victoria came to the throne and in which David Fletcher and Joseph Payne brought the Denmark Hill Grammar School into being. There were also significant variations among those of England, Ireland, Scotland and Wales. One new phenomenon were the Sunday schools which had developed rapidly from the 1780s. Although the Sunday school movement was to prove strongest in Wales, by 1841 1,679,000 children and young persons (together with some adults) were enrolled in English Sunday schools. This figure constituted nearly 50 percent of those aged between five and 15.[10] Day schools included various charity and parish schools, dame and private adventure schools (private schools run largely by and for members of the working classes) and a range of endowed or "free" schools which might cater to children from a variety of backgrounds. These schools educated both boys and girls (although sometimes in separate establishments) as did the schools of the two great societies, which provided a substantial part of nineteenth-century elementary schooling. These were the National Society for promoting the education of the poor in the principles of the Established Church, founded in 1811, and the British and Foreign School Society, created in 1814 to replace the Royal Lancasterian Society of 1808. In 1870 the National Society controlled three-quarters of the state-aided elementary schools in England and Wales. In contrast, the endowed grammar schools, many of which dated from the sixteenth and seventeenth centuries, were almost always for boys. This was particularly true of the "great" schools, as the leading grammar schools of England were called. Eton and Westminster were the great schools of the later eighteenth century; by the middle of the nineteenth, Charterhouse, Harrow, Rugby, Shrewsbury, Winchester, and two day schools, St. Paul's and Merchant Taylors', had joined their ranks. By the end of the century the term "public school," which had replaced that of "great school," was being applied to a much wider range of establishments.

Many nineteenth-century public schools, including the nine identified by the Clarendon Commission in 1861, were ancient grammar schools which had shed most or all of their local connections, including the duty to educate poor scholars at no charge, and had become boarding schools with regional or national reputations. This process was facilitated by the rise of the railways. Other public schools, however, were nineteenth-century foundations. These included proprietary schools, established by companies but not for profit. Some were day schools, like those of King's College and University College, London; others like the Anglican schools of the 1840s, Brighton, Cheltenham, Hurstpierpoint, Marlborough and Radley, were for boarders. Some schools were founded for the sons of particular professional groups: Cheltenham for colonial officers, both civil and military; Epsom for doctors; Marlborough for the clergy.

Private schools were schools run by private individuals for profit. They were the norm for the schooling of girls of the middling and upper ranks of society, but private schools for boys faced greater competition—from endowed, grammar, proprietary and public schools. Their selling points might be curricula and entry requirements, which were not restricted by ancient statutes or custom, and a more closely supervised regime in which young boys were not so much at the mercy of older ones. On the other hand, private schools might suffer from their owners' need to make a profit—there being no guaranteed endowment income—and from poor premises and staff. They also lacked continuity. Whereas a grammar or public school would have the apparatus of an endowment, freehold premises and a board of governors, private schools were often in leased or rented premises and dependent upon the good health, willpower, financial acumen, organizational ability and teaching prowess of a single individual.[11]

It is impossible to give accurate numbers of private schools. Some indication, however, is provided by the Education Census of 1851 which received information from 29,425 establishments. Some 4,956 of these were classified as "superior," schools which might provide study of the Classical languages, take in boarders, be organized on a proprietary basis, and make a genuine attempt at producing young ladies or gentlemen. "Middling" schools, of which some 7,095 were recorded, might concentrate more upon arithmetic, English grammar and geography, their pupils being destined for the commercial world. Below these came the so-called "inferior" schools, private adventure or dame schools, where reading and possibly writing formed the staple fare. A further 3,495 schools were listed as "undescribed."[12]

Camberwell Schools

At any period of substantial population growth, as happened in Camberwell in the nineteenth century, it was likely that the supply of such services as churches and schools would be found wanting. The traditional school for boys in Camberwell was the Free Grammar School, founded in 1615 by the then Vicar of Camberwell, Edward Wilson, and often referred to as Wilson's Grammar School. A board of governors was established, and the first master was a Cambridge graduate, Edward Wilson. Whether this was the founder himself or, as seems more likely, a relative, probably his nephew, is not clear.[13] There was no limit on the number of scholars but they were to be born or resident in Camberwell "whereof twelve shall be freely taught, and shall be the children of such of the inhabitants of the said parish as shall be poor."[14]

In the second decade of the nineteenth century, instruction of the free scholars in Latin and Greek, which had been discontinued, was resumed. In 1818 the master of the school was William Jephson who, in addition to the 12 local free scholars, had from 25 to 30 boarders at £42 per annum.[15] In 1821 English, reading and arithmetic were added to the curriculum for the foundation scholars. These curriculum changes were symptomatic of several similar attempts throughout the country to resolve the central dilemma of the free grammar schools of the day. If such a school continued to focus on the Classics then few poor children would attend. On the other hand if substantial numbers of poor children were admitted then the school would have to concentrate upon basic subjects and forfeit its claim to be a grammar school. In many cases, and particularly where the value of the endowment had declined, masters found it necessary to recruit private scholars who were willing both to study the Classics and to pay fees, and to neglect, or even to exclude, poor scholars.

At Camberwell such problems were compounded by difficulties in the governing body, by the ill-health of the master and by an expensive lawsuit. The school flourished for a while in the later 1820s and early 1830s, but the opening of the Camberwell Collegiate School in 1835 appears to have had a significant effect, if only because the local clergy and influential parishioners were attracted to support this new proprietary school. Matters came to a head with the great conflagration of 7 February 1841, when the entire structure of St. Giles Church was burned to the ground. Although the school itself escaped the fire, a decision was taken to raze the school buildings too. The new St. Giles, built at a cost of some £24,000 to a cruciform plan from a design by George Gilbert Scott, then in partnership with W. B. Moffatt, was consecrated on 21 November 1844, but the school remained closed until the 1880s. The land on which it had stood was let out for grazing purposes at a nominal rent.[16] In the 1860s the Taunton Commission simply reported that the Free Grammar School at Camberwell had been "in abeyance for more than 20 years."[17]

With the Grammar School in difficulties in the 1830s, the closest competitor to the Denmark Hill Grammar School was undoubtedly the Camberwell Collegiate School, which stood on the eastern side of The Grove. This was an Anglican proprietary school founded under the patronage of the Bishop of Winchester, and which also had the strong support of the local incumbent, J. G. Storie. Its collegiate character—it was indeed in union with the newly founded King's College, London—was emphasized in the buildings, completed in 1834 to a design from Henry Roberts, the architect of Fishmongers' Hall. They constituted a substantial and expensive pile, constructed in white brick with stone dressings, with a frontage of some 300 feet and a depth of nearly 250. The grounds comprised some two acres, and the principal schoolroom measured 67 by 33 feet. The most noteworthy feature of the building, however, was its "fine cloister." The school opened on 26 January 1835 but appears to have been but moderately successful. Blanch attributed its difficulties to "the proximity of Dulwich College and other educational establishments."[18] The school closed in 1867 and its land was sold for building purposes. Dulwich College, founded in 1619 by the actor Edward Alleyn for the education of 12 poor scholars and up to 80 fee-payers, was indeed substantially endowed, but itself was beset by problems until its reconstitution into Upper and Lower Schools under the Dulwich College Act of 1857.[19]

Camberwell and its near neighbour Peckham were particularly known for the number of girls' private schools, a circumstance which continued at least until the third quarter of the nineteenth century. For example, although the Grove Hill House School appears to have closed soon after the Paynes' departure,[20] in the Grove area alone, Blanch who wrote in 1875 noted Surbiton House in Grove Hill run by a Mrs Dransfield, two schools in Camberwell Grove under the care of a Miss Cusworth and a Miss Bishop and the academy of the Misses McDowall in Grove Park.[21]

Just as Eliza Payne was a schoolmistress both before and after her marriage, so many of David Fletcher's female relatives taught in neighbouring schools. One such establishment was the Pelican House School on the Peckham Road, so named from the pelicans which stood on brick pilasters at the entrance gates. This was founded in the 1820s and managed by a series of Miss and Mrs Fletchers. In 1851 it was under the control of a 56–year-old Miss Fletcher, with five teachers and 20 resident pupils aged from 14 to 18 years, though there was also one of nine years. In

1875 Blanch found it under the direction of a niece of Miss Fletcher, whom he identified as "Miss Dixie," and thriving with some 75 pupils. In fact this was probably Charlotte Fletcher Dixon who, aged 14 and listed as a scholar, was resident with her parents at Pelican House in 1851.[22]

Thus in 1837 Camberwell was a propitious place in which to found a boys' private school or, in the case of Fletcher and Payne, to expand and develop an existing institution. The area was fashionable, and Denmark Hill amongst its most favoured locations. The population was rising, but as yet the tone was still set by those of the middle classes who wanted access to the City by day, but rural tranquillity by night. The traditional means of supplying grammar school education, Wilson's Grammar School, was in poor shape, indeed was soon to disappear. Both local residents and others who would wish to send their sons to board at a school that, while keeping the traditional word "Grammar" in its title, would provide a more "modern" approach to the curriculum, suitable for a business career, might be attracted by the new establishment at Denmark Hill. Such a school might particularly appeal to members of the Dissenting community.

Denmark Hill House

One of the major problems for those about to set up a private school was to find suitable premises. The capital cost of a purpose-built establishment was beyond the reach of most. One answer, particularly for smaller schools, was to provide education in the house of the master or mistress. Such schools might well be seen as examples of the domestic system of industry. Another solution was to lease or rent a substantial property which, although it might also provide accommodation for the proprietor and teaching staff, was principally devoted to the boarding and teaching of pupils.

By any standards the property in which David Fletcher and Joseph Payne were to launch their new venture was an imposing one—indeed it could claim royal connections. Nevertheless there is no incontrovertible evidence as to the origin of the building which housed the Denmark Hill Grammar School. Tradition had it that the house was built by Sir Christopher Wren for Prince George of Denmark, who in 1683 married Anne, the younger daughter of James II, who became Queen in 1702. Certainly Denmark Hill is supposed to have derived its name from this connection. The attribution was widely assumed in Payne's day (though Charles Mason declared that he could not substantiate it) and on one occasion in 1870, when other members of the Danish royal family were visiting Princess Alexandra, wife of Albert Edward, Prince of Wales, the future Edward VII, the cavalcade stopped at the school while several features of the building were pointed out to Princess Alexandra.[23] It would appear that the house, even before its later additions, was sufficiently imposing to have been used as a royal residence.

By 1800 the property, which had passed through several hands in the eighteenth century, had come into the possession of John Perkins, the well-known brewer. Perkins was a wealthy man, even his salary as manager at Thrale's Brewery, which he subsequently bought, was £500 a year. Perkins traded for some time on his own before forming the successful Barclay and Perkins partnership. At his death he bequeathed the property to his wife during her lifetime, and thereafter jointly to two of his sons, Alfred and Charles. On the death of their mother they sold out to two other brothers, Henry and Frederick, in a deed dated March 1821. It was these sons, Henry and Frederick Perkins, who on 25 December 1837 let the house to David Fletcher for 21 years at a rent of £210 per annum. On 4 October 1858 it was let to Charles Mason, the then headmaster, at the increased rent of £400 per annum.

The house stood on the eastern side of the lower slope of Denmark Hill, at its junction with Coldharbour Lane. It was an imposing edifice, constructed in red brick, and panelled and picked out with Portland stone. The main building, which appeared from the outside to be three storeys high, stood back a short distance from the road and was approached through iron gates hung on pillars which bore the legend "Denmark Hill Grammar School," via a circular drive. The front doors opened into an impressive entrance hall, measuring 28 by 14 feet. Two flights of broad oak steps led to the main first floor landing. Frescoes on the ceiling and walls depicted scenes which, though drawn from Classical times, might not have been considered particularly appropriate for the improvement of adolescent boys. That on the ceiling showed Mars and Venus being caught in the net placed around their bed by Vulcan, the husband of Venus. On the left-hand wall was portrayed the Rape of the Sabines; on the left the Judgement of Paris, although the fair forms of Juno, Minerva and Venus had been modestly covered by petticoats at the insistence of one former female resident of the house. From the outside the house appeared to be symmetrical, indeed the only exterior differences between the front and the back were that the one porch had Ionic columns, the other Corinthian. The inside of the house, however, was a veritable warren, partly as a result of alterations. To the right of the entrance hall and entered via carved folding doors, were two high-ceilinged rooms with large fireplaces of white marble. To the left were several smaller rooms, one with a recess in which might have been fitted a small stage. Short staircases abounded, so that storeys in different parts of the house were not on the same plane. Generally the boys slept in dormitories, some eight to a room, but there were some single and double rooms at the top of the house.[24] When in the early 1870s the house was open to viewing prior to its demolition, on the top floor at least one long room "appeared to have been somewhat recently divided by partitions into small bedrooms."[25]

In 1837 when Fletcher and Payne first took occupancy of the house, they might have supposed that it would be large enough for a school as it stood, especially as there was a substantial range of outbuildings which lay to the southeastern corner of the house. Nevertheless pupil numbers must have necessitated both conversions and additions, and classrooms were subsequently added to both sides of the main house.[26] One of the main features of the property was its extensive grounds. These extended to Grove Lane on the eastern boundary and to Love Lane on the southwest, an area of some six acres. More than half of these were laid out as playgrounds and a cricket field which was large enough to accommodate two matches at a time.[27] Another useful feature for a private school which included a large number of boarding pupils was that some of the property was enclosed by a high brick wall. Within the grounds, in addition to a large lawn, were tall elms and cedars, hawthorns and laurels. One sacred spot was known as "Dr Johnson's walk." Samuel Johnson, the great lexicographer, critic and poet who died in 1784, was a friend of both the Thrales and of the Perkins. When John Perkins worked at Thrales he had a mezzotint of the doctor on his wall. Barclay and Perkins subsequently took a picture of the head of Johnson as their trademark. Another possible literary connection is that the house was represented by Charles Dickens in *Martin Chuzzlewit*, published in 1843.[28]

In 1873 the building was demolished, having been purchased by a Mr Churchwarden Strong for a sum of £11,000 for the house and the estate. Two years later the area was converted into building plots. Daneville and Selbourne Roads were laid down and some 198 houses built, so that within those two years the value of the whole had increased to £100,000.[29]

The School

Fletcher and Payne's new school, though called a grammar school, was a private school. The word "grammar" was used to show that this was a school where the Classical languages were taught. Fletcher was clearly in many respects the senior partner. He controlled the finances; he and his family lived on the premises. He was the proprietor. But Joseph Payne was, in an academic sense, the headmaster, although he was cautious about his use of the term. When in 1865 Lord Taunton asked him point blank, "In this school you were head master, not assistant master?" Payne replied, "In this school I had the entire charge of the children's education."[30]

It is unfortunate for our knowledge of the early years of the Denmark Hill Grammar School that in giving evidence to the Taunton Commission Payne concentrated upon his work at his next school in Leatherhead. This was understandable, given that Payne spent 19 years at Leatherhead, as opposed to seven at Denmark Hill, and that there he was to be both proprietor and headmaster. Nevertheless, the Census of 1841 shows that by that date the school was flourishing. In addition to Fletcher and Payne (who was still living at Grove Hill House) there were four young resident assistants: two masters, Robert Clarke, aged 30, and Richard Weymouth, aged 20; and two mistresses, Frances Vines, 25, and Sarah Welsh, 20, who taught the junior forms. It is possible that Weymouth accompanied or followed Payne to his next school at Leatherhead. There were 57 resident pupils, all boys, whose ages ranged from five to 15, although the majority, some 37, were between 11 and 14. There is no way of knowing whether any day boys were attending in 1841. In 1865 when Payne gave evidence to the Taunton Commission, he said that before he left Denmark Hill in 1844 it had become a school of "between 70 and 80 boys."[31]

At the end of 1844 Joseph and Eliza Payne, together with their two young sons and baby daughter, left Denmark Hill for Leatherhead. David Fletcher appears to have carried on the school alone for a while, but by 1850 had found a new partner in Charles Mason. Mason, born in 1820, was a graduate and fellow of University College, London, who was to become well known as a textbook writer—he had particular success with an English Grammar, published in 1858, which reached its thirtieth edition by 1887. After some three years of partnership Mason succeeded Fletcher and ran the school until its closure, probably in 1873. In 1865, like Payne, he was called to give evidence before the Taunton Commission and described in detail the nature and state of the school at that time. It would be unwise to presume that there were no substantial differences between the school in Mason's day and that some 20 years before. But the similarities between the Denmark Hill Grammar School as described by Mason, and the Mansion Grammar School at Leatherhead as described by Payne, were striking. Mason's account, therefore, may be taken as being not only an important piece of evidence in respect of the school of his own day, but also as indicative of the earlier period, and more generally of this type of first grade boys' private school of the middle years of the nineteenth century.

In the 1860s there were, according to Mason, some 120 pupils, of whom a slight majority, 64 or 65, were boarders. Fees for boarders were 40 to 60 guineas per year according to the age of the pupils, with a further five or six guineas per annum for such extras as drawing, music, drilling, washing and pew rents. Day boys were charged from 16 to 20 guineas per year, with an additional four or five guineas for midday meals. The boarders came mainly from London and the surrounding area, but there were also a number from Lancashire, where Mason had local connections. Mason's calculations of his annual expenses, averaged over a three-year period with 62 boarders and 50 day pupils, including rent, taxes, rates, housekeeping, wages and salaries, and board and lodging for his wife and himself and three children (but making no allowance for his own salary, books or disbursements to individual pupils) was £3,400. Since Mason's receipts from school fees probably totalled in excess of £4,000 per annum, as proprietor and headmaster he was left with a possible profit of about £500. Indeed Mason estimated that were he to make no charge for his services, the cost to a day pupil would be about £15 per annum and that of a boarder about £43. Nevertheless, there were three items which contributed to the relatively high fees at Denmark Hill Grammar School. One was the considerable capital expenditure to which both Fletcher and Mason were put in enlarging and adapting the premises and providing specialist equipment. A second was the substantial rent of some £400 per year in Mason's day, nearly double that of the Fletcher and Payne period. The third was the small size of classes: on average one teacher to every 14 or 15 boys.[32]

In 1865 as in Payne's day the school was divided into two halves: upper and lower. Twenty-eight boys were in the lower school and 92 in the upper. All teaching in the lower school which catered to pupils aged seven to ten, apart from any supervision or intervention by Mason himself, was carried out by mistresses and not masters. In general he strongly favoured the employment of mistresses to teach the younger boys, for he found them to be "more careful, patient, and persevering with young children than men are."[33] No doubt they were also paid less. Boys in the lower school had separate classrooms, a separate playground and separate bedrooms.

Given the size of the fees it is not surprising that the great majority of the pupils were drawn from the upper ranks of the middle classes—the sons of businessmen, manufacturers, merchants, gentleman farmers, lawyers, doctors. To Mason's knowledge, during his time at the school there had been only three sons of Anglican clergymen, though in 1865 some two-thirds of the pupils were Anglican. The school, however, was open to all; there had been Roman Catholic and Unitarian pupils and one Jew. Mason himself was an Independent, and he implied that of the other third the great majority of the pupils were either Independents or Baptists, with very few Wesleyans. Interestingly, Mason stated that "When I first joined it, it was almost exclusively a Nonconformist school, and now it is becoming one of the opposite kind, as far as the pupils are concerned."[34]

The boys ranged from seven to 18 years of age, but pupils arrived at all stages. Some remained for nine years, others came at 17 and stayed for merely a year. Mason calculated that on average boys stayed for about three and a half years. He was generally scathing about their accomplishments when they arrived at the school, and argued that once boys came to Denmark Hill the tuition they received there was so good that unless they were day boys who moved to other neighbourhoods, they continued there for the rest of their schooling: "I do not suppose that during the 15 years that I have been there. . .a dozen of the boys have gone to any other school."[35] Boys generally left the school at age 16 or 17. Very few indeed proceeded to Oxford or Cambridge, though some went to the University of London. The main destination of the pupils of the Denmark Hill Grammar School according to Mason was business—"chiefly merchants' offices."[36] This was not, however, the only outcome. Some became architects or surveyors. Others proceeded to such learned and traditional professions as medicine and the law, for which a period of study at a university might be required.

Assistant teachers at the school were usually aged between 22 and 45. In 1865 there were five regular assistant masters who taught the upper school and two mistresses for the lower school. Unfortunately the questioning of the Taunton Commissioners concentrated upon the masters rather than the mistresses, so the latter remain rather shadowy figures. Although graduates of Oxford and Cambridge were employed at the Denmark Hill

Grammar School, it appears that they were not in the majority: There was but one Cambridge graduate on the staff in 1865. Nor had a clergyman ever been employed as a master. Nevertheless, although Mason himself was a Nonconformist, in 1865 all five assistant masters were members of the Church of England. Four of the five assistant masters (all bachelors) were resident, the fifth, the senior assistant master who taught mathematics, was married and nonresident. His salary was £130 per annum. That of the lowest paid assistant was £80 per annum but he as well as all resident staff received free board and lodging in return for supervisory duties.

Some assistant masters including those at Denmark Hill could and did make extra income by private teaching and by writing. Mason's personal opinion however was that this would be difficult, for the job of an assistant was laborious and irksome in the extreme, and one which really able men would only take up as a short-term occupation. Masters at the Denmark Hill Grammar School had to teach for 28 hours a week and to supervise boys who were preparing lessons for a further four, in addition to their own preparation and marking. Though they might have overall responsibility for a particular class, essentially they were engaged to teach a subject or group of subjects. Resident masters, moreover, were required to undertake general supervisory duties for two days per week. Such duties were not always conducive to the maintenance of a lively and inquiring mind, and many of those who entered permanently upon the role of assistant master, Mason believed, tended "to vegetate in an extremely unprogressive condition."[37] Indeed Mason himself confessed that "I must say there is hardly any calling in life which I myself should be so slow to accept as that of an assistant master in a school."[38] In addition to its full-time masters and mistresses, the Denmark Hill Grammar School also had visiting teachers. Although one of the full-time masters taught French and some German, a French lady attended twice a week to teach French to the junior school, while another mistress was employed three days a week to teach music. Visiting masters included two music teachers, one for the piano and another for singing, and one to teach drill.

Mason used two methods to oversee the work of his assistants. The first was to take each class himself at least once a week for a "repetition" lesson; the second was to inspect the exercise books of one class each day. The senior school was organized into six classes, the junior into two, and boys proceeded from one to another according to merit. A daily record was kept as to progress, and official places in class were determined monthly. Formal examinations took place twice a year. Boys generally moved up a class after the summer holidays.

The curriculum of the Denmark Hill Grammar School reflected a most interesting amalgam of tradition and of parental and pupil choices. Most but not all of the boys learned Latin; a few of the older ones learned Greek. Parents were not usually keen that their sons should study the Classics. "As a general rule," Mason observed, "it is a struggle on my part to get Latin at least learnt. . . . They accept it . . . as a sort of inevitable necessity."[39] Indeed, he judged that were the school to abandon Latin altogether, "I doubt if I should have a dozen remonstrances from the parents of pupils."[40] Mason, who himself taught Classics to the top class, justified the study of Latin as a mental training, "for the general development of the boys' faculties, and as enabling them to understand their own language properly."[41]

At the heart of the Denmark Hill curriculum lay arithmetic and mathematics (which included algebra and Euclid), English grammar and composition, and modern languages. All pupils took at least one foreign language, either French or German; many took both. Invariably they began with French, for which provision was made in the junior school. This was the core curriculum for which parents of the middling classes, many of them from industrial and commercial backgrounds themselves, were prepared to pay substantial fees. The emphasis upon modern languages, which Mason personally regarded as inferior to Latin for the purpose of training the young mind, came from the parents. Mason confirmed that given the background of many of his pupils and their probable future careers, "a knowledge of either French or German I consider of great importance; because, with reference to business, it seems to be universally demanded now-a-days."[42] Other subjects on the

Denmark Hill timetable included history, geography, mechanics, natural philosophy and chemistry. This last subject, which Mason taught himself, was approached both by lectures and by practical work in a laboratory. There was also a small observatory and telescopes for the pursuit of astronomy, and an occasional class in surveying. Bookkeeping was taught only at the insistence of parents; Mason believed a sound knowledge of the principles and application of arithmetic to be of greater importance for the schoolboy mind. Music was a popular subject, and there were many opportunities for sport: football in the winter and cricket and fives in the summer. There was a large shed in the playground for use in wet weather.

In common with many public schools, the Denmark Hill Grammar School appreciated the value of physical exercise. In the summer in addition to drill, Wednesday and Saturday afternoons were given to cricket, and on other days play was allowed for an hour before lunch, from half-past four until six, and from half-past six until a quarter past seven. Additionally, in the summer months boys went swimming twice a week in baths attached to the nearby canal. Camberwell was healthy, the site and surroundings of the school were healthy, schoolrooms and bedrooms were healthy, the curriculum allowed for substantial healthy exercise. Small wonder that Denmark Hill was not subject to those epidemics which caused the temporary closure of so many schools of the period. Mason could assure the Taunton Commissioners that "Our boys are unusually healthy."[43]

The curriculum of Denmark Hill was not merely a compromise between the traditional and the new, the Classical and the modern, it was also a compromise between the elementary and the secondary. Thus a boy who entered the lower of the two classes in the junior school would begin with English subjects (reading, spelling, writing), elementary arithmetic, geography and English history, a curriculum very similar to that of a good National or British Society school. In the upper class, however, while the elementary curriculum continued, elements of the modern and Classical curricula appeared, as all boys would begin to study French, and some would start to study Latin. What of religious instruction, which played a central role in so many nineteenth-century schools? Prayers were said morning and evening, and there was a daily scripture lesson. Sunday was a solemn day but no doctrinal instruction was ever given. On Sundays boys attended the church or chapel of their choosing for both morning and evening service. Boys preparing for confirmation in the Anglican Church would attend the evening classes of a local clergyman. Gentle discipline and ordered purposefulness were the hallmarks of a good private school. Mason painted an ideal picture of the Denmark Hill Grammar schoolboys, escorted each evening by masters upstairs to their small dormitories or single bedrooms in the old house, where all would observe five minutes silence, kneel down and reverently say their prayers. No fagging (younger boys acting as servants for their seniors) was permitted, nor was there any prefect system, as emerged in the public schools. Nor did the top class enjoy any special privileges, indeed Mason's penchant for promoting according to ability meant that the youngest boy in the top class was only 13 years old. Although all boys were encouraged to exert a good influence, especially over those younger than themselves, the major responsibility for good order, outside the classroom as well as in, remained with the staff. In accordance with the spirit of the private (as distinct from the public) school, at Denmark Hill there was "a master with the boys at all times of the day."[44] Masters were not allowed to inflict any form of corporal punishment whatsoever, not even "a box on the ears."[45] Mason reserved this right to himself but said that he used it "very rarely. Frequently for months together I never have occasion to touch a boy."[46]

Textbook Writer

One final dimension of Joseph Payne's period at Denmark Hill should be mentioned here—his emergence as an author of textbooks. Payne's interests as a teacher and writer, coupled with his relatively straightened circumstances and dependent position, naturally led him to the writing of books for use in schools. Not only were the books successful in scholarly and financial terms, they also provided him with further status and reputation in discussions and correspondence with a variety of educationists and authors. Thus in 1841, he was in earnest exchange with Alexander Allen, master of the Madras House Grammar School in Hackney, about the use at the Denmark Hill Grammar School of some of Allen's publications, notably the *Constructive Greek Exercises* (1839), and *A New Latin Delectus* (1840).[47] In 1845 Payne sent a copy of his latest volume of collected poems to James Silk Buckingham, social reformer, journalist, lecturer and publisher of travel books, for the library of the British and Foreign Institute in London's Hanover Square, which had been founded some two years earlier, largely as a result of Buckingham's exertions.[48] Another correspondent on the subject of (possibly mislaid) books was James Kay Shuttleworth, the first secretary to the Committee of the Privy Council on Education.[49]

Select Poetry for Children, first published in 1839, was a simple collection of poems suitable for children. In addition to the poems themselves, Payne provided brief explanatory notes. The collection, as was customary at that time, was aimed at both "schools and families," and was intended for children between six and 12 years of age. Payne believed that an early acquaintance with poetry would develop taste and moral character, exercise and strengthen the memory, and cultivate "the graces of elocution." In the preface he declared that if the book were to be successful he intended to produce a sequel entitled *Select Poetry for Youth*. The book was indeed successful and in 1845 the sequel duly appeared, though by then its notional title had been changed to *Studies in English Poetry*.

Select Poetry for Children, which was published by Rolfe and Fletcher in Cornhill, and priced at 2s. 6d. cloth and 3s. gilt-edged, soon proved to be a runaway bestseller. It was widely and enthusiastically reviewed as the following selection indicates.[50]

> "A very nice little volume, containing a charming collection of poetry" *Spectator*
>
> "A rich selection of pieces" *Congregational Magazine*
>
> "A very pleasing and suitable selection" *Westminster Review*

"No school or nursery, mother or teacher, ought to be without it" *Manchester Chronicle*

"A nice little book" *Tait's Magazine*

"A very good selection . . . judiciously arranged" *Patriot*

"It is really a treat to see anything so simply good as this little volume before us" *Metropolitan Magazine*

"The selection . . . reflects great credit upon his judgement and tact as a caterer for children" *Sunday School Teachers Magazine*

"This selection displays taste and judgement" *Wesleyan Chronicle*

"Well adapted to secure the attention and deeply to interest the juvenile reader" *Eclectic Review*

"An excellent selection" *Christian Witness*

Two further editions were produced while Payne was still at Denmark Hill, and the work remained in use throughout the remainder of the nineteenth century. The fourth edition of 1845, and the first produced after Payne's move to Leatherhead, contained some substantial revisions. The number of pages was increased from 276 to 310. New poems were added, including the previously unpublished *William Tell* by J. H. Gurney. In 1874, two years before his death, Payne produced a final revision and enlargement. Additions included poems by Browning, Kingsley and Tennyson, in the 342 pages of the eighteenth edition.

Payne attributed the success of *Select Poetry for Children* to the fact that children have an instinct for the intellectual and beautiful, prefer what is above rather than below the level of their understanding, and "reject what it merely childish."[51] Payne argued, and stated that in so doing he drew upon experience rather than theory, that children had more ability "to think, and to enter into the thoughts of others, than is usually entertained."[52] There is no doubt that towards the end of his life, as the preface to the 1874 edition showed, Payne found it gratifying to believe and to some extent to know, that many thousands of children had found delight in his collection.

Studies in English Poetry was advertised on its title page as a "textbook for the higher classes in schools and as an introduction to the study of English literature." It was divided into two parts: the first miscellaneous poems and extracts; the second a chronological selection of poems and extracts from Chaucer to Burns. Payne's purpose here was to provide a history of the English language, a theme in which he was to take a particular interest. Accordingly brief biographies of the authors, and explanatory and critical notes on their works, were also included. This meant that *Studies in English Poetry* was more didactic and substantial than its predecessor. It was not, however, as successful. In 1859 when a revised third edition which ran to 466 pages was published, *Select Poetry for Children* had reached its thirteenth edition. This might have been because the *Studies* was aimed at the school, rather than at the school and domestic markets. Nevertheless, many copies were sold. There were complimentary reviews in such journals as the *Baptist Magazine, British Quarterly Review, Christian Witness, Eclectic Review, Tait's Magazine, The Student, Watchman* and *Youth's Magazine*.[53] Five years after Payne's death demand was still high, and a revised eighth edition was published in 1881.

The Death of John Dyer

Though there were many successes and joys for Joseph and Eliza during their life together in Camberwell since 1837, in 1841 tragedy struck in a very public way with the death of John Dyer. John Dyer was not an original or a profound thinker. He was cautious, methodical and meticulous, a man of duty and of stern Christian devotion. He refused to have his portrait painted and, though awarded a doctorate by a reputable American university, refused to use the title.[54] He was humourless, and "in his anxiety to discountenance sin, he would unnecessarily frown on the innocent gaieties of youth and administer reproof in a tone of severity disproportionate to the fault."[55] He was a gloomy man. Edward Steane euphemistically declared that he was possessed of an "unusual seriousness . . . [which] . . . connected as this was with a certain want of freedom in social intercourse, gave him the appearance of reserve." John Dyer was a severe rather than a joyous Christian, his character was invested "with those attributes which show rather how awful goodness is than how

lovely . . . rather disposed to pensiveness than hilarity."[56] One of
the most distinctive features of his diaries was that at the end of
each of the slim black volumes, under the heading "Necrology,"
he set down a list of his friends and acquaintances who had died
during the year, with a brief comment upon their lives. Two
extracts from the 1837 diary give a flavour of this morbid
collection:

> In her 97th year *Mrs Fletcher*, mother of our friend Joseph
> Fletcher Esq. of Tottenham. She had long been reduced to
> a state of second childhood. *Anne*, only daughter of good
> friend *Freeman* of Bow, of consumption, about 23 or 4. She
> was at school for some time at Battersea, but I have seen
> little of her since.[57]

What finally drove John Dyer to take his own life is not
clear. For years he had been considerably overworked, and
members of the committee of the Baptist Missionary Society
were well aware that some assistance was required. The problem
was that while Dyer himself sought subordinate, secretarial help,
the committee members were keen to appoint a joint secretary
and to effect a distribution of the work between the two. The
most natural division would have been between the Society's
foreign and domestic business. Eventually a compromise was
reached, and at the annual meeting at Exeter Hall on 30 April
1840 an announcement was made that the youthful Joseph
Angus was appointed as cosecretary. Dyer, however, was to be
referred to as the "senior" and Angus as the "junior" secretary.[58]

In the early days of July 1841 John Dyer's mental state was
giving increasing cause for concern. On 9 July he collapsed in his
office, and though he insisted on returning to Fen Court for the
committee meeting of 15 July was persuaded not to participate
but to remain in another room. Mary and he were then living in
Sydenham, together with his youngest son Henry. For a week
John Dyer was attended daily by John Gay, a surgeon and family
friend, who observed his changing moods which oscillated
between rationality and delusion. Gay ordered leeches to be
applied to Dyer's head, pronounced him much better on
Tuesday, 20 July, and thus did not visit on the succeeding day
when Henry Dyer described his father as being "much excited"
and "walking from room to room in a restless manner."[59] Mary

Dyer suspected that her husband might try to commit suicide, a suspicion which led her to remove and hide his razor and other sharp implements. As a further precaution, since Gay had not prescribed a keeper, Henry volunteered to sleep in the same room as his father, which he did on the night of Wednesday, 21 July. At seven the next morning Henry was awakened by the cries of Jane Marshall, one of the servants, who had found John Dyer, clad only in his nightshirt, drowned in a water cistern which stood in an archway at the back of the house. Henry Dyer rushed downstairs. Although his father's legs were protruding from the cistern, he had to enlist the aid of a passing coalman, Joseph Hall, to get the body out.

These melancholy details emerged at the inquest held on the afternoon of 23 July at the Greyhound Inn, Sydenham, in a room which, ironically enough, John Dyer had himself booked for a meeting of the Religious Tract Society at that very time. Henry Dyer, Jane Marshall, Joseph Hall and John Gay appeared as witnesses. Henry attributed his father's state of mind "to anxiety, he having been extensively engaged in public business for the last month." The jury returned a verdict "that the deceased gentleman destroyed himself, being in a state of temporary insanity." The suicide of so prominent a Baptist by drowning naturally attracted newspaper attention: *The Times* carried reports of the inquest on both 24 and 26 July. F. A. Cox, the historian of the Baptist Missionary Society, who some 35 years before had heard Dyer's first sermon as a minister, gave the graveside oration at the burial ground in Little Wild Street. His poignant words included one observation particularly applicable to Eliza and Joseph, namely that "Many of us, that filled the relation of children lately, have now only to fill that of parents."[60]

NOTES

1. Charles Stanford, *A Memorial of the Rev. Edward Steane, D.D.* (London, 1882), p. 21.

2. H. J. Dyos, *Victorian Suburb: A Study of the Growth of Camberwell* (Leicester, 1961), p. 29.

3. *Ibid.*, p. 37.

4. *Ibid.*, p. 31.

5. *Ibid.*, pp. 38–9.

6. *Ibid.*, p. 39.

7. *Ibid.*, pp. 66–7.

8. *Ibid.*, pp. 72–3.

9. *Ibid.*, p. 55.

10. Thomas Walter Laqueur, *Religion and Respectability: Sunday Schools and Working-Class Culture, 1780–1850* (New Haven, 1976), p. 44.

11. See *Taunton Report*, i, p. 229 for a summary of the strengths and weaknesses of private schools.

12. John Roach, *A History of Secondary Education in England, 1800–1870* (London, 1986), p. 105.

13. For Wilson's see D. H. Allport, *A Short History of Wilson's Grammar School* (London, 1951).

14. Blanch, *Camberwell*, p. 251.

15. Margaret Bryant, *The London Experience of Secondary Education* (London, 1986), p. 255.

16. Blanch, *Camberwell*, p. 254.

17. *Taunton Report*, x, p. 108.

18. Blanch, *Camberwell*, p. 307, stated that it stood on the west side of The Grove, but contemporary maps placed it on the east side.

19. Dyos, *Victorian Suburb*, p. 165,

20. In 1851 it was occupied by a musical instrument maker, Thomas Key, his wife Amy, and five children aged between 27 and 18. The birthplaces of these children suggest that the Keys had previously lived at Charing Cross and in Camberwell New Road.

21. Blanch, *Camberwell*, p. 265.

22. Census Enumerators' Returns, 1851; Blanch, *Camberwell*, p. 266.

23. Blanch, *Camberwell*, p. 308. Details of the house are to be found in Blanch, *Camberwell*, pp. 307–10.

24. *Taunton Report*, iv, p. 348.

25. Blanch, *Camberwell*, p. 309.

26. *Taunton Report*, iv, p. 352.

27. *Taunton Report*, iv, pp. 351–2.

28. Olive M. Walker, *A Tour of Camberwell* (London, 1954), p. 108.

29. Blanch, *Camberwell*, p. 310.

30. *Taunton Report*, iv, p. 663.

31. *Ibid.*, p. 663. There is no firm evidence on Weymouth, but there was a "Mr Weymouth" living in The Mansion in 1845 or 1846, and in 1848 the *Educational Times* published a series of letters on such diverse topics as the Classics, physical exercise and etymology, from "R. F. W.," a London graduate, resident in Leatherhead. An R. F. Weymouth was recorded as master of the Portland Grammar School, Plymouth in 1849, *Educational Times* III, 27 (December 1849), p. 69.

32. *Taunton Report*, iv, p. 358.

33. *Ibid.*, p. 345.

34. *Ibid.*, p. 347.

35. *Ibid.*, p. 332.

36. *Ibid.*, p. 333.

37. *Ibid.*, p. 343.

38. *Ibid.*, p. 342.

39. *Ibid.*, p. 336.

40. *Ibid.*, p. 337.

41. *Ibid.*, p. 340.

42. *Ibid.*, p. 340.

43. *Ibid.*, p. 352.

44. *Ibid.*, p. 350.

45. *Ibid.*, p. 349.

46. *Ibid.*, p. 349.

47. Allen to Payne, 7 June 1841, Allen to Payne, undated, Author's Collection.

48. Buckingham to Payne, 23 April 1845, Author's Collection.

49. Kay Shuttleworth to Payne, 10 April and 31 May (1843?), Author's Collection.

50. These reviews were included, with others, at the back of the fourth edition of *Studies in English Poetry*, published in 1859. By then *Select Poetry for Children* had reached its thirteenth edition.

51. Preface to the eighteenth edition, 1874, p. ix.

52. *Ibid.*, pp. ix-x.

53. Included in *Select Poetry for Children* (London, 13th edition 1858).

54. Ernest A. Payne, *First Generation*, p. 125.

55. Steane, *A Sermon*, p. 24.

56. *Ibid.*, p. 24.

57. John Dyer's diary, 1837, 1/4/1C, Angus Library, Regent's Park College, Oxford.

58. Cox, *History of the Baptist Missionary Society*, II, p. 380; Ernest A. Payne, *The Great Succession*, p. 14.

59. *The Times*, 24 July 1841, carried a long account of the inquest. See also Stanley, *Baptist Missionary Society*, p. 212.

60. Steane, *A Sermon*, p. 40.

CHAPTER THREE

From Leatherhead to Kildare Gardens

Proprietor

In the 1820s at Gowring's school in the New Kent Road, Joseph Payne was an assistant master. At that time he had been largely self-taught, had no formal qualifications and few prospects. It was the publication of the pamphlet on Jacotot which, in the 1830s, made it possible for him to become first a tutor and then a partner, albeit a junior partner, in the school at Denmark Hill. Study of Jacotot, no doubt, convinced him of the importance of the will in human achievement. Neither as an assistant nor as a junior partner was Payne fully satisfied with his role. He was never prepared to vegetate. To the end of his life his was an active spirit.

Accordingly, in the 1840s he determined to establish his own school, as sole proprietor and headmaster. Although as yet precise evidence is lacking, there were probably two factors which influenced his decision to leave the Denmark Hill Grammar School in 1844. The first was his growing family. John Burnell Payne was born on 24 October 1838, a mere ten months after his parents' marriage; Joseph Frank on 10 January 1840; and Mary Eliza came next on 31 March 1842. Like her two elder brothers Mary was born at Grove Hill House in Camberwell. William Payne was to be born on 4 March 1845 at Leatherhead, some three months after his parents had moved their young family there. Assistant masters in boys' private and public schools were invariably single men. Payne was more than a mere assistant at Denmark Hill, but he was not the sole proprietor. It was David Fletcher to whom the house had been leased and it was David Fletcher and his family who actually lived on the premises. A second factor might well have been the success of *Select Poetry for Children*. Capital was needed to establish a new school. No clear indication of the source of Payne's finance has yet been found, but it seems likely that the success of one textbook and the prospect of another made a significant contribution towards strengthening his financial position and prospects.

Leatherhead

In the 1840s Leatherhead, some 18 miles to the south of London in the county of Surrey, was a large, self-contained village which was in the process of becoming a small country town. In 1841 there were a mere 1,740 inhabitants. This figure had increased to 2,042 by the next Census in 1851, but in 1861 shortly before Payne left it stood only at 2,079. Thus, unlike Camberwell, Leatherhead would retain its rural nature throughout the nineteenth century and beyond. There were many substantial properties in the vicinity and many wealthy residents: the Bethunes of Thorncroft Manor, the Boultons of Givons Grove and the Corries of Vale Lodge. In 1841 apart from servants agricultural workers formed by far the largest single group of employees. Local trades included coachbuilders, saddle and harness makers, tanners and shoemakers, brick and tile makers, and brewers.[1] Some of these occupations reflected Leatherhead's position at an important crossroads. Here the east-west route from Croydon to Guildford crossed the highly unpredictable River Mole by means of a brick bridge of 14 arches, and was itself traversed by the main coaching route from London to Bognor and Worthing on the Sussex coast. In the 1830s and 1840s some eight public coaches per day passed along Leatherhead's turnpiked roads. By the early 1850s, however, omnibuses were replacing coaches. The railway reached nearby Epsom in 1847 and was extended to Leatherhead in 1859. Though Leatherhead was then connected directly both to London Bridge and to Waterloo, not until 1867 was the line extended southwards to Dorking and Horsham.

Why did the Paynes choose Leatherhead? It was and remains a most pleasant residential location. It is possible that Joseph and Eliza had come to know it through John Dyer, who would have travelled via Leatherhead on his visits to Mary Jackson at Dorking. Perhaps it was simply the result of one or more country excursions into the extrametropolitan part of a county in which they already lived. Another possible connection was the family of de Crespigny, who lived in Champion Lodge adjacent to the Denmark Hill School, and who for a time owned The Mansion in Leatherhead. Perhaps it was specifically because in 1844 the ownership of The Mansion, one of Leatherhead's finest houses, passed to Nathaniel Bland of Randalls Park who was seeking a tenant.

One other feature of Leatherhead might have been important. In the 1840s there appears to have been neither a grammar school nor any substantial boys' private school in the area. In 1791 Thomas Hopkins kept an "Academy for Young Gentlemen" in Leatherhead, while a day school for boys run by Thomas Hill was referred to in directories of 1832 and 1838. From 1838 Emmanuel Marter kept a boys' boarding school, but this could not have been very successful, for in 1851 he was manager of a brick and tile works and subsequently became chairman of the Leatherhead Gas Company.[2] Thus in its day, the Mansion Grammar School was by far the most prestigious and important school in Leatherhead and the surrounding area. Not until 1872 did St. John's School, which had been started in 1851 by Ashby Haslewood, Vicar of St. Mark's Church in St. John's Wood, London, arrive in Leatherhead. This school for the sons of clergy came with 65 boys. By the end of the century there were some 300.[3] Other Leatherhead boys' schools of the 1870s were the Leatherhead Road Boarding School, a preparatory school which still exists as Downsend School, and the Surrey House School in Church Street, almost directly opposite The Mansion, which possibly was started to cater to boys from the Mansion Grammar School when it closed around 1878. The headmaster of Surrey House, which took 28 boarders, was George Alcock. In 1893 Surrey House was closed and he opened a new school, Cameron House, in the premises next door. Such developments, however, lay in the future. In 1845 when the Paynes moved to

Leatherhead the most prominent boys' school for some miles around would be that at The Mansion.

The Mansion

The word "Mansion" was derived not from the house itself, but from the term "minchin," the Middle-English word for nun. The land on which The Mansion stood was bounded by Bridge Street to the north, Church Street to the east, Vicarage Lane to the south and by the River Mole to the west. In 1366 some 40 acres of land between the River Mole and the Leatherhead to Dorking Road were granted to the Prioress and Convent of Kilburn by one Roger de Apperdele, from which date it was known as the manor of Minchin. Five years after the dissolution of the convent in 1536, the manor was granted to Thomas Stydolf of Mickleham.[4] F. B. Benger has suggested that in the later sixteenth century, Edmund Tylney, Master of the Revels to Elizabeth I, lived at The Mansion and entertained the Queen there in 1591.[5] What is certain is that the property passed into the possession of the Howard family. In 1642 Tylney's cousin, Charles Howard, second Earl of Nottingham, third Baron Howard of Effingham (a son of the admiral who fought the Spanish Armada) and Lord Lieutenant of Surrey, called a meeting at The Mansion to commit the county to the Parliamentary cause. Though Howard died at The Mansion in the same year, his widow continued to live there until her death in 1651. The old house, however, which survived the Civil War and the incursion of a Royalist troop in 1643, was demolished some time in the early eighteenth century. The present house which Payne was to occupy in 1845 was almost certainly built in 1739. In 1786 William Wade, an illegitimate son of Field Marshal General George Wade, best known for his exploits in pacifying and disarming the Scottish clans and building military roads in the Highlands, became sole owner of The Mansion. From 1769 Wade had achieved some fame, notoriety indeed, as the master of ceremonies at both Bath and Brighton, though he was forced to leave the former in 1777. Wade died at his Brighton home in 1810, and The Mansion subsequently passed to one of his daughters, Emilia, wife of

Philip Champion de Crespigny. In the 1830s a Colonel W. H. Spicer owned The Mansion and died there in 1841. In 1844 it was purchased at auction by Nathaniel Bland and leased to Payne.

The house was broad and substantial and built in Flemish bond of warm red brick. With large windows, it stood in a prominent position within Leatherhead. On the other side of Church Street on the road running southwards to Dorking was the parish church of St. Mary and St. Nicholas. To the front of the house was a high brick wall which continued along Vicarage Lane and where evidence of an earlier flint wall, part of the original house perhaps, is still visible. To the rear pleasant grounds, laid out by Hamilton of Pain's Hill, sloped down to the River Mole. Unlike the house which accommodated the Denmark Hill Grammar School, The Mansion still stands. In 1950 it was purchased by the Surrey County Council and today is best known as the seat of the Leatherhead branch of the County Library. Although the area to the north of The Mansion has been built upon (Minchin Close perpetuates the original connection), to proceed southwards along Church Street is to pass quickly into Green Belt fields and countryside, and to enjoy the views westwards to Fetcham Downs and southwards towards Box Hill, which the Paynes and their pupils would have experienced. The size and quality of the house and its attractive setting were emphasized in the school stationery. One surviving sheet shows a fine engraving of the rear of the school, with a broad path leading down to the tree-lined banks of the Mole and bearing the legend, "The Grammar School from the Island."[6]

The School

Joseph Payne continued at Denmark Hill until December 1844. On 14 December and 4, 11, 18 January 1845, he placed substantial advertisements on the front page of the local newspaper, the *Sussex Agricultural Express*, a paper which also covered the counties of Surrey and Kent. The school would open on Wednesday, 29 January 1845. Prospectuses were available from Mr Thompson, Chemist, Leatherhead; from Messrs Dyer, 24, Paternoster Row, London; or from Payne himself, who in

December was still resident at Grove Hill House in Camberwell. Fees would be high, from 40 to 60 guineas per year according to age, inclusive of minor extras. The preparatory department, for boys aged nine or less, would be under the direct superintendence of Eliza Payne. As the founder of a new school Joseph Payne had no formal qualifications to offer. He never obtained a university degree, nor was he in holy orders. At that date there was no recognized form of training for teaching in secondary schools. His advertisements, therefore, drew attention to

> an experience of twenty years in the work of education seconded by the careful study of the best authors on the subject, and an earnest zeal and respect for his profession.

The curriculum would be broad and the moral tone secure. The new headmaster assured parents that

> he advocates no exclusive system, but aims to adopt the most valuable features of all, combining with the solid instruction of the Old Grammar School a liberal infusion of sound mathematical and scientific knowledge.... To moral discipline Mr Payne attaches great value, and will endeavour by all the arrangements of the family, as well as of the school, to cultivate a high tone of principle and feeling among his pupils.[7]

Whatever misgivings the Paynes might have felt about their new venture, by common consent the Mansion Grammar School (sometimes referred to as the Mansion School the Mansion House School and even the Mansion House Grammar School) was a considerable success. In his obituary of Payne Charles Mason declared of the Leatherhead period that: "Here he laboured with great energy and success for about eighteen years, his school taking rank as one of the very first private schools in this country."[8] Pupils from the school were prominent in the pass lists of external examinations, particularly those of the University of Oxford, and in 1865 Payne was chosen to give evidence to the Taunton Commission. The 21 volumes of the report of this Commission provide a wealth of information about mid-nineteenth-century secondary schooling. Indeed the mass of data has been called "the most complete sociological information pertaining to education ever assembled in this country."[9] The evidence which Payne presented on 14 June 1865 remains the most important single source about the school, although it must be viewed with caution as possibly painting an overcomplimentary picture.[10]

Another useful source is the Census of 1851 which details all those resident on the Census day, together with their occupations, ages and places of birth. It shows that on the night of 30 March of that year in addition to the Payne family, one governess, three assistant masters and eight servants—all unmarried—were in residence at The Mansion. Seven were females: a cook, a parlour maid, two house maids, a nurse, a kitchen maid and a laundry maid. There was one groom. It is possible that there were other nonresident servants. These catered to the needs of 51 resident pupils (all boys) and possibly some day scholars as well. In his evidence to Taunton, Payne said that the average number of boys was "about 70."[11] Of the three assistant masters Joseph Wilson, aged 38, the eldest son of a farmer from Donegal, taught mathematics and had graduated in 1840 from the University of Glasgow.[12] A second Irishman and farmer's son was Wyndham Armstrong, aged 27, born in Limerick, and educated at Dungannon School and Trinity College, Dublin. A letter of recommendation from his tutor, James Henthorn Todd, the Regius Professor of Hebrew, described Armstrong as being "an excellent Classical scholar, of mild and gentleman-like manners" who, though short of funds, had supported himself during his studies by taking pupils and "has therefore had considerable experience as a teacher and is of diligent and steady habits."[13] Armstrong taught Classics, as did Robert Ibbs, aged 23, a nongraduate who came from Kimbolton in Huntingdon. Ibbs was successful in the teachers' examinations of the College of Preceptors, and was later to join Payne as a member of its Council. Understandably Payne did not require his masters to be university graduates: his principal concern was their "aptitude for teaching."[14] On Payne's retirement in 1863 Wilson and Ibbs became joint proprietors of the school. At the time of the 1871 Census, Ibbs, who by then had a wife, five daughters and a son, was listed as head of the household and the bachelor Wilson as his partner. Wilson left Leatherhead in 1874 and in the following year moved to south London as a master at the Blackheath School for the Sons of Missionaries. He retired from that post in 1880 and died on 1 March 1902.[15] In his evidence to Taunton Payne said that he paid his staff £150, £110, £90 and £80 per annum, exclusive of board and lodging, but there is no evidence as to the salaries paid specifically to Wilson, Armstrong and Ibbs.

Of the 51 pupils listed in 1851, there was one aged 16, nine of 15, eight of 14, ten of 13, twelve of 12, seven of 11, two of 10 and two of 9. In his evidence to Taunton Payne said that the school was divided into three sections. Boys came to the junior department at age eight or nine. Those in the next grade, aged 11 to 15, paid 60 guineas, and those who entered after 15, 70 guineas per annum. Although Payne stated that some boys stayed until age 18, and it is possible that in 1851 the relative newness of the school meant that there was a preponderance of younger boys, in none of the 1851, 1861 or 1871 Censuses was any pupil recorded above the age of 16. In 1871, 46 resident pupils were listed: their ages ranged from eight to 16. In 1872 a notice about the school, printed in the well-known handbook *Our Schools and Colleges*, indicated that it catered to 65 pupils, nearly all boarders, between the ages of 8 and 17, with fees of 40 to 60 guineas per year. The same publication showed the Denmark Hill Grammar School charging an identical range of fees for its 50 or so boarders, but with a further 50 day pupils also in attendance.[16]

The Census of 1861 was doubtless taken during the Easter vacation, as indicated by the presence of the Paynes' two elder sons, John Burnell, then a student at Trinity College, Cambridge; and Joseph Frank, who was at Magdalen College, Oxford; as well as their daughter Mary Eliza and youngest son William. No resident masters were recorded and only a dozen pupils, although there were 11 servants. Two other family members present were Eliza's 12–year-old nephew, Samuel Dyer, who might well have been a pupil at the school, and a cousin, also Eliza, who had been born on 25 July 1815 in far-off Samarang in Java, the daughter of intrepid Baptist missionary parents, Thomas and Eliza Trowt.[17]

The pupils who attended the Mansion Grammar School must have come from wealthy families. Though there were some sons of shopkeepers, Payne himself categorized the fathers as being in the main "merchants, professional men and private gentlemen."[18] It is interesting that Payne did not mention parents with a literary, scientific or artistic bent. One such was the artist, author and inventor Isaac Taylor. Between 1848 and 1852 Payne engaged in a lengthy correspondence over nonpayment of bills with the impecunious and voluminous Taylor, who lived at Stanford Rivers in Essex and who in 1838 had himself written a book entitled *Home Education*.[19] Taylor had 11 children, but no pupil of that name was listed in the Census of the Mansion in 1851. Though Taylor's life was characterized by a series of financial disasters, his was by no means an isolated case, for the collection of outstanding debts was a substantial item in the work of most private school principals. No doubt many of the boys proceeded to business and commercial occupations, but Payne stated that the Mansion Grammar School provided "A classical education for the most part" (a third of the boys learned Greek as well as Latin), and that many boys subsequently went on to universities.[20] Sons of Anglicans and Protestant Dissenters were admitted, but there appear to have been neither Roman Catholics nor Jews, though whether by chance or design is not clear. Daily religious education was based directly upon the Bible; no catechism or other doctrinal formulary was employed. As at Denmark Hill, on Sundays all boys were required to attend the church or chapel of their choosing, and some pupils paid pew rents in the parish church.[21]

The ethos of the Payne household, however, and possibly of the school, as at Denmark Hill in Payne's day, was Independent. Evidence on this point comes from the records of the Leatherhead Congregational Church.[22] It would appear that shortly after they arrived in Leatherhead Joseph and Eliza, who were listed as "Mr and Mrs Payne from churches in Camberwell," were received into membership. Payne became one of the 13 trustees of the Church, which had a substantial new building capable of seating 250. In May 1846 he was appointed deacon (a lay office), while a list of Church members from the following year was headed by the names of "Mr and Mrs Payne of The Mansion." In addition to members of the Payne family, servants and pupils of The Mansion also attended the Leatherhead Congregational Church. Sarah Heffer, the cook, and Jemima Line, the nurse, were among the former category. Members of the teaching staff also followed the headmaster to his place of worship. In 1845 or 1846 a "Mr Weymouth" of The Mansion was received into the Church, and Joseph Wilson was to occupy a most prominent position. When in August 1863 the Paynes were about to leave Leatherhead, a "Mr Wilson" was unanimously elected in his place. This was probably Joseph Wilson, although an entry for 1860 in the Church Record Book suggests that Joseph Wilson left Leatherhead at the end of that year to enter the ministry of the Irish Presbyterian Church. Certainly Joseph Wilson was still teaching at the Mansion in 1871, and his connections with the Leatherhead Congregational Church continued even after he left the school and the area. In December 1876, when the Church revised its trust deed of 27 January 1845, Wilson, then teaching at the Blackheath School for the Sons of Missionaries, was appointed one of 12 new trustees. Another of the trustees of 1876 was the headmaster of the Blackheath School, Rev. Edward Waite,[23] who had been the minister of the Leatherhead Congregational Church from 1852 to 1865. In 1852 it was Joseph Payne and his two fellow deacons who wrote to Waite inviting him to become minister. At least one of the Waite children, Edward Wilkins Waite, born in 1854, who subsequently became a well-known painter, attended the Mansion, although his father's stipend was never more than £150 per annum.

Although Waite and Wilson proceeded to the Blackheath School for the Sons of Missionaries, and John Dyer had been secretary to the Baptist Missionary Society, the extent to which the Mansion Grammar School itself had a missionary connection is not clear. Certainly the only boy recorded in the 1851 Census as having been born overseas, in Macao in China, was the 11-year-old Benjamin Stephen Hobson, the son of Dr Benjamin Hobson, an eminent medical missionary. Hobson left the Mansion in 1855 and rejoined his parents in China in 1857.[24] The 1871 Census included five pupils who were not British-born. There were three boys named Harris, presumably brothers, who had all been born in India, one Chinese-born, Russell Endicott, and a David White, born in British Guiana.

As to the secular curriculum, lessons were timetabled for a formidable 42 hours per week. Payne reported to the Taunton Commission that of this total, Classics occupied 43 percent, mathematics 30 percent, French and German 14 percent, history and geography 10 percent, spelling 2 percent, and reading 1 percent. Such precise calculations, however, seemed to be at odds with other evidence which indicated that the curriculum varied considerably according to the ages and interests of the boys. For example, although all pupils took Latin and French, Greek and German were optional, a situation which to a considerable degree mirrored that of Denmark Hill. With respect to the learning of Latin, however, Payne, unlike Mason, assured Lord Taunton that parents of boys at his school did not generally have "an indisposition to their sons being taught Latin."[25]

In addition to the curriculum as reported to Taunton, there were other "subsidiary" subjects, including science. Payne himself had a longstanding interest in science, and the school had a chemistry laboratory which could manage seven or eight pupils at a time. A visiting teacher from London was engaged to give practical chemistry classes in the evenings, for which parents paid an extra fee. These classes were only open to older pupils. No extra charge was made for the more orthodox and bookish science teaching which was required for pupils preparing for the matriculation examinations of the University of London. Some indication of Payne's flexibility in curriculum matters was given by his statement that he allowed some boys, sons of gentlemen and farmers, to give up Latin a year or two before the end of their time at the Mansion and to devote more time to science with particular reference to its agricultural application. Payne's emphasis upon chemistry, and particularly upon practical chemistry in a laboratory, stemmed from his belief that it was both a valuable discipline of the mind, and a source of much useful information. It also appears to have spilled over into technology and was commended by Payne as making boys "much more handy." This, no doubt, resulted from Payne's insistence that boys who broke pieces of equipment should mend them themselves, a requirement which led to "a considerable facility which they had not had before in using their hands and in using their wits." He noted with some satisfaction the good performance of his pupils in science subjects in external examinations, and that "boys who learnt chemistry and became interested in it, almost invariably, as I found afterwards, when they left school, pursued it themselves."[26]

It is also possible that there was a general programme of visiting speakers. In 1852 James Sheridan Knowles, the Irish dramatist and actor turned Baptist preacher and teacher, responded to an invitation to give a course of lectures or lessons, while in 1858 Clara Balfour, arguably the most active female professional lecturer of the nineteenth century, agreed to speak on "England in the Sixteenth Century."[27] Attention was also paid to physical, as well as mental, exercise. Though Payne frequently condemned what he believed to be the excessive time devoted to games at some boys' schools, at the Mansion as at Denmark Hill there was a playground and sporting facilities. Payne, whose evidence to the Taunton Commission included the judgement that "generally speaking, boys who work well also play well, though the converse is by no means necessarily true," declared his pupils to have been "capital cricketers."[28]

In 1866, three years after his retirement from Leatherhead, Payne produced a curriculum scheme for boys aged 8 to 16 years which indicated some divergence from that actually practised at the Mansion. Latin, though occupying some half of the time between ages 12 and 14, was absent before that age and reduced to a quarter after 14. No place was found for Greek.[29]

While the private schools could rarely compete with the great public schools in terms of size and reputation, they could offer a more domestic and kindly environment. H. A. Giffard, who reported for the Taunton Commission on schools in extrametropolitan Surrey, placed the Mansion Grammar School in the top class of private schools. His comments on accommodation were not specific to any school, but indicated one of the most appealing elements about such schools, although expressed in the grudging and mocking tones which characterized the Taunton approach to private establishments:

> The accommodation, both in respect of day-rooms and sleeping-rooms is, in the upper class of private schools,

with few exceptions, satisfactory. In fact the domestic arrangements are always looked after by the parents when they place a boy at a school, and these and the diet often form the sole objects of their attention. The proprietors of private boarding schools are generally very ready to show a visitor over their establishments, and are for the most part very proud of the extent and comfort of their houses. One of the boasts of the good boarding schools is that boys are treated as if they were at home.[30]

Although the youngest boarders at the Mansion Grammar School slept in a dormitory which could take up to 11 pupils, a nurse slept close by. The largest room for older boys held a maximum of eight pupils. There were several double rooms, a useful facility since many pairs of brothers attended the school, while some boys even had separate rooms.

Corporal punishment, or the supposed lack of it, was another distinguishing feature of the private school. There was a general belief that private schoolmasters were less likely to use the birch or cane for fear that parents might remove their sons from the school. The opposite view was that private schools were "oriental despotisms," run by a succession of Wackford Squeers, and that flogging in a public or grammar school was at least carried out in a traditional, open way, with a public tariff of blows for each offence. In July 1860 the issue came to the fore when Thomas Hopley, a private schoolmaster at Eastbourne, was sentenced to four years penal servitude for beating to death a 15-year-old boy, Reginald Cancellor.[31] Giffard found that of 22 first-class private schools in Surrey and Sussex, six had dispensed with the birch or cane altogether, while in the others corporal punishment was stated to be "very rare."[32]

There is no evidence as to the extent of corporal punishment at the Denmark Hill Grammar School in Payne's day, but it is clear from Mason's evidence to Taunton that in 1865 he was still using (however sparingly) the birch on little boys and the cane on older ones. In neither case was such punishment restricted to blows on the hand.[33] Payne's regime at the Mansion Grammar School appears to have been milder. Although in the early years of the Mansion Grammar School corporal punishment was used occasionally, subsequently, Payne assured Lord Taunton "I gave it up entirely."[34] Instead

Payne came to rely upon moral and personal influence, and he stated that "I found in the end that I did very much more by a word or a look in that way than I had done by using corporal punishment."[35] This reliance upon moral rather than physical persuasion made Payne rather wary of accepting boys from public schools who had become accustomed to a more barbarous regime. On one occasion such a pupil lasted barely a quarter of an hour at the Mansion before Payne expelled him for his use of foul language in the playground. Payne's considered views upon corporal punishment were expressed in a lecture given on 20 February 1861 at the College of Preceptors in London and printed in the *Educational Times* of March of that year. On that occasion he advised his audience that he had "long since given up the notion of beating boys into a love of learning."[36]

Examinations

The middle years of the nineteenth century saw the founding and proliferation of examination systems for schools. From 1862 grant-aided elementary schools were, under the terms of the Revised Code of that year, subject to the rigours of the system of "payment by results." Pupils were examined annually by Her Majesty's Inspectors, initially in the three subjects of Reading, Writing and Arithmetic, and according to six prescribed Standards. Payments from government funds were made according to the success of pupils. Levels of attainment in secondary schools could be measured by pupil performance in the examinations of the College of Preceptors, and in the "Local" examinations of the universities of Oxford and Cambridge.

It was in 1850 that the College of Preceptors, to the great dismay of many of its members including its first president, Henry Turrell, decided to institute an examination of school pupils. Opposition to the scheme came from those who feared that the College would be diverted from its primary aim of training and examining teachers. Support came from those who believed that school examinations would provide a useful test both of pupils and of their teachers, and enable private schools to be measured against grammar and public ones. In 1851 the admission of girls to the examinations allowed males to be measured against females. The great success of the system, which was fully adopted in 1854, two years before the examinations of the Society of Arts and four years before those of the universities of Oxford and Cambridge, also helped to place the finances of the College on a sounder footing. The first formal examination took place in December 1850 when the pupils of Messrs Goodacre and Cockayne in Nottingham were examined on behalf of the College. Nevertheless, in March of that year there was an examination in Classics of the pupils at the Mansion by William Smith, the well-known editor, schoolmaster, lawyer and lexicographer. Smith's prowess as a Classical scholar—as a student at University College, London, he won first prizes in both Greek and Latin and later returned as Classical examiner—was confirmed by the fame of such works as the *Dictionary of Greek and Roman Antiquities* (1842), and the *Dictionary of Greek and Roman Biography* (1849). Nevertheless, Smith reported that the boys of the Mansion "acquitted themselves in a manner most satisfactory to me and most creditable to themselves and their teachers."[37] Subsequently Preceptors' examinations were held twice a year, unlike those of the universities which were held annually. In consequence, by the 1860s, some 2,000 pupils sat the College's examinations each year, considerably more than took the Locals of Oxford and Cambridge. Moreover, the first-class certificates of the College were recognized by the legal and medical professions as guarantees of a good general education and were accepted as exempting candidates from the preliminary examinations required for entry to such professions.

As to the Local examinations of the universities of Oxford and Cambridge, these provided both for those aged up to 15 or 16, as did the Preceptors, and for older candidates up to 18. These two levels were designated as "junior" and "senior." In his report to the Taunton Commissioners, Giffard advised that in the private schools of Surrey and Sussex, overall, the examinations of Cambridge were preferred to those of Oxford for two reasons. The first was that Cambridge allowed a later age for junior candidates. The second was that while Oxford simply announced the subjects for examination, Cambridge supplied information as to which authors and portions of texts were to be studied.[38] Although Payne entered his pupils for a variety of external examinations, from the 1850s the Mansion Grammar School concentrated upon the Oxford examinations.

In his evidence to Taunton, Payne stated that each year about a quarter of the whole school was entered for the Local examinations. Payne then pronounced himself to be a strong supporter of the Locals. He reported that although selected boys rather than a whole class were entered, this did not mean that at the Mansion the slower boys were neglected. All pupils in a class would cover the same fields of study, but those entered for the examinations would be given extra work. On balance, he argued, "The attention both of masters and boys is quickened, and the great majority gain by the process, which at last issues in the selection of a minority for examination."[39]

Although nineteenth-century league tables of examination results were susceptible to even more criticisms than those of today, a national cumulative table of junior and senior passes in the Oxford examinations for the four years 1858 to 1861 showed that the Mansion Grammar School stood 9th, with 30 passes. No allowance was made for size of school, and the Denmark Hill Grammar School, which was much larger than the Mansion, was placed fourth with 41, having secured the highest number of passes of any school in 1860.[40]

In the Oxford examination of June 1858 the successful Mansion pupils included E. M. Baines, J. K. Doulton, R. F. Pechey and W. R. Price—all at junior level.[41] At Christmas of the same year, Payne's successes in the Cambridge examination for pupils under 16 years of age included C. J. Wilkins, who was placed in the first class with distinction in chemistry. P. Hickson and H. S. Stronach[42] were placed in the second class, with the latter achieving a distinction in Latin. Unclassified passes included those of T. M. Cross, J. K. Doulton again, R. S. Hunt, with a distinction in French, and R. S. Pontifex. As with the Oxford examination of that year there were no Mansion pupils listed in the senior, or under 18, category.[43] Whereas it has been possible to trace only four of the five successful scholars of 1858, all 11 successful candidates in the Oxford Local Examination of 1859 have been identified. They included, at senior level, both

Cross, though only 14 years old, and Price, who was 15. Other seniors were five 16–year-olds, P. Hickson, G. W. C. Mawson, S. Pontifex,[44] C. J. Wilkins and W. H. Woolston. The full range of subjects is not clear, but the Mansion pupils appear to have been successful in several areas. For example, both Cross and Price were noted as having additionally satisfied the examiners in the "Rudiments of Faith and Religion," Wilkins was classified in the three subjects of English, mathematics and physics, while Mawson shone in languages. Two rising stars were R. W. O'Grady and W. Hickson, both aged 14, who were placed in the first division of the junior candidates. Another 14–year-old Mansion scholar to appear in the junior pass list, though in the second division, was William Payne, the youngest of Joseph and Eliza's children, together with C. J. Angus who was only 13.[45]

Increased success in the Oxford examinations did not, however, lead Payne to abandon Cambridge entries altogether. Although at Christmas in 1859, W. Hickson failed to repeat his Oxford achievement, being placed only in the second class on this occasion, F. E. Tucker of the Mansion Grammar School achieved an outstanding result at junior level. Tucker was placed in the first class and was one of only two pupils to achieve four distinctions—in English, French, Greek and Latin. Other Mansion results at this examination included J. Attlee, who was in the third class.[46]

Another list in which Leatherhead pupils featured prominently was that of the matriculation examination of the University of London. For example, in the examination of July 1860 both Stronach and Tucker were placed in the first division.[47] Although there were fewer Oxford successes that summer—O'Grady and T. W. Hill at senior level, H. E. Golding and J. J. Gurney at junior[48]—the quality remained high. Both O'Grady and Hill were among the 11 senior prizewinners (out of a total pass list of nearly 200) who received their awards at the first public distribution for the London centre. The ceremony was held on 5 November 1860 at the Court of the Queen's Bench, Guildhall, where the Lord Mayor presided and distributed the books and certificates which were given as prizes. Although Mason and the Denmark Hill Grammar School supplied two of the five junior prizewinners, Payne, no doubt, took considerable

satisfaction that at senior level Mason had only one.[49] The North
London Collegiate School, whose master was the Rev. W. C.
Williams, was the only other school to have two prizewinners at
senior level.

In 1861 the numbers of Oxford passes rose again. At junior
level W. R. Fox was placed in the first division and seventeenth
in the overall list of merit, with A. Adamson, R. I. Jenks and H. T.
Wade in the second, and W. R. Lee, J. B. Perks, C. E. Ridley and
F. E. Sheffield in the third. At senior level the 16–year-old
Hickson was placed in the first division and sixth in the overall
list of merit, with A. McHinch in the third division. At this
examination there were 648 entries at the junior level, of whom
628 were actually examined and 415 passed. Senior figures were
320 entries, 310 examined and 184 passed.[50]

The fifty years preceding 1860, before the reforms of the
public and endowed schools which followed the reports of the
Clarendon and Taunton Commissions, may be seen as a classic
period in the history of the boys' private school in England. The
most significant feature of the first league tables of examination
results was the success of the private schools, many of whose
masters were members of the College of Preceptors. Payne, no
doubt, took pride in the fact that the two schools which he had
founded should feature so prominently in the Oxford lists for
1858–1861. Unfortunately, as a result of an oversight, the
Mansion was one of the schools which was not credited properly
in the tables appended to the report of the Taunton Commission.
In July 1868, no doubt as a consequence of the protests of
aggrieved masters of the excluded schools, this error was
publicly acknowledged by Henry Roby, the Commission's
secretary.[51]

Retirement

It is not entirely clear as to why Payne left the Mansion in 1863,
but three possible reasons may be adduced. The first was the
sheer burden of his duties. His life at Leatherhead was one of
unremitting toil. He commenced work at six o'clock and
frequently continued until the early hours of the next morning.

The second was a sense of achievement. He had accomplished much and could retire in the knowledge of a job well done. One tangible tribute (listed in Joseph Frank's will) was the handsome silver cup and silver inkstand presented to him by former pupils. Though not a wealthy man, he had by teaching and writing secured a modest financial independence. Third, after some forty years of classroom work, other horizons beckoned. The early years of his retirement were spent principally in travel, in recharging his formidable intellectual batteries, in publications and in pursuing a variety of long-held and cherished educational interests.[52]

The Paynes moved back to London and took a house in Kildare Gardens, Bayswater. The first edition of another bestseller, *Studies in English Prose*, appeared in 1868. There was a spate of pamphlets and articles in learned journals, copies of which were once again liberally distributed. Old acquaintances were renewed and new ones made. For example, in December 1868, the 21-year-old Robert, second of Kay Shuttleworth's sons, came to stay, and his father, on the point of departing on a visit to Italy with his eldest son Ughtred, wrote effusively to Payne in terms which show the respect accorded by the educational administrator to the true pedagogue. "I am always anxious about my children until their principles and powers of self guidance are *fully developed*, and should be deeply grateful to you for that kind vigilance and for such advice as your experience may suggest to Robert."[53] Literary interests could be pursued with renewed vigour, and linguistic studies followed with greater precision. There was correspondence with William Aldis Wright, librarian of Trinity College, Cambridge, Shakespearean and Biblical scholar, editor of poetry collections and of the *Journal of Philology*, about one of Wright's joint publications, *The Bible Wordbook*. He also corresponded with Alexander Ellis about philological issues, not only in respect of their mutual interest in the pronunciation of early English but also over Ellis's schemes for phonetic spelling and orthographical reform.[54] Payne's growing stature in this field led to his becoming chairman of the Philological Society in 1873.

Not that Payne was in any danger of declining into obscurantism and pedantry. His interest in commercial studies continued, and in 1874 he sought advice from John Yeats, author of books on technical instruction and commercial training, who provided Payne with a brief digest of a three-volume work by a former director of the Trade School in Berlin.[55] He also served as a member of the Councils of the Social Science Association and of the Girls' Public Day School Company, and as chairman of the Women's Education Union. But, above all, Joseph Payne now had the freedom to build upon his earlier work as a founding member of the College of Preceptors. This association of teachers, begun in 1846 and granted a Royal Charter in 1849, provided the context for much of Payne's educational career. He had long been its chief examiner in the theory and practice of education. Now in the 1860s he became a Vice-President, and in 1873 achieved his greatest distinction as its first Professor of Education, the first such appointment in Britain.

As for the Mansion Grammar School, though for a while after Payne's retirement it continued under Ibbs and Wilson, it eventually went the way of most nineteenth-century private schools and closed around 1878. One of the great characteristics of Joseph Payne was his love of books. Though Payne, who died on 30 April 1876, would no doubt have regretted the demise of the school he had founded and the fact that the rooms, corridors and staircases of The Mansion no longer echoed to the sounds of schoolboy voices and feet, he would, one suspects, have thoroughly approved of its current function as a public library.

Kildare Gardens

After the spacious premises and grounds of Grove Hill House, Denmark Hill House and The Mansion, 4, Kildare Gardens, Bayswater, a narrow terraced house on four floors with a basement, might have seemed rather cramped and austere. Nevertheless there were compensations. Kildare Gardens as the name implies was a small garden square at the southern end of Kildare Terrace. The house was relatively new (it did not appear on a map of 1855) although the Paynes were not the first occupants. At the time of the Census of 1861 it was occupied by Nathaniel Dindley, a practising barrister aged 32, his wife Sarah aged 30 and their seven-month-old son, John Edward. There were three female servants: a cook, nurse and house maid. The Payne household of 1871 was somewhat similar and comprised Joseph, who was described as a "retired schoolmaster," Eliza, their second son Joseph Frank then a practising physician aged 31 and two unmarried servants: a cook, Martha Herring, aged 26 who had been born in Berkshire; and a 30–year-old housemaid, Sarah Clarke, who came from Northumberland.[56]

In the middle years of the nineteenth century, Bayswater, which as late as 1820 was no more than a small hamlet in the parish of Paddington about a mile to the west of London, was much developed with substantial and fashionable houses. Communications were good, both within London and without (Paddington Station was close) and nearby residents included not only Beata Doreck but also Herbert Spencer. In October 1862 Spencer was living in Gloucester Square, by 1864 he had moved to 88, Kensington Gardens Square, and from 1866 until 1889 he lived in a hotel at 37, Queen's Gardens, Bayswater. Payne and Spencer shared many interests and also some acquaintances, including the American educationist, Edward Youmans.[57] Although there is little evidence to link Payne and Spencer directly, certainly in 1877 Hodgson bracketed them together, when he wrote to Dr Strachan apropos of didactic teaching that, "This is just what Payne, as well as Spencer, specially condemns and deplores."[58] Joseph Payne's public career was to blossom from Kildare Gardens, and he also managed to involve his two elder sons in the work of the College of Preceptors: John Burnell as a lecturer and Joseph Frank as an examiner. But this final period also was tinged by tragedy, in particular the death in 1869 of his eldest son, John Burnell.

John Burnell Payne was, by all accounts, a young man of great talent, but his short life was characterized by uncertainties and changes of direction, in terms of his education, his faith and his career. His early schooling, understandably, was at the hands of his parents, and he then proceeded to University College, London, gaining a B.A. degree in 1858. After further study in London he was admitted as a sizar at Trinity College, Cambridge, on 18 June 1860, no doubt to the delight of his father who had come so close to studying at that ancient university.

Trinity, however, must have seemed uncongenial, for on 16 June 1862 John Burnell migrated to Downing College, in 1864 achieving first-class honours in the Moral Science Tripos. Joseph Mayor, then fellow and tutor of St. John's College, whose lectures he attended, wrote that John Burnell possessed "great intelligence and an unusual amount of information," and in May 1864 recommended him for the post of Professor of English Literature at St. David's College, Lampeter in Wales.[59] Nothing appears to have come of this recommendation, however, and for the next two years John Burnell Payne taught as an assistant master at Wellington College in Berkshire, the nation's monument to the great Duke, the victor of Waterloo. Its original purpose was the education of the orphaned sons of army officers, though it soon became a substantial public school. The school had opened in January 1859, with the 29–year-old Edward White Benson, a Fellow of Trinity College and former master at Rugby, as its first headmaster.

Benson, a future Archbishop of Canterbury, was a man of great energy and resolve, an autocrat who possessed a "volcanic temper."[60] His will and anger were visited upon his staff as much as upon his pupils. Arthur Christopher Benson, his eldest child and biographer, born in 1862 in the Master's lodge at Wellington, acknowledged that

> as a schoolmaster my father was, I suppose, one of the sternest and severest disciplinarians that ever ruled a school. . . . There is no exaggeration in saying that boys and even masters were greatly afraid of him.[61]

The young Arthur who feared his own father by contrast recorded that the assistant masters "were very kind to us as children," but suspected that "the emphatic and dominant temperament of my father tended to obscure and even submerge their individuality."[62]

It was Benson's firm belief that a master could not properly fulfil his duties unless he were in holy orders, and this possibly explains why on 21 December 1865, John Burnell Payne was ordained deacon at Oxford, especially as he did not subsequently proceed to the priesthood. Benson's major aversion, however, was to tobacco, which he could not abide, and of 17 letters which survive from Benson to John Burnell

Payne many are concerned with the vice of smoking.[63] But even more heinous in Benson's eyes was dereliction of duty. One afternoon in the summer of 1866, Payne closed the library in order to watch a school cricket match. Benson personally hauled him over the coals and followed up with a missive, dated 21 July, which left John Burnell in little doubt as to the precariousness of his position:

> I am afraid that the Library is too troublesome to you, and that you will be obliged to resign it, but in any case I am surprised that you did not speak to me first, after what I lately said on the subject. Of course I should be sorry to lose your services, but I must not be left to find out departures from our rules by accident. Nothing can more destroy confidence.[64]

Not surprisingly, Payne departed Wellington shortly afterwards. His entry in the *Wellington College Register* under "Assistant Masters" was suitably brief.

> Appointed 1865. The Rev. J. B. Payne, B.A. Scholar of Downing College, Cambridge. Left 1867. Dead.[65]

In October 1867, having left Wellington, John Burnell Payne became curate of Christ Church, St. Marylebone, in London, not far from Kildare Gardens, Bayswater, but by 1869 he had "from scruples of conscience, given up the clerical profession, and was devoting himself ardently to art-criticism."[66] It would appear that John Burnell had as many problems as a clergyman as he did as a teacher. W. B. Hodgson, who heard one of his early sermons, while finding it "admirable in thought, in feeling, in arrangement, in composition, and in delivery," had also to inform Joseph Payne that he found much of it inaudible, "while Mrs. H., who was with me, could not hear at all."[67]

John Burnell's literary contributions, notably articles on art, literature and religion in such journals as *Macmillan's*, the *Pall Mall Gazette* and *Vanity Fair*, indicated the broad spread of his interests and expertise. Perhaps the most revealing of his writings, however, was a short review of R. H. Quick's, *Essays on Educational Reformers* (1868), published in the *Fortnightly Review*.[68] Herbert Quick was to become a friend and colleague of Joseph Payne. As a boy he had lived at Denmark Hill and, having graduated from Trinity College, Cambridge in 1854, taught successively at Hurstpierpoint, Cranleigh and Harrow. In 1875 he stood in for Joseph Payne as a lecturer at the College of Preceptors,[69] and subsequently, from 1879, gave a course of lectures in the history of education at the University of Cambridge. When Payne died he accorded to Quick his most precious possession, the pick of his library, with its first editions of Brinsley, Comenius, Elyot, Mulcaster and Hoole.[70] Quick remained in contact with Joseph Frank Payne after his father's death and contributed an introduction to the first volume of the collected works.[71] It is possible, indeed, that the offer to review the Quick volume was sent first to Joseph who passed it on to his son. It is also possible or even probable that the review was written jointly by father and son.[72] Certainly, the following reference to public schools was not inconsistent with Joseph Payne's views on this topic:

> It is a somewhat suspicious circumstance that the special "tone" of public schools is described so variously and so vaguely by those who attach most importance to it. Mr Quick borrows from Miss Davies the term "open airiness" to describe this mysterious moral-intellectual-physical something, which I believe to be merely a form of the traditional bearing common to all the European aristocracies, occupying very unsuitably the place of simplicity and docility in those who are still in fact un-emancipated members of the family.[73]

John Burnell's tentative and brief entry into the literary world of London in the later 1860s can be followed in the correspondence of the novelist, George Eliot.[74] Since July 1854 George Eliot had been living with George Henry Lewes,[75] and their home at The Priory, North Bank, Regent's Park, not far from Bayswater and St. Marylebone, became a place of pilgrimage for John Burnell. At this time George Eliot was at the height of her power and fame, with such works as *The Mill on the Floss* (1860), *Silas Marner* (1861), *Romola* (1863) and *Felix Holt* (1866) to her credit. Lewes, himself the founder and former editor of the *Fortnightly Review*, was also very productive in this period. Books on the *Life and Works of Goethe* (1855), *Studies in Animal Life* (1862) and *Aristotle* (1864), give some indication of the range of his interests. The unconventional nature of George Eliot's life meant that she was shunned by many elements of Victorian society, but enjoyed instead the visits and admiration of young intellectuals, many of them bachelors like John Burnell.

It would appear that John Burnell came to know George Eliot as a result of his interest in her poem, *The Spanish Gypsy*, published in 1868.[76] Both John Burnell and Joseph Frank visited The Priory in January and February 1869.[77] On Friday, 29 January, they visited again, at George Eliot's invitation, to enjoy a musical evening.[78] Sunday, 14 February saw another visit, when it would appear that George Eliot was less than forthcoming in response to John Burnell's request for information about her writing of the poem.[79] Later that day Eliot, prompted by Lewes, wrote to John Burnell inviting him to take tea with her at a quarter past eight on the following Wednesday, 17 February, when they might have a more private discussion of *The Spanish Gypsy*. John Burnell's notes of the meeting indicate that although he introduced the subject with "some nervousness," he received a full account of "how the subject occurred to her and continued to be developed in her mind. She talked perhaps for half an hour with an eloquence and fervour which I shall never forget."[80]

Both John Burnell and Joseph Frank came to be fascinated by the Eliot-Lewes circle. One connection, soon discovered, was that George Eliot had been educated in Coventry at the school of a Miss Franklin who was the daughter of Rev. Francis Franklin and his wife, Rebecca Dyer, Eliza's aunt. On 15 February 1869 George Eliot wrote to Sophia Hennell:

> I forgot to tell you that in two young men named Payne, who visit us—one, a physician of promise, the other a clergyman who writes a great deal—I have discovered second cousins of Miss R. Franklin's, whom I have often heard speak of their mother, once Eliza Dyer.[81]

Whether John Burnell Payne had found his true calling, however, was never to be put to the test, for on 27 August 1869 he died of enteric fever at his parents' house in Kildare Gardens. His death naturally affected the whole family most deeply. In his obituary of Joseph Payne, W. B. Hodgson wrote that "the death, a few years ago, of his eldest son Burnell, almost at the opening of a brilliant literary career, gave him a great shock, from which he never fully recovered."[82] For his part Joseph Frank discussed consolation with George Eliot, as he was to do again on the occasion of Eliza's death in 1875.

Joseph Frank's early education mirrored that of his elder brother, first at home and at the Mansion Grammar School, but he proceeded not to Cambridge but to a demyship at Magdalen College, Oxford, matriculating on 25 October 1858. In 1862 he also graduated with a first class in natural science. This led in 1863 to the award of the Burdett-Coutts scholarship for geology, the Radcliffe travelling fellowship in 1865 and a Magdalen College fellowship which he kept until his marriage in 1882. In 1906, four years before his death, Magdalen elected him to an honorary fellowship.

Joseph Frank had a thorough academic and professional grounding for his medical career. He took a B.Sc. degree from the University of London in 1865, an M.B. at Oxford in 1867 and M.D. in 1880. Under the terms of the Radcliffe fellowship he visited Berlin, Paris and Vienna where he made good use of the many pathological facilities, and his experiences were described in articles published in the *British Medical Journal* in 1871. He held appointments at many of the major London hospitals, at St. Mary's, at the Children's Hospital in Great Ormond Street and at the Hospital for Skin Diseases at Blackfriars, but his name was chiefly associated with St. Thomas's where from 1871 he was successively assistant physician, physician and consulting physician. It was George Lewes who, on 25 May 1871, wrote to John Simon, who was then surgeon at St. Thomas's Hospital, on Joseph Frank's behalf:

> Dr Payne who is a candidate for a post at your Hospital wishes me to say a word in his favour, and although I cannot speak as one having authority I can't refuse to bear conscientious testimony to the real worth and ability concealed under his modest and unimpressive exterior. You will be the best judge of his qualifications professionally. I can only say that I believe him to be a thoroughly good man with honest work in him. That is a kind of man rare as you know![83]

During this period of his life Joseph Frank continued as a member of the Eliot-Lewes circle. If the character given above was an accurate one, he must at times have seemed rather dull in contrast to some of the other members of that group. For example on Sunday, 23 April 1871 he attended a glittering and varied gathering at The Priory which included two eminent novelists, Anthony Trollope and Ivan Turgenev, the painter Edward Burne-Jones and Michelle Viardot, one of the most famous operatic sopranos of the day.[84]

In September 1875 Eliza Payne fell ill with enteric fever. She died on 12 October; the death certificate was signed by Joseph Frank. Payne himself never recovered from the shock, and it became Joseph Frank's sad duty to write a series of letters informing various organizations that his father would no longer be able to discharge his several responsibilities. Charles Mason, who must have known Eliza well, characterized her as "a lady of great energy of character, of tact and method in the conduct of affairs. . . . Her intellectual powers. . .were of an unusually high order."[85] Joseph Frank sought solace outside the family circle. Like his elder brother he had serious doubts about the Christian faith, and one of his first actions was to write a long letter to George Eliot, penned almost immediately on 17 October, but not sent until January of the following year. He had admired the way in which in *The Legend of Jubal* (1869) she had written of the value of death in heightening the importance of love and wedded bliss, and of encouraging human beings to seek immortality through creativity. But, in the despair of bereavement, he begged for further comfort:

> If you can say one word to lighten this dark subject, how happy I should be. But let me not put it as an individual wish. It is the longing of all freethinkers now that I am trying to express, and this, as traditional religion decays (if it does) will be the yearning of all mankind. Death is the great problem which man will have to grapple with again; unless we are to believe, not in no God, but in a bad one.[86]

The reply, written on 25 January 1876, has been called "the most revealing statement George Eliot ever made about the role of her art in the quest for values."[87] She did not expand upon the extent to which "the religion of the future must be one that enables us to do without consolation," but she did declare that her writing was "simply a set of experiments in life—an endeavour to see what our thought and emotion may be capable of."[88]

Joseph Payne did not long survive his wife's death. For some months he had been suffering from Bright's disease of the kidneys. Complications arose, and on 30 April 1876 he died at Kildare Gardens. Once again the cause of death was certified by the ever-present Joseph Frank who also, no doubt, was responsible for placing a notice of his father's demise in the columns of *The Times*.[89] At the time of Payne's death, William, the youngest son, then an "indigo broker," appears to have been living at 4, Kildare Gardens. He and Joseph Frank, whose address in the 1870s was variously given as 4, Kildare Gardens and 6, Savile Row, were the executors.[90]

Payne's last will and testament, dated 30 December 1875, was a modest affair of five clauses which, together with a codicil, occupied barely a page. He bequeathed £200 to the College of Preceptors for the endowment fund for a professor of education and £50 to "Thomas John Barnardo or the Treasurer of the East End Juvenile Mission." The remainder of his estate was divided equally between Payne's two surviving sons. The codicil gave Herbert Quick first choice of 50 books from his library; the rest of his "educational books and books relating to education" were left to the College of Preceptors for their library.

After the deaths of his parents Joseph Frank gave up any connection with Kildare Gardens and threw himself into his medical work. Unassuming as he was, he became a person of both fame and fortune, who died a wealthy man. His interests in pathology, epidemiology and dermatology brought him into the public eye; for example in 1877 he was the chief medical witness for the defence in the trial of Louis Staunton and others for the murder of his wife, Harriet. He also gained recognition for his work with plague epidemics, in Russia in 1879 and in India in 1905. He was a frequent lecturer on public occasions, his delivery characterized by a "curious jerky manner of expressing emphasis,"[91] a prolific writer of books and articles on medical matters, and he played a full part in the public and professional life of his day. His posts included Fellow of the College of Physicians, its Harveian Librarian from 1899 and Senior Censor in 1905; President of the Epidemiological Society, 1892–1893; the University of Oxford's representative on the General Medical Council, 1899–1904; and member of the Senate of the University of London, 1899–1906.

Like his father Joseph Frank had a great interest in books. He was on the committee of the London Library and gave many valuable books to the Library of the College of Physicians. At his death, although some particularly valuable manuscripts and books were bequeathed to the Royal College of Physicians and others to his wife and children, the sale of the remaining medical volumes in his collection realised some £2,300.[92] He was also, like his father, passionately interested in the history of his subject. Thus in 1894 his contemporary interest in plague led him to research, edit and publish, with an introduction, the *Loimographia* of the apothecary, William Boghurst, who had witnessed the London plague of 1665. Other historical writings included a life of Thomas Linacre, the founder of the Royal College of Physicians, which was published in 1881, and of Thomas Sydenham, "the English Hippocrates," in 1900. He also wrote long articles on the history of medicine for the *Encyclopaedia Britannica*, and several lives for the medical entries in the *Dictionary of National Biography*. In 1903–1904 Joseph Frank followed in his father's footsteps once again, in delivering the first FitzPatrick Lectures on the history of medicine at the College of Physicians. The first course was on English medicine in the Anglo-Saxon period, the second on the Anglo-Norman period. In 1909 he delivered a course of lectures on Galen and Greek medicine at the University of Oxford. There can be no doubt whatsoever that Joseph Frank was fully conscious of the extent to which his professional life and personal interests overlapped with those of his father.

Joseph Frank married at the age of 42, on 1 September 1882. His bride was Helen Curtis Macpherson, daughter of John Alexander Macpherson, an Australian politician who had retired to England. Joseph Frank and Helen had one son and three daughters: John Burnell, Evelyn Mary, Helen Sylvia and Olive Margaret. All were alive in 1910 when, on 16 November, Joseph Frank died at Lyonsdown House, New Barnet, to which he had retired upon giving up his practice at 78, Wimpole Street.

Joseph Frank inherited all of his father's industry. In addition to his own busy professional and family life he also found time to collect, edit and secure the publication of the great majority of his father's papers and lectures. The first of these was Joseph Payne's short account of *A Visit to German Schools*, published in 1876 with a second edition in 1884. The second was the substantial edited collection, entitled *Lectures on the Science and Art of Education. . . .*, which appeared in 1880, with a second edition in 1883. This was to form the first volume of Payne's collected works. The second volume, entitled *Lectures on the History of Education . . .* was published in 1892. By this act of filial piety Joseph Frank ensured that his father's work would become known to succeeding generations, not only in Britain but also in the United States of America, where full and abridged editions of Payne's writings soon appeared.

NOTES

1. For Leatherhead see Edwina Vardey (ed.), *History of Leatherhead: A Town at the Crossroads* (Leatherhead, 1988).

2. For Leatherhead's independent schools at this period see Linda Heath, *Of Good Report: The Story of the Leatherhead Schools* (Leatherhead, 1986), pp. 93–9. Gas was introduced into Leatherhead in 1851, although the street lights were put on only from October to March, and even then not on moonlit nights, Vardey, *Leatherhead*, p. 174.

3. For the early history of St. John's see Richard Hughes, *St. John's Foundation School, 1851–1872: The Founding and Early History of St. John's School, Leatherhead* (Leatherhead, 1987).

4. For The Mansion see F. B. Benger, "The Mansion, Leatherhead," *Proceedings of the Leatherhead and District Local History Society*, I, 7 (1953), pp. 7–12.

5. *Ibid.*, p. 8.

6. Engraved by W. T. Harris of London and published by T. Hill of Leatherhead. I am most grateful to G. D. Powell for this reference.

7. *Sussex Agricultural Express*, 14 December 1844. If Payne had been teaching for 20 years he would have begun in 1824–5 at the age of 16–17.

8. *Educational Times* XXIX, 182 (June, 1876), p. 57.

9. Brian Simon, *The Two Nations and The Educational Structure, 1780–1870* (London, 1974), p. 320.

10. *Taunton Report*, iv, pp. 663–74.

11. *Ibid.*, p. 666.

12. W. Innes Addison, *The Matriculation Albums of the University of Glasgow from 1728 to 1858* (Glasgow, 1913), p. 417.

13. Todd to Payne, 7 February 1850, Author's Collection; G. D. Burtchaell and T. U. Sadleir (eds.), *Alumni Dublinenses. A Register of the Students, Graduates, Professors and Provosts of Trinity College in the University of Dublin, 1593–1860* (Dublin, 1935), p. 21. Another possible candidate for a teaching post at the school was an Edinburgh graduate, Mr Eason. Robert Redpath to Payne, 28 December 1849, Author's Collection. Redpath, himself an Edinburgh graduate, was minister of a London church for over 40 years and frequently examined at Nonconformist schools and colleges in and around the London area.

14. *Taunton Report*, iv, p. 672.

15. Addison, *Matriculation Albums*, p. 417.

16. F. S. de Carteret-Bisson, *Our Schools and Colleges* (London, 1872), pp. 254, 279, 515. See also Crockford's, *Scholastic Directory for 1861*, p. 107 which listed the school simply as "boarding."

17. Census Enumerators' Returns, 1861; Thomas Trowt to his parents, 25 July 1815, SEA/1, Baptist Missionary Archives, Angus Library, Regent's Park College, Oxford.

18. *Taunton Report*, iv, p. 666.

19. Taylor to Payne: 27 July 1848, 28 July 1848, 22 May 1849, 24 July 1849, 1 November 1850, 13 December 1850, 2 November 1851, 29 April 1852, 12 May 1852, 15 May 1852, Author's Collection.

20. *Taunton Report*, p. 664.

21. I am most grateful to Linda Heath for this information.

22. The Leatherhead Congregational Church was formed in 1829, and the Church Record Book covers the period 1829–1883. I am most grateful to John Henderson, secretary to the Christ Church Leatherhead United Reformed Church, who is currently responsible for the Book, for making this information available to me. See also Edward E. Cleal, *The Story of Congregationalism in Surrey* (London, 1908), pp. 415–6, and Duncan Smith, *A Short History of Christ Church (United Reformed)*

Leatherhead (Leatherhead, 1979). I am grateful to Jana Sims for this last reference.

23. Edward Waite was headmaster of the Blackheath School from 1875 to 1892. For Waite's headmastership of the school, which subsequently became Eltham College, see Clifford Witting (ed.), *The Glory of the Sons: A History of Eltham College School for the Sons of Missionaries* (London, 1952), pp. 30–42. I am most grateful to John Waite for information about his family, and particularly for allowing me to take copies of the photographs of Joseph and Eliza Payne contained in his family album.

24. He died in Inyati, Zimbabwe, in 1869. I am most grateful to John Hobson for this information.

25. *Taunton Report*, iv, p. 665.

26. *Ibid.*, pp. 666–7.

27. Knowles to Payne, 15 June 1852; Balfour to Payne, 14 September 1858, Author's Collection. Though it is possible that these invitations were on behalf of another organization, or shared with the school.

28. *Taunton Report*, iv, p. 673.

29. Payne, *Works*, I, p. 282.

30. *Ibid.*, vii, p. 160.

31. See D. P. Leinster-Mackay, "*Regina v. Hopley*: Some Historical Reflections on Corporal Punishment," *Journal of Educational Administration and History* IX, 1 (January 1977), pp. 1–5.

32. *Taunton Report*, vii, p. 159.

33. *Ibid.*, iv, p. 349.

34. *Ibid.*, iv, p. 671.

35. *Ibid.*, iv, p. 671.

36. *Educational Times* XIV, 162 (March 1861), p. 53.

37. Report by William Smith, 27 March 1850, Author's Collection.

38. *Taunton Report*, vii, p. 170.

39. *Ibid.*, iv, p. 664.

40. *Educational Times* XIV, 7 (October 1861) p. 152.

41. *Educational Times* XI, 132 (September 1858), pp. 202–3. Not all candidates were attributed to a school. Possibilities for confusion were legion. The most successful school, 1858 to 1861, was the Mansion House School at Exeter, while there was a Classical school at Reigate, Surrey, whose master was J. Payne.

42. Also given as "Stonach."

43. *Educational Times* XII, 138 (March 1859), pp. 64–5.

44. Possibly the same as R. S. Pontifex.

45. *Educational Times* XII, 144 (September 1859), pp. 207–8, and 145 (October 1859), pp. 233–4.

46. *Educational Times* XIII, 150 (March 1860), p. 59.

47. *Educational Times* XIII, 155 (August 1860), p. 186.

48. *Educational Times* XIII, 156 (September 1860), pp. 206–8.

49. *Educational Times* XIII, 159 (December 1860), p. 274.

50. *Educational Times* XIV, 6 (September 1861), pp. 125–8.

51. Henry Roby to the editor, July 1868, *Educational Times* XXI, 89 (August 1868), p. 108.

52. Correspondence with Hodgson in the late summer of 1866 suggested that at that time Payne was marooned in a rain-swept Lake District. Hodgson to Payne, 8 September 1866, J. M. D. Meiklejohn (ed.), *Life and letters of William Ballantyne Hodgson* (Edinburgh, 1883), p. 378. Meiklejohn, like Hodgson, was Edinburgh born and educated. In 1875, the year in which he joined the College of Preceptors, he was living near Payne at Orme Square, Bayswater Road, *Paddington, Kensington and Bayswater Chronicle*, 25 September 1875.

53. Kay Shuttleworth to Payne, 10 December 1868, Author's Collection.

54. Wright to Payne, 9 June 1866; Ellis to Payne, 21 October 1871, and an undated fragment from Ellis to Payne about a visit by the latter, Author's Collection. Although the librarian of Trinity from 1863 and senior bursar from 1870, as a Nonconformist Wright was prevented from taking up a fellowship until 1878.

55. Yeats to Payne, 10 April 1874, Author's Collection.

56. Census Enumerators' Returns, 1861, 1871.

57. For Youmans see John Fiske, *Life and Letters of Edward Livingston Youmans, comprising correspondence with Spencer, Huxley, Tyndall and others* (London, 1894), p. 220, where Youmans refers to his "personal contact with a good many members of the College of Preceptors." His account of the lecture on "The Scientific Study of Human Nature" which he gave at the College on 12 October 1866, and of the comments of Payne, who chaired the meeting, are on pp. 224–6. See also the report of the meeting in the *Educational Times* XIX, 68 (November 1866), pp. 167–70.

58. Hodgson to Strachan, 27 December 1877, Meiklejohn, *Hodgson*, p. 278.

59. Testimonial on behalf of J. B. Payne supplied by Joseph Mayor, 27 May 1864, Author's Collection. By that date Mayor had left St. John's and was master of the Kensington School in London.

60. David Newsome, *A History of Wellington College, 1859–1959* (London, 1959), p. 89.

61. A. C. Benson, *The Life of Edward White Benson* (London, 2 vols. 1899–1900), I, p. 202.

62. A. C. Benson, *The Trefoil. Wellington College, Lincoln and Truro* (London, 1923), p. 39.

63. Newsome, *Wellington College*, p. 153.

64. *Ibid.*, p. 155.

65. J. L. Bevir and A. H. Fox-Strangways (eds.), *Wellington College Register, 1859–1888* (Wellington, 1890), p. x.

66. Obituary notice supplied by Evelyn Murphy, quoted in Gordon S. Haight (ed.), *The George Eliot Letters*, (New Haven, 9 vols. 1954–78), V, p. 12.

67. Hodgson to Payne, 6 October 1867, Meiklejohn, *Hodgson*, pp. 379–80.

68. *Fortnightly Review* IV (Old series X) (October 1868), pp. 465–7.

69. F. Storr (ed.), *Life and Remains of the Rev. R. H. Quick* (Cambridge, 1899), p. 479.

70. Storr, *Quick*, pp. 104–5. The Quick Memorial Collection is currently housed in the University of London Library.

71. Storr, *Quick*, p. 263, refers to a conversation between Quick and Joseph Frank on 11 February 1879.

72. In April 1869 Joseph Payne wrote to Quick congratulating him on the volume. Payne to Quick, April 1869, a letter in the possession of Anthony Quick to whom I am most grateful for this reference.

73. *Fortnightly Review* IV (October 1868), p. 466.

74. George Eliot was the pen name of the novelist Mary Ann (or Marian) Evans, 1819–80.

75. George Henry Lewes, 1817–78, author, editor and founder of the *Fortnightly Review*.

76. Early in 1869 she wrote to her publisher, John Blackwood, "A young man who has lately been introduced to us is writing an elaborate article on *The Spanish Gypsy*. I don't know where it is to appear. He has a

considerable position as a journalist, but whether it is deserved I cannot judge for I know nothing that he has written." Eliot to Blackwood, 19 February 1869, Haight, *Eliot Letters*, V, pp. 15–16.

77. George Lewes's diary for 17 January 1869 listed John Burnell and Joseph Frank as callers at the house on that day, Haight, *Eliot Letters*, V, p. 5.

78. Haight, *Eliot Letters*, V, p. 7.

79. *Ibid.*, pp. 12–13.

80. *Ibid.*, p. 13.

81. *Ibid*, p. 14.

82. *Journal of the Women's Education Union* IV, 42 (June 1876), p. 87. Members of the Council of the College of Preceptors sent a letter of condolence to the Paynes, College of Preceptors' Rough Minute Book, 1854–73, 25 September 1869. The minute books of the College of Preceptors have been in the care of the author during the writing of this book and have now been deposited in the Library of the Institute of Education, University of London.

83. Haight, *Eliot Letters*, V, p. 148 and IX, p. 17.

84. Haight, *Eliot Letters*, V, p. 143.

85. *Educational Times* XXIX, 182 (June 1876), p. 57. Ernest A. Payne, who appears to have had some access to material held by Evelyn Murphy, including a diary of John Burnell, concluded an article on the correspondence of George Eliot with the judgement that Eliza Payne was "a remarkable woman, who should be remembered along with Mrs Trinder, the Misses Franklin and Mrs Todd among the Baptists who advanced the cause of female education." Ernest A. Payne, "Gleanings from the Correspondence of George Eliot," *Baptist Quarterly* XVII (1957–8), p. 181.

86. Haight, *Eliot Letters*, VI, p. 216.

87. Bernard J. Paris, *Experiments in Life: George Eliot's Quest for Values* (Detroit, 1965), p. 117.

88. Haight, *Eliot Letters*, VI, p. 216.

89. *The Times*, 3 May 1876.

90. Will of Joseph Payne, and Post Office *Directories* for 1874, 1875, 1876, 1877.

91. *Dictionary of National Biography.*

92. Will of Joseph Frank Payne, and *Dictionary of National Biography.*

CHAPTER FOUR

The College of Preceptors

Origins

The College of Preceptors was founded in 1846. Its origins lay in the desire of a group of Brighton schoolmasters to raise the standards and standing of the teaching profession. Private schoolmasters and their assistants were suffering a bad press, not least from the pen of Charles Dickens. *Oliver Twist* began publication in 1837; *Nicholas Nickleby* in 1838. Government concern for the training of teachers for elementary schools found expression in the pupil-teacher system established under the Minutes of 1846.

In February 1846 a provisional committee was formed, with Henry Stein Turrell, a young teacher of modern languages and principal of Montpelier House School, Brighton, as chairman.[1] Other members included Reverends W. H. Butler, R. Lee, and Messrs J. Andrews, J. T. Coleman, D. Gunton, J. D. Hall, J. Sansbury, R. Stokes and J. Wharton. During the next few months the group met in both Brighton and London and called a general meeting at the Freemasons' Tavern in Great Queen Street in London for 20 June. At this assembly, which may be counted as the foundation of the College, and which, according to one report, was attended by 300 schoolmasters,[2] some 60 members were enrolled and the following 4 resolutions (among others) were adopted:

1. That, in the opinion of this meeting, it is desirable for the protection of the interests both of the scholastic profession and the public, that some proof of

qualification, both as to the amount of knowledge and the art of conveying it to others, should be required, from and after a certain time to be hereafter specified, of all persons who may be desirous of entering the profession; and that the test, in the first instance, should be applied to Assistant Masters only.

2. That, in the opinion of this meeting, the test of qualification should be referred to a legally authorized or corporate body, or college, consisting of persons engaged in tuition.

3. That for the purpose of effecting this object—viz., the formation of a corporate body—the members of the profession who enrol their names at this meeting, do resolve themselves, and are hereby resolved, into the College of Preceptors; and that those persons now enrolled, or who may hereafter be enrolled, shall incur no liability beyond the amount of their respective annual subscriptions.

4. That a Council, consisting of the members of the Provisional Committee, with power to add to their number, be now appointed for the purpose of conducting the business of the institution, and that Mr Turrell be appointed President of the Council.[3]

It is not clear exactly what part Payne played in the foundation of the College, though he was undoubtedly present at the Freemasons' Hall meeting and one of the original 60 subscribers. On 17 December 1868 in a paper entitled "On the past, present, and future of the College of Preceptors,"[4] Payne— with undue modesty according to another founding member in his audience, Stephen Freeman, the College's second president and master of a school at Baker Street in Enfield—simply stated that he was "present at the birth of the institution."[5] He also acknowledged that "before that important event I was in attendance, taking my part, more however as a listener than as a talker, in the gossip which generally goes on when a birth is expected."[6]

Weaknesses

Whatever part Payne played in the foundation of the College, in looking back from the vantage point of 1868 he was to regret several features in its early history.

The first was that the College failed to enforce a universal test of competence. If the purpose of the College were to be the testing of schoolteachers for the protection of both the profession and the public, then all members should have been subject to such a test. Instead, the resolutions allowed the founding members to be admitted without the test, as were schoolmasters subsequently, so that in consequence over a period of 22 years only some 500 teachers were actually certificated by the College. In the first year these numbered 24, but the yearly average of the period 1860–1867 was only four.[7] Bylaws of 16 July and 30 December 1846 declared that all schoolmasters who joined the College before the first day of January 1847 should have the highest rank of MCP, Member of the College of Preceptors. All assistant masters who passed the highest test, either in Classics or mathematics, should also be accorded the rank of MCP. Assistant masters who passed in other subjects would be entitled to the lower rank only, namely ACP, Associate of the College of Preceptors. These arrangements became permanent. Today, the membership of the college is of two kinds. The qualifications of ACP, LCP and FCP (Associate, Licentiate and Fellow) may be gained by study and examination, though annually the College also confers some eight Charter Fellowships upon distinguished educationists. The designations, F.Coll.P. and M.Coll.P., on the other hand, are conferred by the College on recommendation, without formal test.

One result of the liberality with which membership of the College was bestowed was that within six months the original 60 had grown to 600, and within a year to more than 1,000. As Payne observed, "can anyone wonder that schoolmasters by hundreds, finding that *high rank* in a learned corporation was to be obtained at the rate of seven shillings a letter . . . should have availed themselves of the golden opportunity."[8] Life membership was available for a sum of ten guineas. Annual subscription rates were one guinea for principals and half a guinea for assistants.

Another development which Payne regretted was the recruitment of an impressive list of patrons. The first patron was the Marquis of Northampton, then President of the Royal Society. Vice-patrons included the Vice-President of the Royal Society, Sir John Lubbock MP, and other MPs, some prominent in the cause of education, for example Aglionby, Brotherton, Ewart, Godson, Ormsby Gore, Hastie, Mackinnon, Romilly and Wyse. A separate Ladies' Department boasted the protection of the Dowager Marchioness of Cornwallis, Lady Charlotte Lyndsay, Lady Domville, Lady Palmer and Lady Wilson.[9] The self-made Payne had little use for such aristocratic connections and trappings. In respect of this impressive list he declared:

> I do not . . . attach much importance to the enrolment of aristocratic names in connection with a literary or educational institution. I have long believed that there is a sort of degradation in receiving *patronage* at all—from a strong conviction, that a man or institution that is really worthy of patronage does not want it, and that one that is unworthy cannot be made worthy by any amount of patronage.[10]

Though Payne's strictures on patronage applied to the Ladies' Department as well, he was a strong supporter of the female element in the College and welcomed the early participation of such well-known promoters of girls' education as Misses Edgeworth, Corner and Strickland. But in 1849, the separation of sexes was discontinued, a move which Payne regarded on balance as regressive. His judgement in this respect was proved correct. Although from 1849 women could become members of the College, the principal offices of the College were always held by men.[11] Not until 1869 were women admitted to the Council. The first to serve in this capacity was Frances Buss.[12] In 1896, when the College celebrated its golden jubilee, five of the 48 Council members were women.[13]

Strengths

Notwithstanding the early problems of the College, there were also many achievements. Some 70 local boards were brought into being, each with an honorary secretary and a central office established in London, initially at 42, Great Russell Street. The first secretary was John Parker who, on taking the post at a salary of £150 per annum together with free accommodation, gave up his principalship of the Trafalgar House Academy in Brighton and came to London. Parker, who had formerly been an assistant master at Ongar Academy in Essex, the school of Richard Stokes who was one of the members of the provisional committee, had a particular interest in the concept of a self-governing teaching profession. By 1848 the College had moved its headquarters to a new location, 28, Bloomsbury Square, for which an annual rent of £100 was paid to the Duke of Bedford. Parker and his family occupied the upper part of the house, while the three principal rooms were used as a library, an office and a meeting room.[14]

Four other significant ventures were established by 1847. One was a Preceptors' Benevolent Institution for "assisting the distressed and aged members of the scholastic profession, in the higher, middle and lower classes, of society."[15] The senior patron was the Marquis of Northampton, the senior patroness Her Royal Highness the Princess Mary of Baden. In addition to providing such assistance, the Institution also envisaged the endowment of a "Provident Retreat" for aged members, and the foundation of some university scholarships for the sons of teachers. A second substantial foundation was the Agency Department, whose books were opened on 3 April 1847, a means whereby school principals might advertise their vacancies and assistants (and some principals) their desire for employment.[16]

A third development was the Preceptors' and General Life Mutual Assurance Company, a venture which received the approval of the College Council on 8 May 1847 and was provisionally registered a week later—in the names of John Parker and David Walker.[17] This venture, which was announced as being "distinct in its operations and responsibilities, but still under the sanction and patronage of the College,"[18] was open to both male and female teachers. On 8 July 1847 there was a meeting of the promoters at 42, Great Russell Street, and, four days later, of the provisional board of directors at the Freemasons' Tavern, when Parker acted as secretary. On 21 August 1848 the Company was incorporated under the terms of the Joint Stock Regulation Act,[19] and the first meeting of the board of directors following the incorporation took place at 28 Bloomsbury Square on 26 August 1848. Present on that occasion were George Thompson MP, chairman; John Neate the deputy chairman; Rev. Dr Richard Wilson of Gough House, Chelsea, one of the College's three Vice-Presidents; William Seggins from Sudbury; David Walker from Maidstone; and John Parker as secretary. The objects of the Company were to enable "educators of both sexes, professional men of all ranks, and the industrious of all classes, to make provision for, misfortune, old age and death." Unfortunately the Company offered terms which were too generous to its members and soon found itself in difficulties.[20]

The fourth development of 1847, and one which was to provide a most valuable service for the teaching profession as a whole and the College in particular, until it was finally outmatched in 1923 by the *Times Educational Supplement*, was the *Educational Times*. The first edition of the *Educational Times*, "A monthly stamped journal of education, science and literature," was published on Saturday, 2 October 1847 at a cost of sixpence stamped or fivepence unstamped, and consisted of 16 pages. From the start it acted as the unofficial paper of the College and is by far the most important single source for its early history, although the formal relationship was not fully cemented until April 1861. From that date, the 163rd issue by the old reckoning but the first in a new series which marked the new relationship, the paper became the organ of the College and bore on its masthead the legend *The Educational Times and Journal of the College of Preceptors*. The price was then sevenpence stamped or sixpence unstamped, for 24 pages.

The *Educational Times* was a serious paper with a serious purpose, although not averse to the inclusion of an occasional humorous piece. It published papers, model answers and pass lists of Preceptors' exams, membership lists and minutes of

Preceptors' meetings, accounts of lectures and publications, advertisements of teaching posts and from those seeking employment. It commented on the great educational issues of the day, and printed earnest correspondence from those who would reform the educational establishment and from those who had suffered at its hands.

The Royal Charter

As early as 20 November 1846 a deputation from the College Council had waited upon Lord John Russell to urge upon the new Prime Minister the need for competent and responsible teachers for schools for the children of the middle classes.[21] Nothing came of this initiative, but in 1847 the Council determined that the best way to secure official recognition of its role was to apply for a Royal Charter. A sum of £500 was required to finance this enterprise and a group of Council members generously offered that once one half of the total had been raised by general subscription they would supply the rest. A first list of 138 subscribers was published in December 1847, with Henry Turrell's name at the head for five guineas. Payne's contribution was a modest half guinea,[22] but early in 1848, prompted perhaps by the knowledge that Turrell had made a second donation of £10, he, too, gave a further contribution, on this occasion of a full guinea.[23]

The College's determination to seek a charter aroused hostility from many quarters. In England the traditional route into teaching in boys' grammar or public schools, and in some private schools, was by attendance and possibly graduation at Oxford and Cambridge, and by ordination into the Anglican Church. Such an education, it was widely believed, supplied both the knowledge of what to teach and how to teach. For traditionalists, therefore, the granting of a charter to the College of Preceptors, a body composed in the main of nongraduate lay persons, many of whom were Dissenters, seemed to be an assault upon the principles and persons of the teaching profession, as currently constituted. Equipped with a charter the College might promote the notions that (with respect to teaching) secular was superior to religious, and the College's own qualifications to the degrees of the ancient universities. Opposition, however, came not only from entrenched interests but also from those radicals who feared the establishment of a new set of privileges and interests. One of the most lively of the Preceptors' local boards was that at Manchester, a city still flushed with the success of the Anti-Corn-Law League, and now pioneering, through the Lancashire (later National) Public School Association, the cause of rate-aided elementary schools. The leading representative of the College in this region was William Ballantyne Hodgson, the Edinburgh-born educational reformer and political economist. In 1847 Hodgson had moved from his previous post as principal of the Liverpool Institute, to become principal of the Chorlton High School in Manchester.

On the evening of Monday, 8 October 1848, the mayor of Manchester, Elkanah Armitage, was in the chair, and Hodgson on the platform, when John Parker and Stephen Freeman spoke to a large audience in the lecture theatre of the Manchester Athenaeum on the objects and plans of the College. It is not clear whether Parker and Freeman had been warned by Hodgson and the local secretary, Makinson, of the hostility which existed towards the charter application, but the responses to their opening speeches soon set the tone for the rest of the evening. Alexander Henry MP declared that "he never knew a chartered body which did not end in intolerance, bigotry and oppression." W. Corns even moved an amendment against the charter application. He chided the Dissenting ministers on the platform and castigated "the State Church, that biggest and vilest of all corporations." He fulminated against the Committee of Council and Her Majesty's Inspectors of Education, "I believe there is not one of them who has ever been a schoolmaster in his life." J. C. Dyer, a member of the College, and William Shuttleworth were others who spoke against the charter application, but at the end of the meeting Corns could find only three persons prepared to support his amendment, and the arguments of those who assured the meeting that the charter would not be exclusive but would enable the College to "put the stamp upon the true and genuine teacher, as Government put a stamp upon gold and silver articles," won the day.[24] Such was the anxiety raised by the

Manchester meeting and the fear of the loss of Dissenting and Voluntaryist support, that the *Educational Times* of November 1848 included an article entitled "What is the Charter? and what it is not," signed only as "F," but written by a "staunch Dissenter." This stated that the College was committed to the "utmost degree of Civil and Religious Liberty for all," and concluded that the Council was seeking a charter essentially as "the just means of affixing a lawful stamp on our board of examination."[25] Whether these arguments convinced the radical doubters is not clear. What is certain is that the College had enough patrons and friends at Court to secure the Royal favour, and the Charter was issued on 28 March 1849.

The Charter's preamble referred to Turrell as the petitioner, and to the main purpose of the College as:

> of promoting sound learning and of advancing the interests of education, more especially among the middle classes by affording facilities to the teacher for the acquiring of a sound knowledge of his profession, and by providing for the periodical Session of a competent Board of Examiners to ascertain, and give certificates of, the acquirements and fitness for their office of persons engaged or desiring to be engaged in the Education of Youth, particularly in the Private Schools of England and Wales.[26]

Under the terms of the Charter, provision was made for the holding of two general meetings per year, for the election of a Council of 48, one quarter of whom were to retire each year, and for the election of a President, three Vice-Presidents, Dean, Secretary, Treasurer and Auditors.

Most members of the College were no doubt mightily pleased with its new Charter and celebration dinners were held. Typically Payne, though he had subscribed to the Charter fund, was critical both of the Charter and of the College constitution. Payne disapproved of the Charter because he saw it as a diversion from the essential purpose of the College. For him the quality of education would not be improved by the purchase of expensive pieces of parchment, but by the training and certification of teachers. He saw the whole process as a waste of time and money, and in 1868 commented caustically:

The fact that it was necessary to pay more than £500 in hard cash to lawyers to procure a sanction from Victoria, Queen, Defender of the Faith, to a body of men seeking nothing for themselves personally, but only "to promote sound learning and advance the interests of education," is one of those strange anomalies which, with a crowd of others, we shall leave for the amusement of our successors.[27]

He disapproved of the constitution of the College as set out under the Charter because, prior to the Charter, Vice-Presidents and Council members were not eligible for reelection until a year had elapsed. Payne believed that the College had become less democratic under the Charter and that it was an example of "a popular constitution aristocratically managed."[28]

The Council

The Council of the College comprised 48 members. This was a large body but, given the fact that its members were widely scattered throughout the country and travel was difficult, and that many had very demanding jobs, not surprisingly there was rarely a majority in attendance at meetings.

In 1849 the Council was composed entirely of males but, in the future, female members would include such notables as Frances Buss and Beata Doreck. Just under half were graduates of British universities. Twelve were Anglican clergyman, two were Dissenting ministers. This did not, however, imply a representation of the priesthood of the Anglican Church as such, but rather that masters of endowed grammar schools, of whom there were 13 on the Council, were usually required to be in holy orders. There was one MP, William Ewart, Liverpool born and Oxford educated, "an advanced Liberal," who had previously represented Bletchingley, Liverpool and Wigan in the Commons, but was now a member for Dumfries. Ewart's educational campaigns included the establishment of schools of design and free public libraries, the admission of "unattached" students to universities, and examination entry for the civil and diplomatic service. All were eventually achieved. Ewart was not to play a substantial role in the College's history, but other members of the Council of 1849 (besides Turrell and Payne) who were to become leading lights were the next three presidents—S. C. Freeman from Enfield; G. A. Jacob, headmaster of the Collegiate School, Sheffield; and E. R. Humphreys from Murchiston Castle, Edinburgh—the dean, Richard Wilson, headmaster of St. Peter's Collegiate School in Eaton Square, London; and W. B. Hodgson, principal of Chorlton High School, Manchester. The largest single category of members was of those, like Payne himself, who were principals of private schools.[29]

Examinations for Teachers

Payne regretted, even deplored, the College's list of eminent patrons, the Charter and the indiscriminate sale of qualifications. Instead he argued that the true object of the College "was the testing of the qualifications of teachers, with a view to the protection both of the scholastic profession and of the public."[30] He, therefore, supported proposals for the formation of an assistant masters' association, for an educational library, for the production of a manual on the theory and practice of education and for a series of lectures on the subject.[31] However, in the early years of the College, only limited progress was made towards the achievement of these objectives. An examination system was established, a system in which Payne played a considerable role.

The College's first examining board was headed by the dean, the Rev. Dr Richard Wilson. He, together with the Reverends Stoddart and Eccleston, acted as examiners for the Classics paper.[32] Other examiners included John Hind, James Wharton and George Boole for Mathematics; Freeman, Seggins and Payne for Commerce; Delille, Wattey and Gassion for French, and Antoine Heyd for German.[33] The first examination was held in January 1847 when 24 candidates passed. There is no record of the total number of entries. Candidates were required to offer Bible History and Theory and Practice of Education. Classics, Commerce, Mathematics and Foreign Languages, etc., were optional. The "etc." covered "any departments of knowledge not previously enumerated," and the June 1847 examination included Geology and Physics.[34]

The College's first examination papers in the Theory and Practice of Education were, in many senses, pioneering. Candidates were no doubt rightly perplexed by the lack of consistency between the successive papers. At the simplest level this was apparent in the numbers of questions set. Over the first four years these ranged from 10 to 25, a real problem when candidates were expected to answer all the questions or as many as they could. Of the three examiners in this period who set the papers, Turrell, Payne and Freeman, only Turrell showed any consistency on this point.[35]

Theory and Practice examination papers, 1847–50

Date	Examiner	Number of Questions
January 1847	Turrell	10
June 1847	Payne	21
January 1848	Payne	18
June 1848	Freeman	18
January 1849	Turrell	11
June 1849	Payne	12
January 1850	Freeman	25
June 1850	Freeman	14

Even more problems, however, arose from the nature of the papers. The first, set by Turrell, put practice before theory.

January 1847[36]

The Theory and Practice of Education

1. In what manner do you consider the religious and moral sentiments can be most effectively cultivated?

2. How does the branch of instruction which you undertake operate upon the intellectual faculties?

3. State what you know of the different systems of teaching, and point out their excellencies and defects.

4. Give an outline of the plan of instruction which you would adopt in communicating a knowledge of the

subjects you desire to teach—what works and what editions would you use?

5. In what way would you arrange the studies of a school (classical and mathematical, or commercial) averaging (25) (40) (100) pupils from 10 to 16 years of age? State the numbers of teachers requisite, and the amount and division of time given to each study, to exercise and to sleep in such an establishment.

6. By what means and upon what principles would you maintain discipline? How would you punish offences against order and against morality?

7. Point out the Educational errors to which inexperienced teachers are most liable.

8. Draw the ground plan of a school-room intended for 25 or 40 or 100 pupils; arranging desks, &c., so as to provide, as far as possible, against the collision of classes, the interference of pupils with each other, and the various causes of confusion and disorder in a school, placing the principal's desk in a position to command the whole.

9. State what you know of the best method of lighting, warming and ventilating a school-room.

10. What do you consider the best course of developing the perceptive, reasoning, retentive, and imitative faculties? and what studies do you deem the best agency for cultivating them respectively?

Turrell's paper required teachers to reflect upon their everyday experience of the schoolroom, and of the school more generally. It did not ask for any specific knowledge of educational history, nor of the theories of the great educators, past or present. There were no specific references to authors or works. One may imagine, therefore, the consternation of those candidates who sat the June examination paper set by Joseph Payne.

June 1847[37]

The Theory and Practice of Education

1. Give a definition of Education in its widest sense, and distinguish it from Instruction.

2. The Germans make a distinction between *Pädagogik*, the science of Education; *Methodik*, the science of Methods; *Didaktik*, the art of teaching. How would you define their respective provinces?

3. What ought to be mental and moral qualifications of an accomplished Schoolmaster?

4. State the leading features of Pestalozzi's, Jacotot's, and De Fellenberg's systems of Education, and point out their several excellencies and defects.

5. What provision should be made, in a comprehensive scheme of Education, for the training of the physical powers?

6. What plans would you adopt for the moral and religious training of your pupils in general? and how would you deal with cases of swearing, lying, or dishonesty?

7. Trace the analogy between the profession of teaching and that of medicine.

8. State the arguments for and against the use of corporal punishment as a means of discipline.

9. Discuss the following educational dogmas:

    1. The faults of the school are to be sought for in the master.

    2. The object of education is to stimulate the pupil to educate himself.

    3. The pupil should never be allowed to leave a subject until he thoroughly understands it.

    4. *On ne s'instruit pas en s'amusant.*

    5. *Non multa sed multum.*

    6. *Festina lente.*

10. Explain and contrast the analytical and synthetical (or constructive) methods of teaching. Illustrate the

application of each to teaching Arithmetic or Latin, and trace their respective moral effects on the mind of the pupil.

11. Describe the course of studies pursued by the Athenian and Roman youths of the times of Pericles and Augustus respectively.

12. What subjects should constitute the curriculum of studies in schools for the middle and higher classes in this country?

13. State the principal arguments for and against making classical studies a prominent part of a liberal education.

14. What is the nature and range of the mental discipline effected by the study of Mathematics?

15. What are the main deficiencies in our common methods of teaching Mathematics? How would you propose to remedy them? As an illustration explain how you would teach Arithmetic to an elementary class.

16. What was Milton's opinion respecting the desirableness of making the Natural Sciences the chief objects of study in elementary schools, as propounded in his *Tractate on Education*? Quote also Dr Johnson's comment on that opinion.

17. Which do you consider, from personal experience, the best books for teaching the following subjects: Greek, Latin, French, German, Algebra, Trigonometry, Arithmetic, Geography, General History, and English Grammar?

18. Give an outline of the plan you would pursue in teaching Greek, Euclid, or History.

19. Point out the errors to which inexperienced teachers are most liable.

20. It is stated that in Germany the teacher would no more think of meeting his pupils without special daily preparation, than a Barrister or a Clergyman would address an audience without careful premeditation. What must be the result of such a habit?

21. Name the works on Education that you have studied, and give an analysis of some one of them.

Substantial though this paper might appear to be, it was not inconsistent with others included in the same examination. There were 25 questions on the Commerce and Political Economy paper, 26 on that for English Language and Literature, 26 on Physics and 20 on Chemistry. Though Modern History candidates were faced with a mere 10, these included not only English history, for example a comparison of the position of the middle classes in the reigns of Henry III and George III, but also detailed questions on the histories of America, Belgium, Canada, France, Holland, Portugal, Prussia and Spain. Nevertheless, there was clearly some feeling, both amongst teachers and in the College Council (and no doubt among the candidates) that Payne was asking a great deal for a compulsory paper, and that whereas the other papers tested knowledge which fell within established areas and disciplines, the Theory and Practice paper, as construed by Payne, did not. Question 17, for example assumed that candidates were actively teaching at least ten subjects, including two Classical and two modern languages; question 9 assumed some familiarity with the Latin and French languages; while questions 11, 16 and 4 required a knowledge of the theory and practice of education which spanned some 2,000 years.

The examination paper of June 1847 may be seen as Payne's contribution to the creation of the very subject of the theory and practice of education in Britain. Few teachers, however, shared his concept or could match his erudition. Payne, therefore, was asked by the Council to supply model answers to the questions posed on the Theory and Practice of Education paper. This he declined to do, although the practice was common in respect of mathematical papers, and indeed a full set of solutions to the algebra paper of January 1847 was published in the *Educational Times* of December 1847. Payne's refusal was based on two premises. The first was that specimen answers for mathematics could not be used by candidates to answer questions on future papers, because although the principles examined might be similar there was an infinite variety of actual problems which could be set. The same was not true of theory and practice of education, and therefore were he to supply "pattern answers" they might be learned by heart and simply repeated in future examinations. As he stated in a memorandum on this issue written on 17 November 1847, "the questions on this subject must, from the nature of the case, be very nearly the same year after year."[38] The second objection was that there was no single right answer to many questions, and that the paper was designed to make individuals responsible for working out the relationship between theory and their own practice. In his November memorandum Payne advised:

> The main object of this particular examination is to ascertain the candidate's own experience in the practice of his profession, and his feeling towards it as well as the amount of reflection and investigation that feeling may have called forth on his part. My own opinion is, that he is but half a schoolmaster who does not regard his own profession as the most honourable—next to the sacred calling of the minister of God—that a man can be called upon to sustain; and he, therefore, who does not evince, by his examination on this subject, that he has read much and thought much upon it, has yet a great deal to learn.[39]

Nevertheless, Payne was not insensible to the great gap which existed between the demands of the Preceptors' examinations and the high-quality profession which he envisaged, on the one hand, and the reality of life for most junior assistants on the other. The very first number of the *Educational Times* carried a letter from a young teacher in Islington who questioned the practicability of the College's advice "that each school in connexion with the College of Preceptors may act as a normal or training school" and asked, in respect of preparation for the examinations, "how is it possible for a young man who fags all day in and out of school to be able to fit himself for such a task?"[40] But although Payne was unwilling to supply model answers he was happy to provide "hints and reference to authorities" for answers to the Theory and Practice paper for June 1847, and these were duly printed in a double-page spread in the *Educational Times* of December 1847.[41]

For question 1 Payne advised the starting point that "Instruction is, of course, only a species of education." He then went on to provide a list of no fewer than 35 publications on the general subject of education. These included works by Plato, Xenophon, Aristotle, Plutarch, Quintilian, Augustine, Montaigne, Fleury, Rousseau, Rollin, Helvetius, Pestalozzi, Jacotot, Degerando, Ascham, Milton, Locke, Edgeworth, together with those of contemporary writers, and publications of the Central Society for Education and of the Society for the Diffusion of Useful Knowledge. The starting point for an answer to question 2, Payne advised, was that "*Pädagogik* is the generic term; *Methodik* and *Didaktik* are species." Recommended reading for this question were two volumes cited in the previous list, Victor Cousin, *Report on the State of Public Instruction in Prussia* and Henry Dunn, *Principles of Teaching*, which Payne commended as "a valuable manual." Dunn, together with other works including one by Thomas Arnold, was recommended for an answer to question 3 on the mental and moral qualities of a schoolmaster.

As for question 4, according to Payne the characteristic feature of Pestalozzi's system was that of "synthesis," that of Jacotot, "analysis." Both, he advised, were essentially adapted to intellectual education "while De Fellenberg's is more comprehensive, and aims to develop all the faculties of our nature, physical, intellectual, and moral." Payne's reading list for this question excluded mention of his own pamphlet on Jacotot but did make reference to the article in the *Quarterly Journal of Education* in which it had been reviewed. For question 5 Payne simply supplied a list of six books on mental and physical cultivation and health, and for question 6 a list of four volumes, including three from the general list for question 1 was given. These were Dunn, Edgeworth, *Practical Education*, especially chapter viii on "Truth," and Abbott, *The Teacher*, in which chapter iv on "Moral Discipline" was singled out as "containing many very valuable suggestions."

Payne's comments on question 7 showed that he was not here referring to a profession as a group of people engaged in a particular type of employment (the General Medical Council would not be created until 1858, and contrasts between the teaching and medical professions in that sense were not so marked), but rather to the actual practice of that employment.

His analogy as to the similarities, rather than the differences, between the two practices was highly revealing:

> It would be well if all teachers could learn to look upon the faults of their pupils as symptoms of mental or moral disease, and as such requiring careful, judicious, quiet and benevolent attention, with a view to their complete restoration to health.

This comment reflected Payne's personal approach towards teaching, that of patient, caring endeavour, but typically he provided other references, including Dunn's rather different view of the analogy, and the works of three writers on the moral treatment of the insane.

For question 8 on corporal punishment Payne, who was himself an opponent of beating, simply provided four references: Knox, Ascham, Locke and Thomas Arnold. Question 9, on the six "educational dogmas," Payne advised "may be left to exercise the ingenuity of the candidate. With regard to most of them, much may be said on both sides." Question 10 on the analytical and synthetical (or constructive) methods of teaching caused Payne to range widely. Both methods were used, though writers such as Pestalozzi and Jacotot had insisted on the predominance of one or the other. The preference of James Kay Shuttleworth, Secretary to the Committee of Privy Council on Education, was for the synthetical method, and the consequent adoption of this approach in works published under the sanction of the government was noted and examples provided of books on the teaching of arithmetic and Classics. The works of two authors, Becker and Barthelemy, were recommended as sources of information about Athenian and Roman education for question 12.

Questions 13 and 14, about the school curriculum with particular reference to the place of Classics, were issues of deep personal concern to Payne and to all teachers in private, grammar and public schools. Payne made a distinction between those authors like Bentham, Combe and Simpson who maintained that the main object of education was the acquisition of knowledge, and those who believed instead that schooling should develop and discipline the faculties. References to the utility or otherwise of the Classics included Angus, *Four Lectures on the Advantage of a Classical Education as an auxiliary to a Commercial Education*; Beattie, *Essay on the Utility of Classical Learning*; and a publication of the Central Society of Education by Long entitled, *What are the Advantages of a Study of Antiquity at the Present Time?* For questions 14 and 15 on the teaching of mathematics Payne provided a list of authors and works, including four articles by De Morgan published in the *Quarterly Journal of Education.* Answers to question 16 would require a knowledge of the *Tractate* and of Johnson's life of Milton.

Question 17 on the best books for teaching specific subjects, Payne advised, "must of course, be answered from personal experience and knowledge." Nevertheless, the full list which he provided—eight for arithmetic, seven for Latin, five each for Greek and history, four for German, three each for algebra, geometry, trigonometry and English grammar, and two for French and geography—suggested both the breadth of Payne's teaching experience and that a mere list of preferred texts, rather than any comment or justification, was required as an answer. It is possible that Payne found the compilation of this list of recommended reading for the teaching of eleven subjects (he included geometry which was not in the original paper as printed in the *Educational Times*) somewhat arduous, for as to questions 18 to 21 he simply stated: "The remaining questions should be answered from personal experience and observation."

Theory or Practice?

Payne's examination paper of June 1847 showed the erudition and application of an able and dedicated person in a relatively uncharted area of knowledge. He declared his list of recommended reading to be "imperfect," but hoped that it would be "augmented at some future opportunity."[42] This no doubt raised further feelings of concern among Council members and in the College more widely. Payne's reading list and advice indicated the extent to which candidates were required to be thoroughly acquainted with a considerable range of literature about the history, theory and practice of education. Was such knowledge necessary or even attainable?

Payne's next paper of January 1848 was in many respects much easier. There were fewer questions: none on educational history and no direct references to specific authors or works on education. The only question which required any reference to theory not grounded on practice was number 17 which asked candidates to "give an analysis of any work on Education that you have studied."[43]

Wilson and Freeman were listed as examiners in Theory and Practice for June 1848 when Freeman set the paper, and Wilson and Turrell for January 1849 when it was devised by Turrell.[44] In the summer of 1849, however, Payne returned to the fold with a searching paper which nevertheless contained only one reference to a specific educational work.

June, 1849[45]

The Theory and Practice of Education

1. What should be the object chiefly aimed at by a Teacher in adopting his profession?

2. What constitutes, in your opinion, a good Education— moral, intellectual and physical?

3. Show that in moral training a Teacher's success mainly depends on the influence which his personal character gives him.

4. Seeing the object of all intellectual training should be the formation of habits and the development of the mental faculties, show how the study of Classics and Mathematics promotes that end.

5. Distinguish between Elementary and Professional Education.

6. What are the advantages and disadvantages of teaching by Lectures as practised in the Continental schools?

7. In what way would you cultivate the faculty of Taste in your pupils?

8. Suppose a class before you ready to commence the study of Modern History, Physical Geography, or Algebra, how would you introduce the subject to their notice?

9. In making arrangements for a school consisting of six classes, what Authors and Exercises should a graduated course of instruction in Latin comprehend?

10. What Systems of Instruction are you acquainted with? State their leading features and discuss their merits.

11. What means do you consider best adapted to ensure proficiency in Prose Composition in Latin and Greek? In what respects does the practice of Versification appear to you to be useful?

12. Defend or impugn Harris' designation of the study of Mathematics as "the noblest praxis of logic."

Some indication of the effect of this paper upon the candidates has survived. In 1850 Freeman and Payne drew up a manual on the theory and practice of education which contained not only all the examination papers to that date but also the full answer papers of three candidates to the June 1849 examination. These answer papers were included, according to Freeman and Payne, "not as first class models . . . but rather as honest and highly creditable illustrations of what can be done by School-Assistants of studious habits and respectable attainments."[46] Although not made explicit by the examiners, it would appear that all three of the candidates (referred to cryptically as J. D., F. A. L. and S. S.) obtained second-class passes.[47] Unfortunately the pass list for June 1849 has no mention of any successful candidates in Theory and Practice. Other pass lists indicate that two of the candidates were probably F. A. Laing of the Grammar School, Kimbolton, Huntingdonshire and S. Sharpe of Castle Meadow, Norwich.[48] "J. D." completed all 12 questions and his answers occupied some four and a quarter sides of the manual; "F. A. L." finished 10 questions which covered just over two sides: "S. S." managed 11 answers in some two and a half sides. Varied and interesting answers were provided to questions 5, 6 and 7. Question 10 was poorly done; question 12 was largely avoided.

Responses to question 1 give some flavour of the purposeful and earnest tone which characterized the work of all three candidates. The answer of "J. D." was expressed in a single sentence:

> The training of the rising generation committed to his charge, to occupy useful and respectable positions in after life.

"F. A. L." began his more substantial answer with:

> To be fully impressed with the importance and religious responsibility of his high calling.

"S. S." emphasized the importance of "sound truth." The object of the teacher should be

> so to direct, improve, and enlarge the minds of youth, as to qualify them for whatever position in life they may be called to by Providence.[49]

Concern about the Theory and Practice examination came to a head in 1850. In May a leader in the *Educational Times* gave grudging praise but argued that an examination was not enough "to produce, or even to test, efficient Educators."[50] Two recommendations were made for improving the situation: the adoption of a "means of ascertaining the practical ability"[51] of teachers (presumably a viva voce or some type of classroom examination) and a series of annual prizes for proficiency in the Theory and Practice examination. The prizes proposed were munificent in the extreme: four of £20, eight of £10 and 16 of £5![52] From 1855 a prize was indeed awarded for performance in the Theory and Practice examination.

On Saturday, 22 June 1850, the issue of how best to promote the theory and practice of education among teachers surfaced at a meeting of Council which accepted the recommendation of the secretary, John Parker, that

> the College Examiners in *The Theory and Practice of Education* should be requested to collect and collate the whole of the hitherto printed papers in their particular department, with power to make such alterations and comments as they might think desirable.[53]

Payne, who was listed as an examiner for the Theory and Practice paper[54] at the summer examination in 1850, was not present at the June Council meeting nor at that held on 20 July when it was resolved that

> Messrs Freeman and Payne, in conjunction with the Examinations Committee be authorized to draw up a suggestive manual on the Theory and Practice of Education with least possible delay in such form and manner as shall to them seem desirable and to print and publish the same at the expense of the College.[55]

Interestingly, although at this meeting Payne, in his absence, was appointed to the Library Committee of the College (the Library was open daily from 10 a.m. to 4 p.m.), unlike Freeman he was not made a member of the "Committee for Examinations, Lectures, Conversazioni and Classes."[56] Moreover, in the summer of 1850 John Dyne, a Council member and principal of Bolton House School, Turnham Green, planned a course of lectures for teachers, on the "Theory and Practice of Education," delivered on 22 June which was given not by Payne but by Freeman.[57] Some 35 lectures were planned, three per day, from 20 June to 20 July, for a course fee of 10 shillings. Other topics included Literature, both English and French, Chemistry, Geometry, Music, Political Philosophy, Vegetable Physiology and Zoology.[58]

Freeman and Payne must have worked quickly to compile the manual, for at the Council meeting held on 24 August, to which Hodgson (then Vice-President) sent a letter declining the office of President (Freeman who was chairing the meeting was elected in his stead), it was agreed that Freeman and Parker should be responsible for the printing and publishing of the "suggestive manual," a task that should be fulfilled "with the least possible delay and expense."[59]

A suggestive manual on the theory and practice of education, published in 1850, was a modest affair of some 50 pages, and priced at one shilling.[60] In their prefatory notice Freeman and Payne stated that the manual was but a first attempt to answer the question, so frequently raised by candidates and others, "What is meant by *The Theory and Practice of Education* and what works they should read, or what courses of study they should pursue on that subject." They disclaimed any attempt to provide a textbook; instead useful starting points were offered. These included the full text of Freeman's lecture given on 22 June 1850, a schedule of the lecture course and examination programme for

June and July 1850, and a copy of the nine-point reference to be supplied in respect of all candidates for the examination, a reference which bore the awesome heading "Dean's Preliminary Moral Test." This was followed by the eight examination papers in Theory and Practice from January 1847 to June 1850, and the three sets of answers to the examination held on 25 June 1849, referred to above.

The next three pages gave details of the Ladies' Department. Though this might seem to have been an incongruous inclusion in such a manual, its purpose no doubt was to show that examinations were open to female candidates. It also reflected the keen interest in female education exhibited by both Payne and Freeman, whose wife, Ellen, was secretary to the Ladies' Committee. The manual was concluded with a section on "books on the theory and practice of education." This began with a reference to Payne's suggestions included in the *Educational Times* of December 1847, when commenting on his examination paper of June of that year, and an acknowledgment that the ferocity of that list and advice had possibly deterred some prospective candidates. Such erudition, Freeman and Payne now advised, might be expected of first-class candidates, but "book theories" were not everything. The most important element was that candidates should be reflective practitioners and provide evidence that they could

> think deeply and act conscientiously in all their professional *practice*. Enlightened private reflection and laborious performance of Educational DUTY amongst living pupils, will always be the most "suggestive manual" and the best *"Text-book"* which can be recommended.[61]

Fletcher and Payne, however, were careful to cover themselves against the charge of lowering standards. Their "Abridged List" of some 30 titles on education, which included works by such female authors as de Wahl, Hamilton, Lewis and Martineau, was concluded with "THE HOLY BIBLE; both testaments," and "Innumerable other works, both Ancient and Modern."[62]

Whether the manual had much impact is not clear. In May 1851 it appeared, together with five other titles, at the head of a review in the *Educational Times*,[63] but there was no discussion of its contents. Though Payne, no doubt, contributed substantially to the book list, the inclusion of Freeman's lecture, his standing as a schoolmaster of some 25 years' experience and his accession in 1850 to the presidency, meant that the manual would principally be associated with his name rather than with that of Payne.

Payne attended the September and December Council meetings in 1850 and was listed as an examiner for Theory and Practice for January 1851 but Theory and Practice and the balance between the two remained controversial. Indeed, at the Council meeting of 28 September 1850 a decision was taken to refer to the Examinations Committee a proposal for "giving more practical efficacy to the testing of candidates in the Theory and Practice of Education."[64]

Though the effect of the manual upon Theory and Practice is not easily determined, one feature of the examination of January 1851 which no doubt delighted Freeman and Payne was the performance of the female candidates. Eleven males and nine females were successful overall. The men, however, amassed 35 certificates among them; the women 40! Of the 35, seven certificates were won by one candidate, Samuel Burrell, who secured second-class passes in English Grammar and Geography, and third-class in Classics, French, Hebrew, Scripture History and English History. One interesting name on the pass list was that of Robert Ibbs, one of only two candidates to secure a first-class pass in Theory and Practice, who also obtained a second class in Scripture History and a third in Classics. Ibbs was, or was about to become, an assistant master at Payne's school in Leatherhead.[65]

In 1851 Payne's attendance at Council meetings was erratic. He spoke at the half-yearly general meeting held on Saturday, 28 June, was listed as an examiner in Theory and Practice in the summer of 1851, and was accorded other duties including that of moderating the papers in Modern Languages.[66] It is noticeable that at this examination Theory and Practice was listed under "Additional Subjects." The most striking feature of the examination overall, however, was that once again, as Dean Richard Wilson remarked in his report, "the ladies have done themselves more credit than the gentlemen."[67] Payne's original concept of the centrality and nature of Theory and Practice was being supplanted. For example, in May, June and July of 1851 the *Educational Times* published three rambling articles written by Henry Turrell, the first president, under the heading "Theory and Practice of Education," articles which dealt with the "cultivation of the intellectual powers by means of the study of language," and concluded by stating that "classical study is the best ground-work for the training and strengthening of the mind."[68] The College, moreover, was broadening its sphere of interests. These ranged from an unsuccessful attempt to gain free admission for assistant teachers, both females and males, to the Great Exhibition, on the grounds that it would be of educational benefit to their pupils, to the College's scheme for another series of pioneering examinations—not of teachers but of their pupils. A still wider world was beckoning. On 8 November 1851 members of the College Council were informed of the contents of a letter from a Mr Cawthorne, secretary of the South Australian Preceptors' Association and master of the Adelaide Grammar School, who inquired as to the possibility of some form of incorporation between the College of Preceptors and "similar societies established in any of the British Colonies."[69]

Payne's vision of the erudite schoolteacher, at the one time learned in the theory of education and distinguished in its practice, was not fulfilled at this time. Practical problems prevailed. There were no training colleges for secondary schoolteachers and no courses of lectures they could attend in the evenings. As Payne's reading list and the production of a suggestive manual indicated, there was a limited range of contemporary textbooks and secondary works on education. Moreover, there were few incentives for teachers to engage in further study. To Payne's great regret the College of Preceptors did not enforce its first resolution of 1846, "that some proof of qualification, both as to the amount of knowledge and the art of conveying it to others," be required from its members. Little wonder that, in the 1850s, he turned to educational matters nearer to home: the education of his own family and of the boys at the Mansion Grammar School.

NOTES

1. College of Preceptors, *Calendar of the College. Instituted June, 1846* (London, 1847); Chapman, *Professional Roots*, p. 11.

2. Chapman, *Professional Roots*, p. 21.

3. College of Preceptors, *Fifty Years of Progress in Education. A review of the work of the College of Preceptors, from its foundation in 1846 to its Jubilee in 1896* (London, 1896), p. 4.

4. Payne, *Works*, I, pp. 309–27.

5. *Ibid.*, p. 309.

6. *Ibid.*, p. 309.

7. *Ibid.*, p. 311.

8. *Ibid.*, p. 312.

9. *Fifty Years*, p. 6.

10. Payne, *Works*, I, p. 313.

11. In 1993 the President of the College was Lady Bridget Plowden, best known for the Plowden Report of 1967 on *Children and Their Primary Schools*.

12. Frances Mary Buss, 1827–94, probably the best-known pioneer of education for girls in Britain. She was buried at Theydon Bois in Essex, where the College of Preceptors is now located. The initials FCP are on her tombstone.

13. *Fifty Years*, p. 22.

14. Chapman, *Professional Roots*, p. 23.

15. *Educational Times* I, 12 (September 1848), p. 257.

16. Payne, *Works*, I, p. 314.

17. Preceptors' and General Mutual Life Assurance Company Minute Book, 1847–9.

18. *Fifty Years*, p. 7.

19. 7 and 8 Vict. Cap. 110. Preceptors' and General Mutual Life Assurance Company Minute Book, 1847–9, p. 11.

20. *Fifty Years*, p. 7.

21. Chapman, *Professional Roots*, p. 24.

22. *Educational Times* I, 3 (December 1847), p. 56.

23. *Educational Times* I, 7 (April 1848), p. 137.

24. *Educational Times* II, 14 (November 1848), pp. 31–3.

25. *Educational Times* II, 14 (November 1848), pp. 34–5.

26. *Fifty Years*, p. 9.

27. Payne, *Works*, I, p. 316.

28. *Ibid.*

29. *Educational Times* II, 22 (July 1849), p. 223, and 23 (August 1849), p. 243.

30. Payne, *Works*, I, p. 311.

31. *Ibid.*, p. 314.

32. *Fifty Years*, p. 6.

33. *Educational Times* I, 1 (October 1847), p. 5.

34. *Ibid.*

35. College of Preceptors, *A suggestive manual on the theory and practice of education* (London, 1850), pp. 30–7.

36. *Suggestive manual*, p. 30.

37. *Suggestive manual*, pp. 31–2. The examination paper was also reproduced in the *Educational Times* I, 1 (October 1847), p. 3, and the reading list and guide in the *Educational Times* I, 3 (December 1847), pp. 40–1.

38. *Educational Times* I, 3 (December 1847), p. 40.

39. *Ibid.*

40. *Educational Times* I, 1 (October 1847), p. 8.

41. *Educational Times* I, 3 (December 1847), pp. 40–1.

42. *Ibid.*, p. 40.

43. *Suggestive manual*, p. 33.

44. *Educational Times* I, 9 (June 1848), p. 196; II, 15 (December 1848), p. 49.

45. *Suggestive manual*, p. 35. Also printed in the *Educational Times* II, 24 (September 1849), p. 285.

46. *Suggestive manual*, prefatory notice.

47. *Ibid.*

48. *Educational Times* II, 23 (August 1849), pp. 259–60.

49. *Suggestive manual*, pp. 37, 42, 44.

50. *Educational Times* III, 32 (May 1850), p. 171.

51. *Ibid.*

52. *Educational Times* III, 32 (May 1850), p. 172.

53. Minutes of the Council meeting of 22 June 1850, College of Preceptors' Council Minute Book, 1848–57, p. 85; *Educational Times* III, 34 (July 1850), p. 238.

54. The paper was printed in the *Educational Times* III, 35 (August 1850), p. 260.

55. Minutes of the Council meeting of 20 July 1850, Council Minute Book, 1848–57, p. 95.

56. Council Minute Book, 1848–57, p. 98.

57. *Educational Times* III, 33 (June 1850), p. 212.

58. *Suggestive manual*, pp. 2–4.

59. Minutes of the Council meeting of 24 August 1850, Council Minute Book, 1848–57, p. 101.

60. See the Auditors' report for 1850, which made a cautionary reference to the sum expended for printing "Mr Freeman's Pamphlet." Auditors' Report, dated 26 December 1850, inserted in the Council Minute Book, 1848–57, between pp. 126 and 127.

61. *Suggestive manual*, p. 50.

62. *Ibid.*, p. 51.

63. *Educational Times* IV, 44 (May 1851), p. 182.

64. Minutes of the Council meeting of 28 September 1850, Council Minute Book, 1848–57, p. 109.

65. *Educational Times* IV, 41 (February 1851), p. 102.

66. Council Minute Book, 1848–57, p. 140.

67. *Educational Times* IV, 47 (August 1851), p. 246.

68. The third article, begun in the July edition, spilled over into that of August, *Educational Times IV*, 47 (August 1851), p. 247.

69. Minutes of the Council meeting of 8 November 1851, Council Minute Book, 1848–57, p. 156.

CHAPTER FIVE

Professor of Education

A New Lease on Life

The purpose of this chapter is to trace the process by which Joseph Payne, having retired from active schoolteaching in 1863, managed within a space of ten years to secure appointment as the first professor of education in Britain. Subsequent chapters will consider how, both before and during his professorship, he developed a critique of much of the educational organization and practice of his day, and advanced such causes as the education of girls and women, the training and status of teachers, the development of a science and art of education and the improvement of classroom practice. Two factors may be identified in the creation of this chair and in the choice of Payne to occupy it. The first was Payne's growing personal standing within the educational world. This was based not only upon his past reputation, writings and activities on behalf of several educational causes, but also upon his willingness to learn. Ever an enthusiast for education, the years after his retirement from Leatherhead were not simply a period in which he repeated former ideas. As Charles Lake observed in 1878, "it was a notable characteristic of his mind this capacity and wish to learn so late in life."[1] During his years as a schoolmaster Payne had remained conversant with the many educational issues of his day; now he had time to reflect and act upon them. As Herbert Quick wrote in 1880 in his introduction to the first volume of Payne's collected works:

The consequence was that when after many years of labour he found himself able to spend his remaining days as he chose, he set himself to work with an enthusiasm and energy and self-devotion rarely found even in young men, to arouse teachers to a sense of their deficiencies.[2]

On 8 January 1867, when chairing the annual meeting of the Scholastic Registration Association at the rooms of the Society of Arts in John Street, London, Payne acknowledged "that in some respects his interest in the cause of education had been intensified since his retirement, as he had now more time to bestow upon it."[3] This dimension of time, an existence unfettered by the daily demands of duty in a boys' private school, which had been the regimen of his life for some 40 years—at the New Kent Road, Denmark Hill and Leatherhead—was characteristic of Payne's new status. His problem now was not how best to make time to advance the cause of education, but how best to spend it. The poor Suffolk boy who, even in his latter days at Leatherhead, found himself entered in directories not under "private residents" but under "commercial,"[4] was now a member of the leisured classes. This was his status while resident at 4, Kildare Gardens, Bayswater, and continued in death as in life. His occupational entries both on his own death certificate and on that of Eliza bore the legend, "Gentleman."

The second factor in Payne's progress to the professorship was his work in reforming the College of Preceptors. The main thrust of this reforming zeal was to remind the College of the importance of the first of its original resolutions, adopted in 1846, "that some proof of qualification, both as to the amount of knowledge and the art of conveying it to others, should be required." This campaign was pursued originally in respect to membership of the College. Subsequently Payne sought to apply it to the education and training of teachers in secondary schools as a whole.

In the 1850s Joseph Payne continued his membership in the College of Preceptors and, for a time, his membership in the College Council, though his attendance at meetings was erratic. He served on the Orthographical Committee, but in this period neither sought nor attained major office. Nevertheless it was at this time that Payne was to achieve some recognition of his own knowledge and intellectual power. At a Council meeting held on 27 December 1851, he was proposed as a Fellow of the College, although a controversy about the whole issue of the appointment of Fellows meant that no progress was then made.[5] Eventually, in January 1854, Payne, together with Freeman and Jacob, were elected Fellows of the College (FCP).[6]

In 1852 G. A. Jacob, headmaster of Christ's Hospital School, succeeded Freeman as President and held the post until 1856. In 1859 Jacob replaced Wilson as Dean and continued in this role until 1873. He was followed by A. K. Isbister, headmaster of the Stationers' Company School, who had been editor of the *Educational Times* since 1861 when it became the official journal of the College. Presidents in this period were E. R. Humphreys, headmaster of Cheltenham Grammar School, who held the office until 1859; Benjamin Hall Kennedy, headmaster of Shrewsbury; and from 1868 William Haig-Brown, headmaster of Charterhouse. Secretaries were John Robson from 1859 to 1865; and John O'Neil until 1874. Throughout the 1850s and 1860s, however, Payne served (with others) as an examiner for the Theory and Practice examination, although the papers now bore little resemblance to his first scholarly formulations. Partly, no doubt, as a consequence of this less ambitious approach, in January 1867 Payne was able to report to the half-yearly general meeting that "he had noticed as Examiner, a manifest improvement from year to year in the Candidates' papers upon the Theory and Practice of Education."[7]

Vice-President

Once his association with the Mansion Grammar School was completed, Payne's determination to play a major role in the College once more was indicated by his becoming a Vice-President in 1862, an office he held until 1868. From 1864 he was a most regular attender at Council meetings and, with Kennedy often absent, Payne frequently took the chair. This was a crucial period for the College, and Payne and Hodgson, who also held the rank of Vice-President, were seen as leaders of "a party of radical reform and innovation."[8]

After Payne's death Hodgson described the qualities which gave Payne his authority, not only among the Preceptors, but also in other associations devoted to the causes of education and scholarship. The following long quotation is taken from a notice in the *Journal of the Women's Education Union* of June 1876:

> Long before I had the privilege of knowing him personally, I used to hear from my late friend, Dr Lancaster, of the School at Leatherhead, and of the encouragement there given to the teaching of physical science, at a time when such instruction was much more exceptional than now. This was effected without any injury to the literary and linguistic side of the School course, in which Mr Payne was not less interested than the scientific. It was about twenty years ago that I first saw Mr Payne, at a Conference of Teachers in the Guildhall, London. Without then knowing who he was, I was much impressed by the speech delivered by a dark-looking, broad-browed man, of short stature, wearing spectacles. "He spoke as one having authority," without assumption, but without hesitation, with unusual clearness, force and accuracy of expression. It was not however till 1863, when I settled in London, that, on the Council of the College of Preceptors, our acquaintance ripened into friendship of unusual intimacy, and that I learned more and more to appreciate the solid and excellent qualities of the man. Singularly pure-minded and high-minded, utterly incapable of meanness and subterfuge, recoiling from them when exhibited by others, sensitive as to the good opinion of his fellows, but firm as a rock in his adherence to what he believed to be right or true, devoid of all pretension, courteous to those who differed from him, prompt, effective, and conciliatory in debate, he grew steadily in the respect and confidence of his colleagues, and inspired, wherever he went, sentiments that might well be envied by some men of higher position and more brilliant reputation. As he was my guest for weeks together at Berkhampstead, Bournemouth, and Bonaly, I had the fullest opportunity of studying his character, and (so far as my own power goes) of judging of his acquirements. His reading had obviously been wide and accurate; and without the slightest approach to display on his part, we often had occasion to admire the range and

preciseness of his knowledge in literary and classical questions; his sympathies and tastes were alike catholic and refined; his love of nature and children was very conspicuous. He was truly an enthusiast for education, ever meditating plans for either its improvement or its extension. It was striking to see how his views expanded, and his interest deepened as his experience in training teachers increased. He was continually revising and improving his lectures, adding illustrations and strengthening his exposition of principle.[9]

Payne's "adherence to what he believed to be right or true" regarding the state of the College of Preceptors was not always appreciated. The official review of the first 50 years of the College of Preceptors, published in pamphlet form in 1896, noted that "Mr Payne in particular played the part—often more serviceable than grateful—of the candid friend. He believed in the value of criticism."[10] There is little doubt that some other members of the College, including Isbister, regretted the scope and tone of Payne's criticisms, criticisms which were focused upon two main and connected themes. The first was that, flushed by the success of school examinations, the College had abandoned its primary responsibility: namely to make teachers into scholars and scholars into teachers. The second was that in consequence, the College was not providing a test of entry which would give the public any confidence in the teaching abilities of its members. One means whereby Payne and Hodgson sought to recommit the College to the cause of teachers was through their support of the Scholastic Registration Association. Prime mover in this cause was Barrow Rule who, having joined the College Council in 1863, pressed the College to apply to Parliament for a Teachers' Registration Act. The establishment of a scholastic register, a register which might be administered by the College of Preceptors were no other body willing or able to do so, was, for Payne, a key means of improving the quality and status of teachers.

Public criticism of the College and of its ineffectiveness in providing a guarantee to the public of the worth of teachers came to a head with the investigations and report of the Schools' Inquiry (Taunton) Commission. John Robson, secretary to the College, a graduate of University College, London, and, before his appointment as secretary, a master at University College School for 14 years, gave evidence on 28 February 1865. Although his replies to questions on the extent and nature of the College's examinations for schools were encouraging, his account of membership was confused and open to criticism. At that time, according to Robson, there were three grades of qualification: 21 Fellows, 153 Licentiates and 33 Associates. Seven of the Licentiates and four of the Associates were women. Even these qualifications, however, were not necessarily awarded as a result of successful performance in the College's examinations, while others who were successful in the examinations had not proceeded to membership. Robson admitted that the College recognized the qualifications of other bodies and "hence frequently confers diplomas without any examination by the College itself."[11] Ordinary members totalled 445 men and 28 women, together with a further 47 honorary members.

Robson began the defence of this position by arguing that "it would be impossible for any private body to exact conditions which the law does not impose."[12] Lord Lyttelton having refuted this statement, Robson fell back upon the argument that "if we had imposed any such restriction we should have gained very few supporters."[13] This, of course, was the exact opposite of the position held by Payne. He believed that the application of a rigorous test would guarantee the standing of the College and, in the longer term, increase its membership. As to the ordinary members, although Robson explained that no one would be admitted who was known to be incompetent or morally suspect, the effectiveness of such procedures was clearly open to question. Indeed Robson referred to a recent statement by Kennedy, the President, who had "distinctly warned the public against supposing that the College by electing a person as a member guarantees his fitness to be a member of the profession."[14] A further problem was of teachers who falsely claimed to be members of the College.

The Taunton Commission's findings on the College, which drew not only upon direct evidence from witnesses such as Robson, Mason and Payne, but also upon the investigations of the assistant commissioners, paid tribute to the intentions of the

College and to the value of its examinations for secondary schools of the second grade. But there were also substantial criticisms, and Payne, from his position as Vice-President, chose to use such criticisms to prod the College towards reform. Thus he specifically drew attention to the comments of Joshua Fitch, assistant commissioner for the West Riding of Yorkshire. Fitch reported that he found "amongst schoolmasters here, considerable distrust of the College of Preceptors." Several "had withdrawn themselves in disgust at the shameless use which was made, in advertisements, of the letters M.R.C.P., by men who were wholly unqualified." Of teachers in the West Riding who claimed the title of Licentiate or Associate, one stated that he had acquired this qualification for having an elementary schoolteacher's certificate, another because he had on three occasions sent pupils to be examined by the College and a third for his "long standing in his profession." Fitch found only three teachers who had ever been examined by the College, one of whom had been sent papers which he answered at home and then returned three days later![15]

Such criticisms were echoed in the press. In November 1867 the *Pall Mall Gazette* launched an attack upon the College because "its members have bestowed upon one another, with great liberality, certain professional titles." It characterized the College as "a Society of Schoolmasters, incorporated for the defence of their own professional interests." It challenged the very name of "College"—"because it has no professors."[16] Payne, no doubt, was exercised not only by the article but also by a reply to it written by the College's secretary, John O'Neil. O'Neil justified the lack of professors by arguing that "the function of the College is to *examine*, and not to *teach*."[17] This was not Payne's position. For him the College should employ all its means to produce well-educated teachers who were good classroom practitioners. Such means might well include the appointment of a professor and the establishment of a regular programme of instruction for teachers, even of a training college.

During 1868 and 1869 Payne's criticisms of the College increased. In April 1868 he wrote a review of a report on secondary education in England and Scotland commissioned by the French Ministry of Public Instruction. The report of the two commissioners, MM. Demogeot and Montucci, paid considerable attention to the College and praised some aspects of its work. Payne sought rather to highlight their observations that the College "*n'institue ni écoles ni professeurs*," and their surprise at the shortage of teachers with the College's diplomas. His review concluded by noting that "the writers dismiss the College by classing it with other inefficient attempts (*tentatives insuffisantes*) to accomplish a much needed reformation."[18] In July 1868 the *Educational Times* published a full account of Payne's paper, read at the evening meeting on 17 June, "On the past, present and future of the College of Preceptors." Payne's criticisms on that occasion: "the direction and management have been sometimes feeble and inefficient;" his condemnation of patrons and patronage; and his disparagement of the Charter culminated in his recital of the criticisms of the College contained in the Taunton Report. His solutions included the proposal that the College should "found lectureships and professorships in education, as well as found, endow or utilize training schools."[19]

There is no doubt that some officers and members of the College thought that the "complaining mood"[20] engendered by Payne at this time was regrettable, to say the least. It was bad enough for the College to have to endure the chiding and jibes of a Royal Commission, of foreign observers and of the press. For its senior Vice-President to add fuel to the flames seemed like an act of betrayal. At a meeting of the College Council held on 26 September 1868 William Haig-Brown, the headmaster of Charterhouse, was elected President in succession to Kennedy. Payne, although not present had been reelected to the Council at the half-yearly general meeting held on 8 July, and indeed had chaired the Council meetings held on 18 April, 23 May, 13 June and 8 July, but was not reelected as a Vice-President. Holden, Pinches and Templeton, headmasters respectively of the Ipswich Grammar School, Clarendon House School and the Collegiate School, Brixton Hill, were the only names proposed.[21] Early in 1869 matters came to a head. On Wednesday, 6 January, at the half-yearly general meeting, Payne (together with others in the reform group such as Hodgson and Barrow Rule) attempted to make changes in the College bylaws which might go some way towards making the College a General Teachers' Council. They were unsuccessful on that occasion, but carried the day at the next half-yearly meeting held on 7 July. The outcome of these changes was that in the future only those "who are engaged in education, and have passed an examination satisfactory to the Council" should be admissible as members. No member should be granted the title of Associate or Licentiate without passing the requisite examinations for such grades. The Council was, however, authorized to admit to the grade of Fellow, without examination, "such members of the College as possess well-attested high classical or mathematical attainments, or are eminent as teachers, or have obtained distinction in science, literature, or art."[22] Another resolution, supported by Payne and agreed to on 6 January, stated that

> the Council be asked to institute, at an early date, a Lectureship in the Science and History of Education, to which persons who wish to engage, or are engaged, in the Educational profession shall be admissible upon the payment of a certain fee to be specified by the Council from time to time. Members of the Council shall have free admission.[23]

On the following day the College organized a great meeting at the Society of Arts, a "Conference of Teachers for the Discussion of the Report of the Schools' Inquiry Commission." Haig-Brown presided and the large room of the Society was filled to overflowing with an audience of upwards of 200 eminent educationists. Men present included Edwin Chadwick, the poor law and health reformer, John Storrar, whose interests included the University of London and girls' education and who had served on the Commission; and both its secretary, H. J. Roby, and registrar, D. C. Richmond. Women present included Frances Buss and Emily Davies. The conference, which began at midday and lasted for six hours, ranged among seven topics: the first, "qualifications of schoolmasters"; the seventh, "education of girls." Resolutions were proposed and debate took place with reference to each of the seven topics.[24] Payne, no longer a Vice-President of the College but still a member of the Council, attended this conference in his capacity as Vice-President of the Scholastic Registration Association. The main thrust of his arguments on this occasion was that all those who taught, including those in boys' public and endowed grammar schools, should be required to provide evidence of their ability to teach. Accordingly, he moved a resolution, which had originated from the Scholastic Registration Association

> that the Universities of Great Britain and Ireland should institute special and professional examinations for Schoolmasters, especially in the "Theory and Practice of Education," and that they should grant to the successful Candidates the title of "Licentiate in Education." And the Conference hopes that hereafter this important subject will be made an indispensable condition of *Certification*.[25]

In proposing this resolution Payne referred to the Commissioners' findings on the preparation of teachers for schools for the middle and upper classes in France, where attendance at a normal school was required, and in Germany where certification depended upon attendance at lectures, examination and successful practice for one year in a good school. He also informed the conference that the universities of Oxford and Cambridge, and those of Edinburgh and Aberdeen, were, at that moment, seriously considering the Association's proposals on this subject. Nevertheless Payne's resolution was not carried. Two main objections were raised. The first was "that a trained teacher did not get his efficiency from having passed an examination in the theory and practice of education."[26] The second was expressed most forcibly by an Oxford graduate, the Rev. Dr Mitchinson, headmaster of the King's School, Canterbury, who declared that "if Oxford is to be taken as a sample, I believe the Universities to be the most utterly incompetent places to test anything of the kind which can be found in the world."[27] Accordingly an anodyne amendment, proposed by Isbister, was adopted, which declared the Conference's approval of "special professional examinations of schoolmasters by some competent board of examiners possessing the confidence of the public."[28]

Lecturer

In his capacity as Vice-President, Payne was on occasion open to the charge that his attitude towards the College was critical rather than constructive. However, the same was not true of another role in which he was engaged in the 1860s—that of lecturer. Until the early 1860s Payne's reputation rested upon three factors. The first was his work as a schoolmaster in two highly successful schools, success at Leatherhead was confirmed in part by the performance of his pupils in external examinations. The second was his position as an educational theorist—the interpreter of Jacotot and the College's examiner for the Theory and Practice of Education. The third was his fame as a compiler of textbooks. Then, in January 1861, the College began a series of monthly evening meetings. The purpose of such meetings was "the promotion of union, sympathy, and friendly communication between schoolmasters and teachers, to the mutual benefit of individual members, and the general benefit of the profession."[29]

The opening talk, given on 16 January 1861 at the College's premises at 42, Queen Square, by Dean Jacob was of an introductory nature and poorly attended. The second, which took place on 20 February, "was much more fully attended than the first, and we were happy to observe that several ladies were present."[30] The subject of the lecture, "On Corporal Punishment as a means of discipline in Schools," was a matter of great public interest, not least as a result of the recent trial and conviction of Thomas Hopley. The lecturer was Joseph Payne. Payne provided a brief history of corporal punishment, referred specifically to the arguments which Hopley had brought forward in his defence, and sought to refute them. He himself argued against the use of physical punishment, either as a means of maintaining discipline or of promoting learning. In conclusion, Payne apologized for the length of his paper and admitted "that it had been scribbled amidst many difficulties, and that if I had had more time I would have made it shorter."[31] In the ensuing discussion, all the speakers condemned the habitual use of corporal punishment, but there was some division between those who believed in total abolition and others who did not. Payne made a vigorous and humorous response to those who had spoken against his views, arguing that those who said that they rarely used corporal punishment were in reality his supporters and could easily find a substitute for it. The company then adjourned to the library for refreshments, where "a very general wish was expressed that the subject of the evening's discussion might be resumed on some future occasion."[32]

During the 1860s, and particularly after his retirement from Leatherhead, Payne emerged as the leading light in the evening meetings. He chaired many sessions; he was a regular contributor to discussions; he himself gave papers. In the later 1860s he contributed a paper each year. Thus on 8 March 1865 he spoke on "Dr. Arnold regarded as an Educator" and on 11 April 1866 on "The proper place of Classics in the curriculum of middle-class examinations," a paper which was continued at the next session on 18 May. On 15 May 1867 he returned to an old theme with "Jacotot: his life and system of universal instruction," and once again further discussion took place at the next session. On 17 June 1868 he delivered his critical bombshell when he spoke "On the past, present, and future of the College of Preceptors." But the paper which caused most interest, and which proved to be of crucial importance in respect of the creation of the professorship and Payne's accession to it, was given on 14 April 1869. On that evening Payne sought to build on the discussion which had taken place at the conference of 7 January upon the report of the Taunton Commission. His paper, "The training and equipment of the teacher for his profession: an examination of certain views on this subject advocated at the recent conference," was a justification for the training of teachers for secondary schools. It may also be seen as Payne's claim, should the resolution of 6 January on the establishment of a College lectureship be implemented, to that position.

It must be acknowledged that there was considerable doubt as to the wisdom of proceeding with the lectureship. Although by that date the evening meetings had continued on a regular basis for nearly a decade, they had not been very successful in attracting large audiences. Many members of the College thought them too theoretical. An alternative suggestion was that those who wished to promote good educational practice, rather than delivering learned papers upon their respective subjects, should give lessons to a class of children brought into the College for the purpose—a real example of "lessoning rather than lecturing."[33] Other College members contented themselves with reading the very full accounts of the papers and discussions as printed in the *Educational Times*. The Jubilee pamphlet acknowledged that the Queen Square premises were "poor and unattractive" for such meetings, the audiences in the early years "rather select than numerous."[34] There was no significant improvement over the decade. For example the Council's report to the half-yearly general meeting, held on 6 January 1867, stated that "the attendance at these meetings is very limited."[35] Payne's own comments characteristically were more forthright:

> Many gentlemen interested in education, both literary and scientific, have from time to time delivered lectures, which had cost them more or less of labour to produce, to audiences composed of from sixteen down to three, or even two, Members of the College.[36]

It should be noted that Payne's use of the word "Member" probably underestimated the audience. Even so it would appear that even when guests, friends and occasional visitors were included the total rarely reached 30. Payne deplored this poor attendance, but attributed it not to a gap between theory and practice but to the whole culture of teachers in Britain. The lecture programme had included many of the leading experts in their respective fields, such as Henslow on the teaching of botany and Mason on the teaching of English grammar. He contrasted their reception with the situation in such countries as Germany, Switzerland and the United States where, he asserted, there were meetings of school teachers "the avowed object of which is mutual improvement in their common art, which are attended by three, four, or five hundred teachers at a time."[37]

The actual process by which the College decided to implement its decision to establish a lectureship and to invite Payne to occupy that office has not previously been disentangled. The Jubilee pamphlet stated quite simply (and inaccurately) that the College "resolved in 1871 to establish a Lectureship in Education, and Mr Payne was unanimously selected to carry this purpose into effect."[38] An entry in the Rough Minute Book which refers to a Council meeting of 13 March 1869 indicates that on that occasion there was a vote on the "Lectureship resolution" which was carried by nine votes to two. Isbister then proposed that Hodgson and Payne should be "empowered to offer a lectureship of £50 a year to certain gentlemen." This, however, was not agreed. Rather Hodgson and Payne were asked to:

> report on the best means of giving effect to the resolution of the Council, and to submit to the next meeting their views on the subject and a list of such persons as may appear to them suitable to undertake the office of Lecturer.[39]

It seems clear, from the (albeit brief) report of this meeting, that there was no certainty at this time that Payne would be chosen for the post, although his expertise (and that of Hodgson) was acknowledged in their being chosen to draw up a short list. It is even possible that Isbister made his proposal as a means of excluding the two leading reformers from the lectureship. Certainly the Jubilee pamphlet singled out Isbister as the chief spirit in the party of "conservative caution" which was most distrustful of the enterprise of Hodgson and Payne.[40] Hodgson was assuredly of professorial calibre: indeed in 1871 the University of Edinburgh appointed him to a chair in Political Economy and Mercantile Law.

What happened at the next Council meeting held on 19 April is not entirely clear. The entry in the Rough Minute Book suggests that Payne had identified two possible lecturers: F. W. Farrar, then a master at Harrow, author of the well-known account of schoolboy life, *Eric; or Little by Little* (1858) and editor of the recently published *Essays on a Liberal Education* (1867); and another public schoolmaster and Cambridge graduate, R. H. Quick, whose pioneering *Essays on Educational Reformers* was published in 1868. The matter then seems to have fallen into abeyance for well over a year, perhaps as a result of uncertainties about the College's financial position. Not until the autumn of 1870 did it emerge again when, at the Council meeting of 29 October, it was agreed "that Mr. Payne be asked to communicate with Mr. Farrar and Mr. Quick in reference to the lectureship."[41]

The crucial decision which led to Payne being chosen first as lecturer and subsequently as professor came at the next Council meeting, held on 26 November 1870. Payne then reported that he had communicated with Farrar who had replied that his engagements were such as to prevent him from delivering any lectures "for some time to come." Indeed Farrar was to become headmaster of Marlborough in 1871. On receipt of this news, and Payne made no mention of an approach to Quick:

> It was then agreed, on the motion of Mr Robson, seconded by Mr Oppler, that Mr Payne be requested to deliver a course of lectures upon an educational subject at the College Rooms: and, Mr Payne having acquiesced in the proposal, the Educational Committee were instructed to make the necessary arrangements immediately.[42]

Chapman suggests that Buss was behind the proposal to invite Payne but, characteristically, provides no evidence to support this statement.[43] Certainly Payne had no shortage of supporters among the 21 members present at the Council meeting on 26 November. Indeed they now even included Robert Ibbs, his colleague and successor at the Mansion Grammar School, who had been elected to the Council on 18 June.[44] At this time Ibbs was a rising star. He chaired the half-yearly meeting held on 11 January 1871[45] and was a member of the College delegation which, on 25 January 1871, pressed upon W. E. Forster, the Vice-President of the Council, the cause of a training college for teachers in middle-class schools.[46] Payne's continued commitment to the cause, moreover, was underlined by two current initiatives. The first, indeed, was the very next item on the agenda of the Council meeting of 26 November: a new scheme of examination in the Science and Art of Teaching to replace that of Theory and Practice.[47] The second was that in less than three weeks' time, at an evening meeting on 14 December 1870, Payne was scheduled to lecture on the subject of "The relation of learning to teaching."[48]

At this time Payne was a member of the College's Educational Committee[49] as were Buss and Hodgson.[50] All three were at a Committee meeting held on 7 December 1870, chaired by Jacob, at which the lecture programme was devised. This programme, adopted by the Council on 19 December and reported at the half-yearly meeting on 11 January 1871, was divided into several parts. These would comprise an introductory course on "Training," and another on "the History of Education and Educational Methods" to be delivered by Payne. Other courses on the teaching of Classics, mathematics, the English language and literature, physical science, and mental and moral science were also planned, with Jacob agreeing to give the course on Classics. In order to maximize the number of teachers able to attend the lectures, the Educational Committee recommended that, whenever possible, lectures should be given "during the regular school vacations."[51] The first lecture under the new scheme on the teaching of the English language was given at the College in Queen Square on Wednesday, 11 January 1871, by the headmaster of the City of London School, Edwin Abbott.[52]

Payne's illness in the winter of 1870–1871 meant that he was unable to deliver any lectures during that Christmas vacation, and he determined instead to do so during the summer holiday of 1871. Though the delay was frustrating both to members of the College and to Payne himself, it did give time both for Payne to prepare his lectures more fully, and for the College's Educational Committee to address the issue of whether Payne's lectures should be held at the Queen Square premises or at a larger and more imposing venue. One other benefit was that the lectures and the lectureship became known both outside the College itself and the secondary education field. For example, in May there was correspondence on the subject between the College and the chairman and secretary of the London School Board.[53]

The three lectures delivered by Payne as the College's lecturer in July 1871 showed some differences from the scheme as originally envisaged and reflected his increasing use of the concepts and terminology of the "science and art of education." All three were given at the Society of Arts in John Street. The first, on the evening of Wednesday, 12 July, was entitled "The Theory or Science of Education." Chairman on that occasion (a most appropriate choice) was Professor Thomas Henry Huxley, a leading member of the London School Board and widely known both for his medical and scientific accomplishments as well as for his position as the quintessential Victorian agnostic: indeed he himself had coined the word in 1869. For his second lecture, on Friday, 14 July, Payne took as his title "The Practice or Art of Education." Chairman on that occasion was Joshua Fitch, former principal of the Borough Road College, assistant commissioner for the Taunton Commission and currently assistant commissioner of endowed schools. For the final lecture "Educational Methods," delivered on 17 July, the chair was taken by the College's President, William Haig-Brown, headmaster of Charterhouse. All three lectures were printed in 1871 by the *Educational Times*.[54] They were also included in a volume entitled *Lectures on Education delivered before the members of the College of Preceptors in the year 1871*, published in 1872.[55]

Although the substance of Payne's lectures will be considered in later chapters, it is appropriate at this point to consider three immediate outcomes. The first was a discussion of issues raised by his lectures which took place on the evening of Wednesday, 13 December 1871. Three topics were suggested:

1. How far practice in teaching is improved by a knowledge of the theory of education.

2. To what extent the teacher should communicate knowledge to his pupil—to what extent require him to gain it for himself.

3. Jacotot's notion of learning something thoroughly, and referring all the rest to it.[56]

From the account of the meeting as given in the *Educational Times*, however, it would appear that discussion was severely limited by the amount of time spent by Payne in introducing each of the three topics. The second was an invitation to other teachers by Charles Lake, who himself taught at the Redcliffe School, to give Payne's principles a trial in their classrooms for a term.[57] The third was that the College decided to move from recruiting lecturers to the appointment of a professor. Crucial in this decision was a conference on 6 July 1872, organized by the College, but held once again at the Society of Arts, with Lyon Playfair, Liberal MP for Edinburgh and St. Andrews Universities, and former joint secretary of the Science and Art Department, in the chair. The second resolution called for the establishment of chairs of the science and art of education in all universities, but the most dramatic moment in the conference came when Playfair himself left the chair to move the last resolution which stated:

> That the study of the science and art of education ought to form a necessary part of the professional training of every teacher, and that examinations to test the proficiency of teachers in that subject are urgently required, and ought to be more generally established.

This resolution was an endorsement of Payne's campaign since 1847, and fittingly he spoke next. The resolution was carried unanimously.[58]

Professor

Throughout 1869 the College Council struggled to face up to the implications of its decision that "After the 1st of January 1870, no unexamined person will be admitted as a member of the College." This did not mean that the College was going to require all of its new members to submit to its own examinations; it would rely in large part upon the examinations of others. There would, however, be a particular problem for female teachers who, as yet, had little or no access to the traditional institutions of higher education. The connection between the issues of teachers' examination and female membership arose during the discussions of a special general meeting held on 29 September, and it was on this occasion that Barrow Rule urged the cause of female members on the Council.[59] This proposal was soon taken up. At a Council meeting on 11 December 1869, when an election was held to fill up vacant places, seven names were proposed for the four vacancies. The one female among them, Frances Buss, headmistress of the North London Collegiate School for Girls in Camden, came to the top of the poll with 14 votes.[60] Though some opposition to the election of a woman, in contravention of established practice and without reference to the membership as a whole, was declared at the half-yearly general meeting held on

12 January 1870,[61] three weeks later, on Saturday, 5 February 1870, Frances Buss attended her first meeting as a Council member.[62] Another female recruit to the Council was Beata Doreck. Nominated in June 1871 by Payne and seconded by Hodgson,[63] Doreck attended her first Council meeting on 23 September of that year. Though the relationship between Payne and the promoters of female education will be considered in more detail in a later chapter, one particular connection between Payne and Doreck may be noted here. Not only did they share many educational principles, they were also for a while near-neighbours. Beata Doreck had founded a school in Kildare Terrace, but a few yards from where Payne came to live in Kildare Gardens.

During the early months of 1872 Payne once more found himself at odds with some members of the Council. A dispute arose over the Theory and Practice examination of January of that year, at which Isbister and Conrad Hume Pinches acted as examiners, apparently because Payne and Lake refused to serve. Since neither appointment had been sanctioned by the Council, Lake argued that the results of the examination were null and void until and unless the Council gave retrospective approval.[64] The issue was raised at Council meetings in February and March when Isbister proposed a counterresolution declaring that the Dean had authority to select examiners "if the regular examiners in any subject decline to act."[65] Payne did not attend the next Council meeting on 20 April. Instead he sent a letter of resignation from the office of examiner.[66] Fortunately the Council, in turn, declined to accept it immediately and asked Payne to reconsider, which he did, and the resignation was withdrawn. At the next Council meeting, on 18 May, there were 15 members present, including those who might be counted as Payne's supporters—Buss, Doreck, Hodgson, Ibbs, Lake and Robson. Notwithstanding the presence of Isbister and Jacob, Payne was voted into the chair.[67]

In the summer of 1872 it appeared that the new initiative in respect of lectures would be allowed to lapse. Certainly plans were made to continue the long-established series of evening lectures at Queen Square, and Payne agreed to give a paper on the teaching of science on 11 December. But at a Council meeting on 19 October, in what was apparently the last item of business, Doreck moved a resolution, seconded by Buss, which was referred to the Educational Committee. This called upon the Council to consider the establishment of substantial "Courses of Lectures in the Theory and Practice of Education."[68] At this time Doreck, unlike Buss and Payne, was not a member of the Educational Committee, but she attended the two meetings held on 26 and 28 October at which her proposal was discussed, and a report was made to the Council meeting on 23 November.[69] An elaborate scheme was now suggested. The Council was asked to approve four courses of lectures within the general field of the theory and practice of education, each with ten lectures, in both 1873 and 1874. Three major sources of finance were envisaged: a sum of £50 per annum originally voted by the Council in January 1868 for educational lectures; fees paid by the students at the rate of £5 for the whole course or £1. 10s. for a single course; and a guarantee fund formed by interested members of the College. It was proposed that the lectures should be extensively advertised "in the *Times, Standard* and *Athenaeum*, at the expense of members interested in the scheme." Buss, Doreck and Isbister indicated their willingness to head a subscription list for that purpose with initial donations of £5 each and the promise of a further £5 each if required. Substantial discussion ensued and significant amendments were made. The most important of these was that the Council only agreed to commit itself to a scheme for 1873, and also referred back to the Educational Committee both the actual details of the lecture programme and three crucial, and as yet unconsidered, questions: "by whom the lectures were to be given, what fee should be paid to the lecturers, and the authority by which they should be controlled."[70]

There is no record of the proceedings of the next meeting of the Educational Committee, but matters were resolved at a Council meeting held on 21 December 1872, a meeting chaired by Charles Mason, Payne's successor at Denmark Hill, who had recently become a Vice-President. The following scheme was then approved. There would be three courses: an introductory lecture and ten lectures on the science of education; twelve lectures on the art of education; and ten lectures on the history of education. The lectures were to be accompanied "by illustrative lessons, exercises, and examinations," by "expository readings of passages from educational authors," and by "discussions." Students were also to be enabled to visit schools "for observing good methods of teaching and of school management." Examinations would be held at the end of each year's course. Successful students would receive certificates awarded in the name of the College, though these certificates would also depend upon a satisfactory report from the "Lecturer" as to attendance and practical work. Student fees were set at a guinea for a single course or £2. 12s. 6d. for all three. Lectures, which would be given in the evenings at Queen Square, would be extensively advertised, but no course should run which did not have a minimum of 20 students. The existing lectures, but not the monthly evening meetings, would be discontinued.

A subcommittee of the Educational Committee, consisting of the Dean (then Jacob but soon to be replaced by Isbister) ex officio and five members, "viz—Miss Buss, Miss Doreck, Mr Ellis, Mr Lake and Mr Oppler," was appointed to manage the lecture course. Doreck was also to be added to the Educational Committee. Three further decisions were taken on that momentous occasion:

> That the Lecturer be styled Professor of the Science and Art of Education.
>
> That the fee of the Professor be £50 for each one of the courses of Lectures that may be delivered.
>
> That Mr Payne be requested to undertake the office of Professor of the Science and Art of Education.[71]

Payne was present at the meeting on 21 December, but on 28 December sent a formal reply to the College's invitation. This reply was included in the Council minutes and subsequently published in the *Educational Times*.[72] In accepting the invitation Payne declared himself sensible of the honour accorded to him. He would do everything in his power to make the venture a success and offered to deliver courses to fewer than 20 students at a reduced fee for himself. He urged Council members to support the scheme by encouraging the participation of teachers in their own employ, and by offering increased salaries to those who passed the examinations. Payne's anxieties as to the size of his audience were ill-founded. The inaugural lecture was given on 30 January 1873 and attracted an audience of some 120 persons, though at the end of the lecture only 15 people gave their names as wishing to join the class. On 6 February when the course commenced, the number still stood at only 17, but on that evening was increased to more than 50. Two weeks later it had reached 70, with about half having entered for the full course. Payne, indeed, was forced to ask the Council for money for secretarial and other assistance and a further £50 was made available to him for this purpose. By March, when there were 72 students in attendance, Payne was personally reading and marking more than 300 answers per week.

Payne also asked the Council to make arrangements with principals and others for the students to visit schools. Not surprisingly the schools presided over by Buss and Doreck, together with such other well-known establishments as Queen's College, Harley Street, Bedford Square College and Dulwich College, were among those to whom Payne urged that application should be made, in the event he himself was charged with making the arrangements of communicating with the schools.[73] The identification of suitable girls' schools was of paramount importance. Among Payne's 70 students there were 64 females and six males! Not all of these were young teachers. Some of them, Payne reported, "have been principals of schools for many years."[74] Though it does not appear that Payne carried out any regular supervision of teachers in schools, some indication of his application of theory to practice in the classroom is provided by his inspection of teaching at the North London Collegiate School in July 1874. Payne spent three days at the school and saw lessons in Drawing, Writing, English Grammar, Dictation, Latin, Arithmetic, Geography and Scripture History. The following extracts from the 13–page report which he sent to Frances Buss, the headmistress, indicate clearly that the fundamental principle which he had drawn from Jacotot some 35 years earlier—namely, the paramount importance of pupils' learning—was as strong as ever.

Drawing

... extraordinary blunders which I witnessed—which were due of course to want of correct observation. The teachers, careful and painstaking as they appeared to be, seemed to me not to have a thorough grasp of the principle that their success in teaching the art of drawing must always be in exact proportion to their success in teaching the art of observing.

Grammar

There was, in my opinion, rather too much telling, too little developing.

Latin

I could have judged better if the girls had been less helped. They were scarcely allowed to translate a single sentence themselves, the moment a difficulty occurred they were helped over it.

Scripture History

She made the pupils do most of the work and required them to justify their statements by references to passages to give an exact reason for what they said. There seemed to me a more distinct recognition of the principles of teaching than I had observed in most of the other teachers.[75]

Lectures were given on Thursday evenings at 7:30 and closely followed the pattern of the normal academic year. The course on the "Science or Theory of Education," which comprised ten lectures, ran from 6 February to 10 April. The second course of 12 lectures was entitled the "Art or Practice of Education," and ran from 1 May to 17 July. The third, on the "History of Education," commenced on 25 September and ended on 11 December. Certificates were given to all who attended 20 classes, and such attendance was also deemed to be the equivalent of one year's teaching experience for the purpose of qualifying candidates for the College's Associateship examination.

Though there were many sneers, there were also admirers and emulators. For example, one of the inspectors of schools for Scotland, W. Jolly, approved of the professorship and of Payne's appointment and, while regretting that Scotland had not been the first to found such a chair, urged on the Scottish universities to do so before any of their English counterparts.[76] Payne himself was fully committed to the founding of further chairs of education and personally supported the Scottish initiatives. In the spring of 1874 the Universities of Edinburgh and St. Andrews announced their intention to establish professorships of education, endowed with money left in the trust funds of Andrew Bell, one of the pioneers of the monitorial system of teaching. At Council meetings in March and April of 1874 it was Payne, who himself had delivered a short course of four lectures in Edinburgh, who proposed resolutions (unanimously adopted) that the Council convey its congratulations to the Senates of the two Scottish universities for their declarations of intent, and urge them to proceed as soon as possible.[77]

The Preceptors' professorship and Payne's appointment to it were initially for one year only. Not until December of 1873 did the Council formally decide "that the Training Course of Lectures and Lessons should be continued for the coming year."[78] Payne was reappointed to the professorship with the same fee of £150 plus expenses. The decision to continue with the course was undoubtedly correct. The experiment had been a success. Some 80 students had enrolled in the courses, exhibitions had been offered to the most successful candidates in the final examinations, and there was talk of linking the lectures with a model or training school—for girls in the first instance. Advertisements were placed for courses for 1874 and these promised that, as in 1873, the purpose of the sessions was "not merely to hear lectures, but to write answers to questions, to discuss orally and in writing controverted points, take part in illustrative lectures &c." The course was increased to 36 lectures but the fees remained the same.[79]

Payne's introductory lecture to the second year's course was delivered on 20 January 1874, a lecture which he concluded by quoting from students' exercises from the previous year as to the beneficial effects which participation in the course had brought to their own teaching and their pupils' learning. The following extracts from five of those exercises indicate the very considerable effect that Payne appeared to be having on at least some of his students:

Before attending these Lectures, my aim was that my pupils should gain a certain amount of knowledge. I now see how far more important is the exercise of those powers by which knowledge is gained. . . .

I have learned that the only education worthy of the name is based upon principles derived from the study of child nature, and from the observation of nature's method of developing and training the inherent powers of children from the very moment of their birth. . . .

What you have done for me I endeavour to do for my pupils. I make them correct their own errors; indeed, do their own work as much as possible. Since you have been teaching me, my pupils have progressed in mental development as they have never done in all the years I have been teaching. Though from want of power and early training I have not done you the justice which many of your pupils have, still you have set your seal upon me, and made me aim at being what I was not formerly, a scientific teacher. . . .

I have learned to reverence and admire the great and good, who in different ages and various countries have devoted their minds to the principles or the practice of education, whose thoughts, whose successes, whose very failures, are full of instruction for educators of the present day . . .

My theories have become based on the firm foundation of principles founded on facts; my practice (falling far short of the perfection that I aim at attaining) is nevertheless in the spirit of it. And although in all probability I shall never equal any of those great teachers whose lives and labours you have described, yet I know that I shall daily improve in my practice if I hold fast to those principles that you have laid down. I consider you have shown me the value of a treasure that I unconsciously possessed—I mean the power of observing Nature, and therefore feel towards you the same sort of gratitude that the man feels towards the physician who has restored his sight.[80]

Naturally Payne was highly delighted with these positive evaluations of his first course. In 1874 not only did he continue with the professorial lectures, but he also regularly took part in the evening meetings and on 11 March presented a paper on

Froebel. In September the *Educational Times* printed in full a paper by Payne entitled *Principles of the Science of Education as exhibited in the phenomena attendant on the unfolding of a young child's powers under the influence of natural circumstances.* This was a discussion paper used in the class, and Payne's avowed purpose in publishing it was to invite criticism and comment from a broader constituency.[81] It might also have been intended as a means of advertising. Student numbers on the second year course were lower, but still eminently satisfactory. In May 1874 Payne reported that so far 51 people had joined the class.[82]

In the autumn of 1874, in the context of the College's worsening financial situation, much thought was being given to the best means of securing the continuation of the course. At a meeting of the College's Finance Committee held on 14 October 1874, which recommended the sale of £600 of stock, it was noted "that for some time past the expenditure of the College has far exceeded its receipts."[83] Consequently, in November 1874, the Council decided to set up a fund to endow the professorship.[84] Payne drafted a statement,[85] and the appeal itself was launched in February 1875.[86] The initial list of 13 subscribers showed Buss and Payne to the fore with sums of £20 each, while in his will Payne was to leave a further £200 to the fund. The fund, however, did not prosper. Government grants to aid the foundation of the Edinburgh and St. Andrews chairs naturally led the Preceptors to seek government financial aid to endow their own chair, but without success.

In the spring of 1875 an alternative suggestion for meeting the needs of the higher education of women, and for establishing education as a subject of university study within the capital, was raised by Hodgson. In March of that year, in a letter of congratulation to Payne upon the publication of his pamphlet on Pestalozzi, Hodgson advised that he was

> in hope that a Chair of Education may ere long be established in University College, and all the more as *there* women are likely to obtain more justice than can be expected from any other University in this country.[87]

Although the course continued in 1875 (numbers indeed reached 67) it appears that some alteration had been made in respect of Payne's salary with a view to making the course largely self-financing. The accounts for 1875 indicate that student fees amounted to £119. 3s. 6d., while the expenditure heading included "Fees of Training Class paid to Professor of Education . . . £119. 3s. 6d."[88] It seems likely that most of Payne's remuneration in that year was based on students' fees, although he also appears to have received the interest on the investment portion of the professorial endowment fund. One interesting feature of the advertisements of the course for 1875 was that while the fees remained at one guinea per term, with a composite fee of two and a half guineas for the whole course, there was also a "reduction in the case of elementary teachers." It is not clear whether many elementary teachers availed themselves of this offer and, in so doing, changed the basic composition of the class. Certainly in September 1875 Payne reported that "several of the members of the class were teachers in the recently established schools of the Girls' Public Day School Company."[89]

In the autumn of 1875 following Eliza Payne's death, Joseph Frank informed the Council that his father "had been obliged to discontinue for the present his lectures to the training class."[90] Herbert Quick nobly stepped into the breach and completed the third series on the history of education, a task for which he was eminently qualified. Worse was to follow. In December 1875 the Council learned with regret from Joseph Frank that Joseph Payne's own illness was such that he would have to resign from the professorship.[91] In 1876 Quick took over the mantle and agreed to give three courses of 10 lectures each. Not surprisingly he began not with the science and art, but with his own speciality, the history of education. Having delivered the first course, however, Quick then withdrew. The second course, which began on 11 May, was given by J. M. D. Meiklejohn, the newly appointed Professor of the Theory, History and Practice of Education at the University of St. Andrews. His ten-week course covered reading, English grammar and composition, geography, history, Classical and modern languages and the general principles of teaching. Even Meiklejohn, however, did not continue into the third term, so that the final course, which began on 5 October, was given by G. Croom-Robertson on the theme of "Mental and Moral Science."

Payne's role as the first professor of education in Britain has received little recognition. Even the College of Preceptors' own Jubilee pamphlet minimized his role and success. It stated quite inaccurately:

> The Professorship was therefore suspended after the delivery of Mr Payne's second course, and in its stead three lectureships were established. Professor Croom-Robertson, of University College, was appointed to lecture on Psychology, the Rev. R. H. Quick undertook a course on the History of Education, and Dr Fitch had for his special subject the Practice of Education.[92]

Payne's professorship did not last for two years, nor was it suspended. He continued for three years, from 1873 to 1875, until forced to give up by illness. What is true is that while Payne was an expert not only on the science and art (or theory and practice) as well as on the history of education, it was extremely difficult for the College subsequently to find any one person with such a breadth of educational knowledge and experience. With his resignation and early death that unique combination was lost. The following chapters are concerned to redeem some of that loss by an examination of the nature and quality of Payne's thought on a range of fundamental educational issues.

NOTES

1. *Journal of Education* 29 (May 1878), p. 194.

2. Payne, *Works*, I, p. 4.

3. *Educational Times* XIX, 71 (February 1867), p. 246.

4. Post Office, *Directory for Surrey, 1862*, p. 1395.

5. Minutes of the Council meeting, 27 December 1851, Council Minute Book, 1848–57, p. 164.

6. *Educational Times* VII, 77 (February 1854), p. 101.

7. *Educational Times* XIX, 71 (February 1867), p. 242.

8. *Fifty Years*, p. 20.

9. *Journal of the Women's Education Union* IV, 42 (June 1876), pp. 86–7.

10. *Fifty Years*, p. 20.

11. *Taunton Report*, iv, p. 2.

12. *Ibid*.

13. *Taunton Report*, iv, p. 3.

14. *Ibid*., p. 4.

15. Payne, *Works*, I, pp. 323–4.

16. *Pall Mall Gazette*, 18 November 1867.

17. *Educational Times* XX, 81 (December 1867), p. 199. The *Pall Mall Gazette* refused to publish the letter or to retract its statements, but a copy of O'Neil's letter was sent to each member of the College.

18. *Educational Times* XXI, 85 (April 1868), pp. 10–11.

19. *Educational Times* XXI, 88 (July 1868), pp. 75–81. It was included in Payne, *Works*, I, pp. 307–27.

20. *Educational Times* XXI, 88 (July 1868), p. 80.

21. College of Preceptors' Rough Minute Book, 1854–73, 26 September 1868. Though Payne might not have been eligible for re-election, having served two terms.

22. *Fifty Years*, p. 21.

23. *Educational Times* XXI, 94 (February 1869), p. 250.

24. A report of the conference was printed as a supplement to the *Educational Times* of February 1869, pp. 269–80. This appears to have caused some confusion over the numbering of the February edition, which was given the same number, 94, as that for January. The March edition continued as number 95.

25. *Educational Times* XXI, 94 (February 1869), p. 273. For the work of the Scholastic Registration Association see the 1957 University of London M.A. thesis of F. L. Massey entitled, "The registration of teachers in England and Wales from 1846 to 1899, with special reference to the development of common interest and professional independence."

26. *Ibid*., p. 275.

27. *Ibid*., p. 274.

28. *Ibid*., p. 276.

29. *Fifty Years*, pp. 16–17.

30. *Educational Times* XIV, 162 (March 1861), p. 51.

31. *Ibid.*, p. 53.

32. *Ibid.*

33. *Educational Times* XXII, 100 (August 1869), p. 103.

34. *Fifty Years*, p. 18.

35. *Educational Times* XIX, 71 (February 1867), p. 242.

36. Payne, *Works*, I, pp. 321–2.

37. *Ibid.*, p. 323.

38. *Fifty Years*, p. 22.

39. Rough Minute Book, 1854–73, 13 March 1869.

40. *Fifty Years*, p. 20.

41. Minutes of the Council meeting of 29 October 1870, Council Minute Book, 1870–89, p. 31.

42. Minutes of the Council meeting of 26 November 1870, Council Minute Book, 1870–89, p. 35.

43. Chapman, *Professional Roots*, p. 72. There is no indication of this in the Council Minute Book and the pages for 26 November are missing from the Rough Minute Book. Chapman is clearly confused at this point. He states (p. 73) that Payne's three lectures were delivered in 1872, rather than in 1871.

44. Rough Minute Book, 1854–73, 18 June 1870.

45. *Educational Times* XIII, 118 (February 1871), p. 249.

46. *Ibid.*, p. 240.

47. Minutes of the Council meetings of 18 June, 29 October and 26 November 1870, Council Minute Book, 1870–89, pp. 22, 31 and 35.

48. The lecture was postponed as Payne was indisposed on that evening. *Educational Times* XXIII, 117 (January 1871), p. 233.

49. He also served on the Examinations and Literary Committees, but not on the Finance Committee. Minutes of the Council meeting of 24 September 1870, Council Minute Book, 1870–89, p. 28.

50. Charles Lake was not a member of the Educational Committee, though he served on the Examinations Committee and, together with Ogle, was added as an examiner for Theory and Practice in 1871. Minutes of the Council meeting of 4 February 1871, Council Minute Book, 1870–89, p. 44.

51. Minutes of the Council meeting of 19 December 1870, Council Minute Book, 1870–89, p. 39.

52. *Educational Times* XXIII, 118 (February 1871), pp. 243–9, 251.

53. Minutes of the Council meetings of 29 April and 20 May 1871, Council Minute Book, 1870–89, pp. 52–3.

54. *Educational Times* XXIV, 124 (August 1871), pp. 95–102, 125 (September 1871), pp. 123–9, and 126 (October 1871), pp. 147–54.

55. Other lectures published in this volume were two by Abbott on the English language, and three by Jacob on Classics.

56. *Educational Times* XXIV, 129 (January 1872), pp. 230–3.

57. *Educational Times* XXV, 137 (October 1872), p. 165. Both September and October issues bore the number 137; November, however, continued as 139.

58. *Educational Times* XXV, 136 (August 1872), pp. 99–108.

59. *Educational Times* XXII, 103 (November 1869), p. 178.

60. Rough Minute Book, 1854–73, 11 December 1869. Hodgson invited Buss to stand and communicated to her the details of the result. Extracts from Hodgson's letters were included in Annie E. Ridley, *Frances Mary Buss: and her work for education* (London, 1895), pp. 294–5.

61. *Educational Times* XXII, 106 (February 1870), pp. 252–3.

62. Minutes of the Council meeting of 5 February 1870, Council Minute Book, 1870–89, p. 1.

63. Rough Minute Book, 1854–73, 17 June 1871.

64. Minutes of the Council meeting of 10 February 1872, Council Minute Book, 1870–89, p. 81.

65. Minutes of the Council meeting of 16 March 1872, Council Minute Book, 1870–89, p. 85.

66. At the Council meeting on 10 February 1872 Payne had been re-elected as an examiner for Theory and Practice, together with Coghlan, Lake, Mcleod, Ogle, Quick and Croom Robertson, with Hodgson as moderator. Council Minute Book, 1870–89, p. 79.

67. Minutes of the Council meeting of 18 May 1872, Council Minute Book, 1870–89, p. 90.

68. Minutes of the Council meeting of 19 October 1872, Council Minute Book, 1870–89, p. 108.

69. Minutes of the Council meeting of 23 November 1872, Council Minute Book, 1870–89, p. 116.

70. Minutes of the Council meeting of 23 November 1872, Council Minute Book, 1870–89, pp. 116–8.

71. Minutes of the Council meeting of 21 December 1872, Council Minute Book, 1870–89, pp. 123–4.

72. Council Minute Book, 1870–89, pp. 126–7. A copy of the letter was included here as part of the minutes of the Council meeting which took place on 28 December—adjourned from 21 December. Payne was present on 28 December and presumably delivered the letter by hand. It was also printed in the *Educational Times* XXV, 142 (February 1873), p. 266.

73. Minutes of the Council meeting of 22 March 1873 which included a letter of the same date from Payne, requesting assistance, Council Minute Book, 1870–89, pp. 142–3.

74. Payne's professorial report to the Council meeting of 22 February 1873, Council Minute Book, 1870–89, p. 137.

75. Copy of a handwritten report, addressed to Buss, of Payne's inspection of the school on 24, 27 and 28 July 1874, Archive box, "History of School, 1850–75," North London Collegiate School Archives.

76. *Educational Times* XXVI, 149 (September 1873), p. 133.

77. Minutes of the Council meetings of 14 March and 18 April 1874, Council Minute Book, 1870–89, pp. 174, 177.

78. Minutes of the Council meeting of 13 December 1873, Council Minute Book, 1870–89, p. 164.

79. *Educational Times* XXVI, 153 (January 1874), p. 221.

80. Payne, *Works*, I, pp. 181–2, Two years later Herbert Quick found the students' work full of "a good deal of stuff and verbiage, but somebody is sure to say something sensible." Quoted in Miriam G. Fitch, "Joseph Payne, first Professor of Education in England," *Journal of Education* 66, 779 (June 1934), p. 390.

81. *Educational Times* XXVII, 161 (September 1874), pp. 123–4.

82. Minutes of the Council meeting of 18 May 1874, Council Minute Book, 1870–89, p. 179.

83. Minutes of the Finance Committee meeting of 14 October 1874, College of Preceptors' Finance Committee Minute Book, 1874–1914, p. 3.

84. Minutes of the Council meeting of 14 November 1874, Council Minute Book, 1870–89, p. 204.

85. Minutes of the Educational Committee meeting of 29 December 1874, College of Preceptors' Educational Committee Minute Book, 1874–1919, p. 1.

86. Minutes of the Educational Committee meeting of 20 February 1875, Educational Committee Minute Book, 1874–1919, p. 4.

87. Hodgson to Payne, 1 March 1875, Meiklejohn, *Hodgson*, p. 275.

88. Council Minute Book, 1870–89. Accounts for 1875 bound in between pp. 239 and 240.

89. Minutes of the Council meeting of 18 September 1875, Council Minute Book, 1870–89, p. 227.

90. Minutes of the Council meeting of 13 November 1875, Council Minute Book, 1870–89, p. 234.

91. Minutes of the Council meeting of 11 December 1875, Council Minute Book, 1870–89, p. 237.

92. *Fifty Years*, p. 26.

CHAPTER SIX

Critic and Reformer

Joseph Payne was an outsider. In terms of British society, including that of education, he was a marginal person. He did not belong to any charmed circle. His way in the world was made by the exercise of his own talents. Though possessed of a strong sense of history Payne did not have an unalloyed commitment to traditional institutions and ways of thought. Even in respect of the College of Preceptors, a body in which he obtained high office and in which he assumed a pioneering role, he was on occasion a stern critic. This chapter will examine four areas of Payne's criticisms and reform proposals with regard to the educational thinking and practice of his day. These were the education of girls and women, boys' public schools, elementary schooling, and the training of teachers.

The Education of Girls and Women

In Payne's day by far the largest group of outsiders in British society were girls and women. Apart from the monarch herself, women were excluded from central government, indeed they were not even entitled to vote in parliamentary elections. Nor were they admitted to such learned professions as the Church, Law and Medicine. One means of calling attention to the injustice of such exclusions was through education, and particularly through examinations. Examinations provided a means whereby the intellectual abilities and attainments of males and females could be measured against each other.

Although the three principal school establishments with which he was personally connected—the Rodney House

Academy, the Denmark Hill Grammar School and the Mansion Grammar School—were private schools for boys only, Payne had innumerable contacts with the world of female education, and his criticisms and reform proposals were made from a sound knowledge of the subject. In his years at Camberwell he gained an immediate, indeed intimate, understanding of the inside of a female educational community from his residence at Grove Hill House where Eliza kept her school. It should be noted that, for the first 30 years of their lives, Eliza Payne's experience as a teacher was quite as substantial as his own, and that this experience continued after their marriage. Although the middle years were spent in heavily male environments, as an examiner for the Theory and Practice of Education for the College of Preceptors Payne received regular confirmation of the attainments of some female teachers. After his retirement from Leatherhead, in the context of the Council of the College of Preceptors, Payne was to work closely with two leading female educational reformers—Frances Buss and Beata Doreck. In 1873 both were awarded Fellowships by the College, and Buss proudly reported to the Governors of her school that "Miss Doreck and I are, as yet, the only women on whom such an honour has been conferred."[1] Thereafter the letters FCP stood proudly after Buss's name both in life and in death. In June 1871 it was Payne who nominated Beata Doreck for membership on the Council of the College of Preceptors,[2] and it was Payne who contributed a substantial appreciation of Doreck to the *Educational Times* on the occasion of her death in 1875.[3] In so doing he paid tribute to Doreck's initiative in the establishment of the professorship: "the honour of bringing it to birth belongs mainly to Miss Doreck; who was, however, warmly supported and aided throughout by her fellow Councillor, Miss Buss."[4] The College of Preceptors established a scholarship in Doreck's memory, to be awarded on the results of the College's diploma examinations for teachers. At the Christmas examination of 1876, the scholarship was awarded to a teacher at the North London Collegiate School, Sophie Bryant, who in 1894 succeeded Frances Buss as headmistress.[5]

Buss and Payne shared many educational experiences. Both were largely self-taught, both had a keen interest in history.

Both were required to enter teaching from an early age and to devote their not-inconsiderable energies to building up highly successful private schools. Through Payne, Buss came to admire Jacotot and to apply some of his principles at the North London.[6] Payne had strong connections both with the North London and with its sister establishment, the Camden School for Girls. He was frequently present on formal occasions. For example in 1871, together with Emily Davies, Edwin Abbott, headmaster of the City of London School, and Joshua Fitch, Payne was on the platform at the Camden School prize-giving.[7] He also attended the prize-giving for the two schools held on 21 October 1872 at Willis's Rooms.

The North London not only had a library for the use of pupils but also a special collection of volumes for teachers, and Payne donated books to both.[8] He also gave courses of lessons and lectures at the school. For example, in 1872 Payne delivered a series of nine lessons on the history of the English language to the children of the first and second classes,[9] and in 1875 a parallel series on the "Development of Early French."[10] The short course of four lectures given in 1874—on "Learning and Knowing," "Attention," "Memory" and "How to Read with Understanding," would doubtless have been equally applicable to teachers and pupils.[11] In July 1874, at the invitation of Frances Buss, Joseph Payne carried out a three-day inspection of the teaching at the North London Collegiate School.[12] This inspection, by no means uncritical, was an instance of the issue which formed the closest bond between Buss and Payne and which led to the establishment of the professorship—the need to improve the quality of education by means of the training of teachers.

Frances Buss's concern for the training of teachers for girls' secondary schools might well have been inherited from her mother who was sufficiently anxious, when establishing her private school in Clarence Road, Kentish Town, from which the North London sprang, to undertake a course of elementary teacher training at the Home and Colonial College. Certainly it was developed by contact with Payne and Maria Grey. Indeed, in December 1871 it was Grey who recommended Joseph Payne as the most suitable person to give a "higher course of professional instruction."[13]

On 13 January 1872, at a Preceptors' Council meeting chaired by Payne, approval was given for such a series of lectures "On the Theory and Practice of Education." The first of these was to be delivered on 25 January at the College, but the course was "to be given in connection with the North London Collegiate and Camden School for Girls," and subsequent lectures were indeed given at the schools themselves.[14] A substantial programme of 30 lectures was constructed, to be delivered by Charles Lake, Payne's collaborator in the reform of the Preceptors' examinations. These lectures would be aimed at

> preparing the student directly for the examination of the College of Preceptors in the "Theory and Practice of Education," and indirectly for the examination in Logic and Moral Philosophy (Higher Proficiency) of the University of London.[15]

The sessions were held in Camden Street on Thursday evenings at 5:00 p.m. They began with a lecture of some three-quarters of an hour and were followed by questions and discussion.[16] Lake's lectures were not repeated in 1873, the year in which Payne launched his first professorial course, but M. A. Garvey, a barrister and one of the schools' trustees, gave a short series of six lectures commencing on 23 January 1873 on "the Science and Practical Art of Teaching" to the teachers of both schools.[17]

At this time, following the reorganization into the North London and Camden Schools, Buss was contemplating turning one house, 202 Camden Road, into a day training college capable of training 100 students at a time. She had already adopted Maria Grey's suggestion of recruiting "student teachers,"[18] and in 1872 secured the support of her governors to appoint the first two, Edith Fletcher and Charlotte Offord, in January of 1873.[19] Her vision of what such a training might include was entirely consistent with Payne's views and with the professorial course which he taught from 1873:

> Our students should learn the history of great teachers, their methods, etc., should learn how to teach and what to teach; how to develop the mental, moral, and physical capacities of their pupils (by moral I mean also spiritual).

> We would affiliate to our College the National Schools, the School Boards of the neighbourhood, and *our own* girls' schools, so that every student in training should have the opportunity of seeing actual schools in work.

> I have not mentioned this last to any one but Mr Payne, for several reasons, one being that I am ambitious for the cause of education and especially for the *mixture* of sexes; if the College of Preceptors would take up the idea, it might be better left to them.[20]

Although in Payne's lifetime the College of Preceptors was unable to establish a training college for secondary teachers, the professorial lecture course had Buss's firm support. The North London Collegiate School was one of seven London schools and colleges to which students from Payne's class at the College of Preceptors were to be sent to experience "the opportunity of good teaching."[21]

Buss urged, indeed as in the case of Fanny Franks, sometimes required, her teachers to attend Payne's course.[22] Doreck also commended the classes and it would appear that they were generally appreciated. Many of those who attended subsequently became headmistresses themselves and attributed their success to Payne's influence. In 1873 Frances Lord wrote approvingly to Buss about Payne:

> I am attending Mr Payne's lectures, as you told me to do. My sister Emily goes too, and, as a teacher, makes remarks that Mr Payne thinks well of. If she ever takes up Kindergarten work (as I want her to do), she will, I am sure, be greatly helped by these lectures. My friends, the Wards, find, as we do, that the questions Mr Payne asks draw largely on common observation such as we have been practising and have been wanting to know the value of.[23]

Indeed, it appears that Fanny Franks and Emily Lord, teachers of younger girls at the North London and Notting Hill High School respectively, were so inspired by Payne's lecture on Froebel that in their holidays they set off to seek further training from Madame de Portugall in Geneva. Madame de Portugall, who had been trained in Berlin and taught in Manchester, and was the examiner for the first London Froebel Society's Certificate, was inspector of schools in the canton of Geneva where Froebel's methods were widely used.[24] Another appreciative student, apparently spurred on by Payne to greater heights, was Sophie Bryant who began teaching at the North London in 1875, and who subsequently recorded:

> When Miss Buss accepted my services to teach mathematics, she sent me also to Professor Payne; and whatever educational science I now possess, the clue to it was put into my hands by him. His lectures had that characteristic of combined originality, lucidity, and suggestiveness which is the fruit of intuitive gift in a strong, sincere nature. His sympathetic discussion of his students' essays after the lecture was a model illustration of the principles he expounded. At the basis of his methodology, as I remember it, lay the foundation principle that, in its ultimate analysis, "all teaching is self-teaching," whence it follows that the primary function of the teacher is to induce in the learner, by sympathetic insight and suggestion, the self-teaching attitude appropriate to the subject in hand. With this master clue to method in their minds, his students were led on to study the learner as normally self-teacher in an interesting world, and to develop ways of teaching particular subjects accordingly.[25]

After completing Payne's course Bryant proceeded to a B.A. in 1881 and to a D.Sc. in 1884. In addition to succeeding Buss as headmistress of the North London, she also served on the Bryce Commission on Secondary Education, the Consultative Committee of the Board of Education and the Senate of the University of London. An enthusiastic mountaineer, she died in 1922 while climbing Mont Blanc.

With respect to education both in Britain and in the United States, Payne the appreciated importance of female educational institutions in which female principals, professors and teachers could provide important role models for girls, but he also saw the advantages of coeducation. The professorial classes which Payne taught in the 1870s, although containing a preponderance of females, were open equally to men and women. Payne reported that "He had not detected the least inconvenience or difficulty in the fact of their meeting together for the purpose of instruction."[26] Indeed it would appear that the mixing of sexes had the potential for some lively exchanges. One of Payne's students, P. E. Japernoux, a private teacher of French, acknowledged that "as regards your lectures I greatly enjoy them and I learn many new ideas by them." He also confessed to being "excessively shy and consequently foolish," and was experiencing some difficulty in getting a nine-year-old girl to translate Charles Dickens's *A Christmas Carol* into French. Japernoux asked that the extra discussion class should be held on Tuesday as he had engagements on every other evening of the week. In addition he stated that, in spite of what Jacotot or other educators or philologists might say or write, "as regards teaching a foreign language, say French, to English pupils, even to beginners, without grammar rules, I do not see how it can possibly be done."[27] Payne would have welcomed such discussion, particularly in a coeducational group. He wished to draw upon a range of teaching and learning experiences, both of males and females. His lectures on the history of education were distinguished by a specific attention to the role of girls and women, an attention which was probably not to be equalled in general courses on the history of education until recent times.

At the heart of Payne's approach to the education of girls and women was a belief that men and women, boys and girls, were essentially human beings with equal mental capacities, and that this basic identity was far more important than physiological differences based upon sex. Payne's classic statement of this belief, which was coupled with a reference to the superior moral capacities of females, was made at Sheffield in 1865 at the annual congress of the National Association for the Promotion of Social Science. The Social Science Association (as it was generally known) founded in 1857 with Henry, Lord Brougham as its first President, provided an important platform for critics and reformers. Payne attended several of its annual congresses and in 1870 became a member of the Association's Council. Education was the theme of one of its five sections, and female education featured prominently in its proceedings. Payne's statement came during a discussion on the topic of better provision for the education of girls of the middle and upper classes, introduced by papers from Dorothea Beale, F. D.

Maurice and Elizabeth Wolstenholme. Payne sought to move the discussion

> from facts to principles. Where we have to deal with a common mind, both the subjects taught and the mode of teaching must be in a great degree common. We are not teaching a different, but the same kind of human being. The mind has properly no sex. It is the mind of the human being, and consequently there must be a similarity of instruction of both sexes. It has been said that the female mind is not by nature so susceptible of attention to what is called truth; I rather think, as regards the point of conscience, the balance must be thrown the other way, and that there is really a more conscientious regard to truth among women than among men.[28]

Payne recognized the differences between the girls' and boys' schools of his day, and believed in the need for greater similarity in curricula and teaching methods. He also, however, acknowledged that all schools (girls' and boys') shared many common problems. Although the Taunton Commissioners had drawn attention to the "want of thoroughness and foundation; want of system; slovenliness; inattention; unnecessary time given to accomplishments; want of organization"[29] in girls' schools, Payne sought to distinguish between those criticisms which were pertinent to girls' schools alone and those which were generally applicable. Payne acknowledged the excessive time given to accomplishments in many girls' schools for the middle and upper classes, and supported Dorothea Beale in her suggestion that there should be a reduction in such spheres as art and music, particularly for girls who had little aptitude for those subjects. On the other hand, Payne was well aware that in some boys' schools games had become an easy alternative to serious study and urged that there was much to be gained by all pupils, girls and boys, in studying difficult but worthwhile subjects, for example those which would promote both "accuracy and reasoning."[30] He believed that other of Taunton's criticisms, for example those relating to deficiencies in thoroughness and system, and the prevalence of inattention in classrooms, were attributable in large part to a failing common to schools for boys as well as for girls—the shortage of properly educated and trained teachers.

Payne's promotion of the education of girls and women took place in various contexts—in lectures, in examinations, in the advocacy of teacher training, in the Society for Home Study.[31] But the most obvious manifestation of his commitment to the cause of improved female education, and of the esteem in which he was held by its supporters, came in November 1872 when Payne was chosen as chairman of the Women's Education Union.

The National Union for improving the Education of Women of All Classes (to give the Women's Education Union its full title) originated from the work of Maria Grey, who had married into one of the leading Whig families, and stood, unsuccessfully, as a candidate in the first London School Board elections. In November 1871 the Women's Education Union was formally inaugurated at a meeting at the Royal Society of Arts. Its several objects, as listed at the front of the first volume of its *Journal*, included:

1. To bring into communication and co-operation all individuals and associations engaged in promoting the education of Women, and to collect and register, for the use of Members, all information bearing on that education.

2. To promote the establishment of good Schools, at a moderate cost, for girls of all classes above those provided for by the Elementary Education Act.

3. To aid all measures for extending to Women the means of Higher Education after the School period, such as Colleges and Lectures for Women above eighteen, and Evening Classes for Women already earning their own maintenance.

4. To provide means for Training Female Teachers, and for testing their efficiency by Examinations of recognized authority, followed by Registration, according to fixed standard.

5. To improve the tone of public opinion on the subject of Education itself, and on the national importance of the Education of Women.[32]

Its first President was one of the daughters of Queen Victoria, Her Royal Highness the Princess Louise, Marchioness of Lorne. She was no mere figurehead; indeed the preliminary meeting of those interested in the formation of the Union "was held, by her invitation, in her dining room at 1, Grosvenor Crescent."[33] Its first list of Vice-Presidents (17 males and 6 females) included such noted names as Henry Austin Bruce, a former Vice-President of the Committee of Council on Education, and the Committee's first secretary, Sir James Kay Shuttleworth. But the real direction of the Union was in the hands of its central Committee, which was composed of 14 men and 14 women. Payne was, from its inception, a member of this Committee, as the official representative of the College of Preceptors.[34] Other male Committee members included Kay Shuttleworth, Canon Alfred Barry, the principal of King's College, London, James Bryce, the historian and politician who in 1895 gave his name to the report of a Royal Commission on secondary education, and Edward Carleton Tufnell, the inspector of poor law schools, who represented the Society of Arts. Female members included Maria Grey, who chaired the early meetings; her sister Emily Shirreff, joint editor of the *Journal*; and Frances Buss, who represented the London Schoolmistresses' Association. At the first annual meeting in November 1872, Maria Grey declined to continue in the role of chairman, accepting instead the post of "honorary organizing secretary."[35] Accordingly Joseph Payne, "whose zeal for education and thorough knowledge of the subject point him out as most fit for this position,"[36] a noted tribute indeed in such a talented company, was called to the chair and occupied the position with distinction until ill-health forced his retirement early in 1876.

Payne's duties were not confined to the chairing of meetings. One way in which the Union sought to improve educational opportunities for girls and women was through the endowment of scholarships and prizes. Payne played a prominent part in this work. In February 1874 he placed a letter in several newspapers, including *The Times*, calling attention to the Union's plan to establish a scholarship of £25 for three years to enable girls to proceed from elementary schools to those of the Girls' Public Day School Company or North London Collegiate Trust. In March he was in correspondence with George Croad, clerk to the London School Board, over the administration of the scheme.[37] The Union had already established five scholarships in connection with the University Locals and other examinations and, in April 1874, a Miss Meson won the prize of £25 offered by the Women's Education Union for the best performance by a woman in the examination of the students in Payne's professorial class.[38]

Payne not only played a leading part in the Women's Education Union, he was also to the fore in the foundation and early work of its sister society, the Girls' Public Day School Company. In June 1872 he was on the platform in the Albert Hall when the Company was inaugurated at a large public meeting presided over by Lord Lyttelton. Payne spoke in support of the Company's first scheme "to open a public Collegiate day school for girls in South Kensington, in which provision will be made for the training of teachers."[39] He was one of the original Company shareholders,[40] a member of its Council, and indeed chairman of the Council in 1872.[41] In January 1873 Payne was present at the opening of the Company's first school in Norland Square, Chelsea, and also attended on 28 March when Princess Louise paid a visit to the school. A further eight schools—those at Notting Hill, Croydon, Norwich, Clapham, Nottingham, Bath, Oxford and South Hampstead—were founded during Payne's lifetime.[42]

Payne was aware of the importance attached to the recruitment of good staff by pioneers of girls' public secondary schooling, and particularly approved of the "provisions made in the school scheme of the Company for the training of teachers."[43] One example of this conjunction of interests came in 1873 when Payne's 26–page pamphlet *The Importance of the training of the teacher* was published as the fourth in a series produced under the auspices of the Women's Education Union.[44] The Union's *Journal* also gave some prominence to Payne's lecturing activities. For example, in 1873 Emily Shirreff used a report on the meeting of the Social Science Association at Norwich to draw attention to Payne's successful professorial lectures in London and also to a short course which he had delivered in Edinburgh.[45] In February 1875 it published a three-column account of the sixth in a series of lectures which Payne had delivered in the lecture theatre of the Royal Dublin Society in connection with the General Association of Ireland, a lecture which had attracted "a large attendance of ladies."[46] In May 1876 the *Journal* included a short notice of his death, when Payne was characterized as a "valued friend and member of the Union . . . one of its earliest adherents."[47] The Committee would particularly miss his expertise and leadership in the recently commenced work of training teachers for girls' secondary schools. In the following issue a substantial tribute appeared, based upon Hodgson's letter published in the *Educational News* of 20 May.[48]

It was not until 29 May 1876, a month after Payne's death, that the Committee of the Women's Education Union approved Maria Grey's draft proposal for a training college to prepare women to teach in secondary schools. The Union's training committee became the provisional committee for the Teachers' Training and Registration Society, which in 1878 opened the College in Bishopsgate that beginning in 1886 was to bear Maria Grey's name.[49] Yet there were firm links between Payne's work and the new college. As Irene Lilley, the historian of Maria Grey College, has written in respect of the relationship between Payne and Grey: "It was his concept of professional education and his analysis of theory which underlay her schemes. His published lectures gave shape to her own opinions."[50] When in 1876 Maria Grey prepared the draft scheme she envisaged three elements: instruction in the subject to be taught, instruction in the science and art of teaching, and practice in teaching. The first, she thought, was being supplied by the women's colleges at Cambridge, through University College, London and the University Extension Movement. For the third she looked to the schools of the Girls' Public Day School Company and others. But for the second, for the core of the new college course, she proposed to draw on "a nucleus which requires only to be more fully developed, the lectures of the Professor of Education at the College of Preceptors on the science and art of education."[51]

Another, and more visible link, one which has continued to the present day, was the Joseph Payne Memorial Prize. When Payne died in 1876, Frances Buss sought to establish a memorial to him:

> Because I have not enough to do, I am working up an attempt to raise a little memorial to Mr Payne, the ablest teacher I have ever known—except Dr Hodgson—and the man who has raised the noblest ideal before the profession. It cuts me to the heart to see his name lost to posterity . . . I want the memorial to be a prize or scholarship in the new Teachers' Training Society.[52]

Naturally Maria Grey was among those who collected money for the fund and herself contributed £5.[53] In 1881 Joseph Frank appears to have made at least two contributions,[54] and the prize was duly established in the following year. In 1883 the winner was Miss Dunlop, who later became principal of the Saffron Walden Training College, and in the following year Miss Walker, who subsequently was principal of the St. George's Training College in Edinburgh. Each received the not-inconsiderable sum of £7. 6s. 2d.[55] The value of the prize varied according to the performance of the capital, which was invested in Consols. For example, in 1899 when Winifred Mercier, who went on to a post as history lecturer at Girton, was the recipient, the dividend had fallen to £6. 12s. 4d.[56] Buss's concern for the future reputation of Payne was justified. Not until 1933 did the College of Preceptors, in conjunction with the newly established Institute of Education of the University of London, launch the Joseph Payne Memorial Lectures.[57]

Two points may be made in concluding this section: The first is that Payne's contribution to the advancement of the education of girls and women was recognized in his own day; and the second is to summarize the nature of that contribution.

Contemporary recognition of Payne's commitment was shown in obituary notices, some of which focused upon two themes: his role as the first professor and his work for the education of girls and women. Thus Payne's local newspaper, the *Paddington, Kensington and Bayswater Chronicle*, declared that "much of the success achieved by the Women's Education Union and Girls' Public Day School Company must be traced to his unflagging zeal,"[58] while the monthly *Educational Guide to English and Continental Schools* began its tribute with a reference to Payne's work for the education of women.[59]

Payne argued for the equality of mental capacity between the sexes and rejected claims of female inferiority. He welcomed the attainment by women of positions of authority in professional spheres such as education and medicine. While recognizing that single-sex schools and colleges might more speedily promote access by women to such positions, he also approved of the development of coeducational institutions. In the 1870s his work to promote the training of teachers and the development of a science and art of education took place largely in a female context, and with the full support of the leading female educationists of his day. Finally, he acted as a link among such bodies as the College of Preceptors, the Girls' Public Day School Company and the Women's Education Union, and had the unique distinction of chairing Council meetings of all three associations.

Public Schools for Boys

In the first half of the nineteenth century, Eton, Westminster, Winchester, Charterhouse, Harrow, Rugby and Shrewsbury, together with two day schools, St. Paul's and Merchant Taylors', emerged as the great public schools of England. In 1861 their status was confirmed by the terms of reference of the Clarendon Commission which investigated these nine schools. Preeminent among them, however, both in terms of size and influence and as a matter for public concern, was Eton, founded in 1440 by Henry VI. One third of the report was devoted to Eton, which had already been subjected to severe criticism at the beginning of the decade and which was attended by one third of the 2,696 boys in the nine schools.

Payne was not a great admirer of the public schools. He acknowledged the contributions of reformers such as Thomas Arnold of Rugby but, on balance, regretted what he saw as the schools' fundamental deficiencies—privilege, custom, corruption and immorality on the one hand; and inefficient teaching, limited curricula, and an over-concern with games on the other. His views, which were probably shared by many other proprietors and teachers in private schools, were strongly confirmed by the unhappy experiences of his eldest son, John Burnell, as a master at one of the new nineteenth-century foundations, Wellington College, under its first headmaster, Edward White Benson. Indeed, in a lecture on the training of teachers delivered on 14 April 1869 to an evening meeting at the College of Preceptors, Payne launched into a virulent attack on Benson for his opposition to the training of teachers for secondary schools and for his criticism (on the basis of one example) of the effectiveness of teacher training in Germany.[60]

Payne's strongest condemnation of the public schools, which appeared in a substantial article entitled "Eton," in the *British Quarterly Review* of January 1868,[61] took as its starting point the report of the Clarendon Commissioners, issued in four volumes in 1864.[62] The *British Quarterly Review*, first published in 1845, continued until 1886. Its founder and first editor was Robert Vaughan, himself a Congregational minister, who believed that the press might be as important as the pulpit. Its basic religious viewpoint was that of Evangelical Nonconformity, but its essential watchword was freedom, "of freedom in the largest sense—freedom in Education, freedom in Trade, freedom in Religion—of freedom and fairness in everything!"[63] As such it provided a perfect medium for the expression of Payne's most radical educational views. Interestingly, neither this article on Eton, nor two other *British Quarterly Review* articles of 1868 and 1870 upon education in the United States, which contained strong denunciations of traditional British attitudes and institutions, were included by Joseph Frank in the collected works. Whether the basis for such exclusion was a problem over copyright, a belief that these pieces were already well-known and easily available, or some concern over their highly critical nature, is not clear.

One of Payne's major problems as a critic and reformer in educational matters lay in the nature and role of the state and of government. He did not have great faith in the quality of government in his own day, either at central or local levels. In 1856 he complained to his member of Parliament, William Evelyn, a Conservative, about his support for church rates, and accused him of being "in opposition to the principle of religious equality." [64] The Leatherhead Poll Book for 1857 shows that in the election of that year Payne voted for two candidates with interests in education: John Briscoe, a Liberal, who would "promote the education of all classes of the people"; and Henry Drummond, a Conservative, the president of the Western Literary Institution, who founded the professorship of Political Economy at Oxford. Payne strongly resented the aristocratic and patriarchal dimensions of government, and its continuation by means of patronage. His alternative concept was of an enlightened "commonwealth" (a concept which owed much to his appreciation of the United States) a commonwealth which would both promote, and be promoted by, the education of all its "citizens" (another of Payne's favourite terms).

For Payne, all children, girls and boys, rich and poor, were entitled to a basic schooling as citizens of the commonwealth and at public expense where parents were unable to pay fees. Good quality schooling for children of the upper classes was also a legitimate matter for public concern. One of the great problems for outsiders such as Payne was to provide a justification for governmental interference, by means of commission and legislation, into institutions such as public schools and universities, which were not dependent upon public finance. Payne, unlike the legislators of 1988 who refused to require independent schools to follow the National Curriculum established in that year, argued that even in public schools "the commonwealth is to have a voice in the matter of the education of those who are to be the *heads* as well as those who are to be the *hands* of society."[65] He thus supported the establishment of the Clarendon Commission and not only welcomed its criticisms of the many weaknesses of the nine great schools, but also drew attention to the dilatory way in which the schools responded to the reforms required of them.

Payne urged the reform of the public schools, but his more radical aim was the destruction of the old-boy network and of the assumption that old Etonians, and other public school products, had a natural right to high positions in state and society.[66] In a powerful and prophetic passage Payne declared that:

> These positions are by right ours—the people's—to give, not theirs by right to receive. . . . We want in every department of public business, really efficient men. We want in every public servant the most perfect combination we can obtain of extensive knowledge, mental ability, and moral character. Does Eton, as we know it now, appear peculiarly qualified for the supply of such men? We think not. Yet, at Eton, perhaps for centuries to come, will the upper classes of English society receive their school training.[67]

Payne's specific criticisms of Eton may be considered under four broad heads: management and finances; curriculum and methods of teaching; moral education; and quality of products.

One of the main criticisms of private schools was that the interests of the pupils were frequently sacrificed to the proprietors' needs to make a living. Payne, no doubt, relished the opportunity to criticize the efforts of the provost of Eton, Dr Goodford, and of the bursar and registrar, Messrs Dupuis and Batcheldor, in this respect. He drew attention to "the £6,385 a year which goes into the private purse of the provost and fellows, instead of into the public chest of the college,"[68] and noted that as a result "the begging box is sent briskly round"[69] to parents and former pupils whenever new buildings or other items of extraordinary expenditure were required. Even when money was raised by this method to build a sanatorium, a large proportion of it mysteriously disappeared. Payne observed that the result of this plundering of the funds by the provost and fellows, a plundering justified by custom, religious duty and the need to exercise hospitality, was that Eton had no laboratory, gymnasium, museum, choir, masters' common room or library for the general use of the school. Worst of all, whereas in the original foundation the provision for board (food and drink) was three shillings per week for the provost, for the fellows eighteen pence and for the collegers tenpence, by the nineteenth century the provost was taking £434 per year, the fellows £92, while the sum allotted for the boys had not been increased. Payne acknowledged that some of the worst privations and abuses in respect of the boys' board and lodgings, for example the notorious Long Chamber, had been corrected, but he still concluded that in regard to management and finances the instances he had cited were sufficient "to show how disgracefully the trust reposed in the college authorities of Eton has been abused."[70]

Withering as were Payne's criticisms of the mismanagement of Eton in general and of its finances in particular, he was equally savage upon the curriculum and teaching methods employed in the school. The curriculum was centred upon the Classical languages of Greek and Latin to the virtual exclusion of everything else, except "the inexorable demands of the boats, cricket, the racket and fives courts, football and the lounging about the streets."[71] Though the actual report of the Clarendon Commission, even when critical, was couched in judicious and diplomatic language, Payne, by hunting through the examination of witnesses, managed to light upon Lord Clarendon's own incredulous and indignant response to the description of the Eton curriculum by the headmaster, Dr Balston, a response which Payne quoted in full:

> Nothing can be worse than this state of things, when we find modern languages, geography, history, chronology, and everything else which a well-educated English gentleman ought to know given up, in order that full time should be devoted to the classics, and at the same time we are told [by Dean Liddell and others] that the boys go up to Oxford, not only not proficient, but in a lamentable state of deficiency with respect to the classics.[72]

As to the quality of teaching, Payne praised the abilities and diligence of the masters themselves but judged that their best efforts were largely frustrated by Eton's traditional usages and methods: the large classes, use of cribs, correction of verses by the tutors and "repetitions" by boys from Classical authors. All such practices, Payne believed, contributed to the negation rather than the promotion of true learning and scholarship. Indeed he pronounced the system of teaching to be "a positive absurdity."

Moral education was another cause for complaint. The general tenor of the school, Payne believed, was set by the excessive number of holidays, taken not only on saints' days and their vigils, but also on a variety of pretexts, such as the appointment of an old Etonian to a colonial bishopric, or a birth in the family of a fellow. It was also influenced by the considerable liberties enjoyed by the pupils, their initiation ceremonies, drunkenness, and bullying, institutionalized in the fagging and monitorial systems.

As to the products of this education, Payne attributed the 'much-praised' gentlemanliness of Eton boys to their families and origins, rather than to their schooling. Though there were some exceptions, even those boys who sought to proceed to the universities frequently were found seriously wanting in academic attainments, while the great majority of the pupils, Payne believed, benefitted but little from a school ethos which was characterized by "enormous idleness, indifference to every kind of intellectual excellence, gross ignorance, habits of drinking, wasteful expenditure of money, and general self-indulgence."[73]

Payne did not advocate the complete abolition of the public schools. Like many a critic, before and after, he was intrigued by their unique nature, and wary of excessive governmental intervention in educational matters. He was, nevertheless, an advocate of root and branch reform, both within the schools themselves and in respect of their position and influence within society and the state.

Elementary Schooling

Many of Payne's criticisms of elementary (he himself used the term "primary") schooling were similar to those which he levelled against the public schools. He castigated the attainments of pupils who had been through the system and attributed the low standards to faults in organization, ethos and teaching methods. Although annual statistics of attainment under the Revised Code of 1862, whereby children were examined in the three Rs of reading, writing and arithmetic, were published under government auspices and freely available, Payne's use of these statistics excited both concern and controversy. This stemmed from two causes: Payne subjected the statistics to further analysis (for example by including pupils who might have been entered in the examination but were not) and by concentrating upon failures rather than successes.

For example, the annual report for 1866 showed that 90 percent of those examined passed in reading, 84 percent in writing and 73 percent in arithmetic, giving an average of 82 percent overall. This appeared to be a highly creditable level of performance. As Payne pointed out, however, the requirements of the tests were minimal in the extreme. Furthermore, of the one million children aged six and over whose names were on the books of government-inspected schools, 196,000 could not be presented because they had made fewer than 200 attendances during the year, while a further 139,000 were simply not presented for examination—probably because they would not pass. Some 231,000 failed to satisfy the examiners in whole or part. Another significant weakness was that while children were supposed to progress through the six Standards of the Revised Code and take a new and higher Standard each year, this was far from being the case. Indeed, about half of the children aged ten or over, who should have been presented in Standards 4, 5 and 6, were actually examined in Standards 1, 2 and 3. Poor as these results were, Payne's analysis of the statistics in the annual report for 1871 showed a decline rather than an improvement in levels of performance, a decline possibly associated with changes which stemmed from the Education Act of 1870. Such calculations indicated that the great majority of children never reached the sixth Standard. This, for Payne, was a travesty, for it was one of his maxims, and applicable to all educational situations, whether for boys or girls, rich or poor, public or private, that "efficient teaching implies the success of the great majority of the pupils, not the success of the small minority."[74]

Payne's indictment of the state-supported elementary school system of his day began as part of a general paper which he read on 3 June 1872 at a sessional meeting at the Social Science Association's Rooms in London. That paper was entitled "On the Importance and Necessity of improving our ordinary methods of School Instruction" and covered middle-class as well as elementary schools.[75] In September of the same year, however, he presented a more forceful case which concentrated upon elementary schooling alone, under the provocative title "Why are the Results of our Primary Instruction so Unsatisfactory?" The tone of this presentation was calculated to shock:

> This, then, is the final result of the working of 15,000 schools, conducted by 26,000 teachers, at a cost of about one million a year. All this stupendous machinery is contrived and kept in motion to send out into the world annually about 16,000 children with the ability to read, write and cipher moderately well; and at least 80,000 furnished with little or nothing "which may better them in life."[76]

How then could such failure be explained? Payne attributed it to two basic causes: the first "the idea of education entertained by the Committee of Council";[77] the second the poor quality of teaching. Payne believed that these two causes were strongly interrelated: the second proceeded in large part from the first. He was a vehement and consistent critic of the Revised Code of 1862: it was the negation of his vision of education.

Payne's following castigation of the Code constituted a classic statement of his concept of the nature of education and contained a warning not only for his contemporaries but for succeeding generations:

> We need have no hesitation in pronouncing it to be mechanical in conception, mechanical in means, mechanical in results. . . . The results which we have seen could not in the nature of things be other than they are. They are the legitimate products of a system which assumes the name without possessing the spirit of true education. Nowhere have I ever met, in the course of long practice and study of teaching, with a more striking illustration of the great truth, that just in proportion as you substitute mechanical routine, drill and cram, for intelligent and sympathetic development of the child's powers, you shall fail in the very object you are aiming at. Making quantity not quality the test of your results, you shall fail in securing either quantity or quality. The experiment which has now been tried for ten years in

England ought henceforth to take a place in the annals of
education as an example to deter.[78]

Payne believed that the Revised Code cast a blight upon all who
came under its aegis: inspectors, teachers and pupils.

The poor quality of teaching, Payne argued, depended not
only upon the Revised Code and its ethos, but also upon the
nature of those who administered it. He was a severe critic of the
inspectorate. For Payne the three qualities required in an
inspector were: "a thoughtful study of education, a thorough
acquaintance with school work, gained by long and successful
experience," and "a knowledge of the best methods of teaching
generally, as practised in other countries as well as in our
own."[79] He believed that these posts, "belong of right"[80] to those
who taught in schools and that inspectors should be recruited
from among the most intelligent, hardworking, experienced and
successful elementary schoolteachers. In fact, however, Her
Majesty's Inspectors were drawn from men whose reputations
rested upon their ability to write Greek iambics, and upon the
proud boast that they had never previously set foot in an
elementary school.

Many inspectors, some of whom had a disdain for their
work, saw their task principally in terms of examining as many
children as possible in a day. The teachers attempted to play
their part in achieving this goal by drilling the children into
mechanical answers. In consequence children were not taught to
read as such, but simply to learn by heart certain passages which
they could parrot forth on the day of the inspector's visit. This
meant that the children fulfilled the requirements of the Code
and the schools received their governmental grants, but in reality
little education had taken place. Payne quoted from the reports
of concerned inspectors, for example that of HMI Jolly of 1870,
which acknowledged that reading grants were given to children
who could not really read. Jolly reported that children were not
taught how to overcome difficulties themselves, for example to
decipher an unknown word; instead, they relied upon the
teacher, whose basic aim was to get all the children to learn by
heart the standard reading text.

There were many critics of Eton in the 1860s, and Payne's
strictures might be located both within that context, and as part

of a longstanding rivalry between those who taught in boys' public and private schools. Payne, however, had few connections himself with the elementary school world, and his criticisms of the national system, as under the aegis of the Revised Code of 1862, provoked considerable controversy and some powerful responses. Such responses came from two sources. The first was from that broad body of opinion which believed that the prime aim of elementary schooling, even under the Revised Code, was still religious and moral. Children should be taught their duty towards God and their betters and to recognize the latter and defer to them. This was in distinct contrast to Payne's belief that the purpose of education was to enable people to better themselves. The second group of opponents were those whose ability and reputation had been directly impugned by Payne: the inspectors and teachers.

The storm provoked by Payne's Plymouth paper of 1872 led to a special conference on primary education on 18 April 1873 in London, convened by the Education Department of the Social Science Association. There was but a small attendance, mainly of teachers, but at least two of Payne's Preceptors' colleagues, Barrow Rule and J. M. D. Meiklejohn, were present. The former stated that he was not prepared to lay the blame for the present unsatisfactory state of primary education upon the teachers; the latter argued that the current division into six Standards was impracticable. Payne, who spoke first, reiterated the points he had made at Plymouth: standards of attainment were lamentable; the main problem was the poor quality of teaching; this quality was the result of the system operated by the Education Department of the Privy Council. As in Plymouth he was followed by Rev. Brooke Lambert who, once again, took exception to Payne's calculations and read from a letter from Joshua Fitch to the effect that Payne's claims as to inefficiency were "very seriously exaggerated and calculated to mislead those of the public who were not familiar with the condition of elementary schools."[81] Later in the meeting, however, it appears that Lambert and other doubters acknowledged the accuracy of Payne's figures.

Though the names of Payne and Fitch had been linked together in several educational causes—for example in College of Preceptors' lectures and in promoting the Girls' Public Day School Company—there were residual differences, and a serious and public dispute broke out between them. Though Fitch had been an early critic of the Revised Code, as a former HMI he no doubt personally felt the force of Payne's denigration of the elementary school system in general, and of the role of the inspectors in particular. Accordingly, in a *Fortnightly Review* article entitled "Statistical fallacies respecting public instruction," Fitch stated that "as I happen to have been an inspector during the year to which Mr Payne's figures refer, and so to have had made some small contribution to the results which he sets forth, I shall venture to offer some reasons for questioning the general accuracy and value of those reports."[82] Payne, in his turn, was hurt by some of Fitch's allegations, but maintained that whatever differences there might be over precise calculations of achievement under the Revised Code, there were many eminent educationists who, to use the words of Edwin Abbott, believed that the principal effect of the Code was to "degrade teaching and perpetuate stupidity."

Another line of attack on Payne was that he had raised the whole issue as a means of castigating the achievements in Church schools. This, too, he was strenuously to deny, arguing that standards were no better in undenominational schools, nor indeed in middle-class schools, whether private or endowed. On this latter point he was able to refer back to his quotation in the paper of June 1872 from Fitch's own report for Taunton on endowed schools in Yorkshire:

> Three-fourths of the scholars whom I have examined in endowed schools, if tested by the usual standard appropriate to boys of similar age under the Revised Code, would fail to pass the examination either in arithmetic or any other elementary subject.[83]

Payne was, by no means, wholly opposed to examinations. He recognized their worth, for example in enabling girls and women to challenge male monopolies and as a means of recruiting to the civil and armed services on the basis of talent rather than of patronage. But he also believed that in schools and colleges excessive examination could be the enemy of true education. In October 1873, at the annual meeting of the Social

Science Association held at Norwich, during a discussion of the effects of competitive examinations upon education, chaired by Hodgson and to which Lake and Meiklejohn had presented papers, Payne deplored the practice "of continually pulling up the plants to see the conditions of the roots, the consequence of which was that all good natural growth was stopped."[84]

The Training of Teachers

Payne's central purpose in life was to improve the quality of education in schools. Central to the achievement of that purpose—and equally applicable to secondary schools for girls, public (and private) schools for boys and to elementary schools for the children of the working classes—was an improvement in the quality of teachers. This theme ran throughout Payne's professional life as it runs throughout this book. His involvement began in 1830 with the pamphlet on Jacotot; from the 1840s it found a new expression in his role as examiner for the College of Preceptors. Once himself retired from teaching, Payne furthered the cause through his several lectures and publications. From 1873 his advocacy was enhanced by his new status as Professor of the Science and Art of Education. Several dimensions of this concern for the quality of teachers have already been covered in previous chapters. The following chapter provides a detailed examination of Payne's concept of a science and art of education, knowledge of which he believed to be essential for every teacher. The purpose of this section is to consider Payne's critique of the lack of quality in teachers and the effect this had upon the status of teaching as a profession.

In Payne's day there was a complete free trade in education. Any man or woman, indeed any boy or girl, however ignorant, however lacking in moral principles or business acumen, could set up a school. Such a situation was justified by the application of market principles. Parents would naturally choose good schools for their children. These would flourish, while bad schools would wither and die. In consequence there was no need to require any prior test of the competence of teachers before they set up schools; "liberty of teaching" could prevail.

The basic purpose of the College of Preceptors, and one with which Payne was in full agreement (though he frequently queried the effectiveness of its methods) was to raise the status of the teaching profession by providing the public with a guarantee of fitness and responsibility. He pursued this end by various means, both through the work of the College and through associated bodies, for example the Scholastic Registration Association, of which he became a Vice-President. Payne's critique of the situation involved two main dimensions. The first was to question the widely held view that no training was either desirable or possible for teaching in secondary schools. The second was to examine the type of training provided in those colleges which prepared teachers for elementary schools.

The traditional means whereby masters in boys' public and grammar schools offered evidence as to their scholastic ability and moral rectitude was through their possession of a university degree and their clerical status. For example Benson, who like other public school headmasters was to progress to a bishopric, and even to the see of Canterbury itself, required his assistant masters at Wellington to take holy orders. It was widely believed, and in many quarters the belief lasted well into the twentieth century, that these masters neither needed to be, nor could be, trained in the art of teaching. Benson himself declared that "only experience can prove whether a man can teach or not" and added that "probably a period of not less than two years would be required to ascertain this point."[85] This belief, which might place pupils in the hands of a succession of incompetents throughout their school careers, was especially galling to those like Payne who had no university degree or clerical status upon which to rely. It provided a particular problem for females who had no access to such qualifications.

When, in 1876, Maria Grey was canvassing support for a women's training college for secondary teachers, she received a stern rebuff from the Bishop of Exeter who declared:

> I am not an advocate, have never been an advocate, for Institutions for the Training of Teachers *above* the

> Elementary. In providing for Elementary schools, such institutions were a necessity. But they are *not* a necessity for teachers of schools *above* the Elementary. And unless a necessity, I think them a great evil.[86]

In contrast, Payne believed that all teachers, male and female, secondary and primary, should undergo training and should acquire a preliminary certificate of competence before being allowed to proceed to posts in schools. Payne sought to base membership of the teaching profession upon such proofs of competence. As a model he described the situation in Germany where intending teachers were required to demonstrate their knowledge of subject matter, attend lectures on the principles and practice of teaching, give classes in front of experts and finally undertake a year's probationary teaching, before becoming full members of their profession.[87]

Herbert Quick, a graduate of Trinity College, Cambridge, and a clergyman, who spent two years in Germany before beginning a teaching career which spanned a variety of grammar, preparatory and public schools, including Harrow, admitted the validity of Payne's arguments. On 13 June 1872, prompted by Payne's recent paper to the Social Science Association, he recorded:

> Mr Joseph Payne has made a vigorous onslaught on the state of education in England. . . . What he would have is a more systematic training of teachers and a stop put to *didactic* teaching. The teacher is to be the guide merely. This theory is undoubtedly the right one, but there are great difficulties in working it in a school, and most school teachers give it up altogether. If intelligent teaching is to be found anywhere in England it ought to be in schools like Harrow, where we have for masters the very pick of the Universities. But, whatever may be the cause, our men here do not take much interest in the theory of their profession, and the results of their teaching, as tested by the average boy when he goes to Oxford or Cambridge, do not seem satisfactory.[88]

Nevertheless, it must be acknowledged that in spite of the efforts of Payne and of others, very few teachers were trained for secondary schools until well into the twentieth century. Among male teachers in public and grammar schools, class and gender prejudices suggested that training was appropriate only for those who taught in elementary schools, or for women teachers at secondary level. Even the day training colleges, though attached to universities, were concerned with elementary training. In consequence in 1909–1910, the first year of the Board of Education's regulations for secondary training, only 35 men and 139 women were recorded as having completed a course of training for work in secondary schools. The corresponding figures for 1913–1914 were 38 and 167.[89]

While Payne's criticisms of secondary schools, therefore, centred upon the contemporary British presumption that no training was necessary, his criticisms of elementary schools, many of which were run by teachers who had undergone training and certification before taking up their posts, and whose pupils were subjected to an annual examination, concentrated not upon the lack of training, but upon its lack of quality. Payne acknowledged that students in training colleges in Britain were subject to a strenuous regime: tested for admission and annually thereafter; visiting model schools to see examples of good practice; giving criticism lessons themselves in the practising schools; and instructed in school management—the keeping of registers and timetables. Indeed, he advocated the setting up of further colleges so that these benefits might be more widely spread, and supported the College of Preceptors' scheme for the establishment of a training college in London for intending secondary teachers. Nevertheless, Payne found two major faults with the colleges of his day.

The first of these was the nature and extent of denominational control. The great majority of the training colleges which existed in Britain in the 1870s came under the auspices of the Anglican Church. Payne regretted the denominational ethos of the elementary teacher training of his day and strongly opposed the use of public money to establish further denominationally controlled colleges or to enlarge those which already existed. In Payne's view, the Elementary Education Act of 1870, with its promise of nondenominational religious teaching in the new board schools, reinforced the need for nondenominational training colleges. Since the school boards were not empowered to create training colleges, national colleges were required, colleges in which "there must be no recognition whatever of the denominations to which the students belonged, nor of the denominational character of the schools which any of them were to enter."[90]

The second feature of existing training institutions to attract Payne's criticism was that the ethos of the Revised Code affected the colleges as well as the schools. Teachers in training were brought up in an atmosphere of mechanical drill and routine, their horizons circumscribed by the limited range of subjects and attainments prescribed under the Code. Payne also believed that there was too much lecturing and not enough lessoning in the colleges. The consequence of this limited approach was that the colleges neither taught, nor professed to teach, the science and art of education. In the colleges, as in the schools, the theory prevailed "that education consists in telling, preaching, expounding, lecturing, cramming the memory, mechanical drilling of the lower faculties, or driving to learn."[91] In opposition to this limited regime, Payne presented his own theory of education as one which was characterized by

> awakening the mind to the consciousness of its power by bringing it into vital contact with facts of daily experience, cultivating by suitable exercises its faculties of observation, perception, reflection, judgment, and reasoning, aiding it to gain clear and accurate ideas of its own; training it, in short, to form habits of thinking.[92]

Payne believed that no person should become a teacher who was not versed in three types of knowledge: a knowledge of the subject of instruction; a knowledge of the nature of the being to be instructed; and a knowledge of the best methods of instruction.[93] Products of existing training colleges, he thought, were restricted, essentially by government policy, to too-narrow a knowledge of the subject or subjects of instruction. Their knowledge of children was limited by their complete ignorance of psychology. Their knowledge of the best methods of instruction was hampered by a national fixation with cramming which left prospective teachers without any appreciation of the great practitioners and theorists of the art of teaching who had lived in previous ages, or who resided in other countries.

Thus Payne's critique of the colleges of his day foreshadowed the creation of a new concept and context for the training of teachers. Payne was not against instruction in the practicalities of school management—the organization of classes and the keeping of registers—nor any of the other useful dimensions of the training regimes of his day. But he additionally wanted students to acquire that which was currently being denied to them—a sound knowledge of the science and art of education. In the 1870s Payne's professorial course provided a blueprint for this new concept. From the 1890s a new context arose, institutions of university rank, unconnected with any denomination, where students might study pedagogy and the psychological, historical and comparative dimensions of education under the guidance of persons of professorial status.

NOTES

1. Report presented on 10 October 1873, Head Mistresses' Reports to Governors, 1871–85, p. 48, North London Collegiate School Archives.

2. Minutes of the Council meeting of 17 June 1871, College of Preceptors' Council Minute Book, 1870–89, p. 56.

3. *Educational Times* XXVIII, 174 (October 1875), pp. 156–7.

4. *Ibid.*, p. 157.

5. Minutes of the Finance Committee meeting of 14 April 1877, College of Preceptors' Finance Committee Minute Book, 1874–1914, p. 20.

6. Sarah A. Burstall, *Frances Mary Buss: An Educational Pioneer* (London, 1938), p. 70.

7. Ridley, *Buss*, p. 108.

8. Minutes of the Governors' meeting of 9 December 1872, Governors' Minute Book, 1870–5, p. 64; Report presented on 7 April 1873, Head Mistresses' Reports to Governors, 1871–85, p 36; Report for 1873, Prize Day Reports and Lists, 1870–80, p. 98: North London Collegiate School Archives.

9. Report presented on 21 October 1872, Head Mistresses' Reports to Governors, 1871–85, p. 27, North London Collegiate School Archives.

10. Report for 1875, Prize Day Reports and Lists, 1870–80, p. 124, North London Collegiate School Archives.

11. Report for 1874, Prize Day Reports and Lists, 1870–80, p. 114; Report presented on 13 April 1874, Head Mistresses' Reports to Governors, 1871–85, p. 53: North London Collegiate School Archives.

12. Copy of a 13–page handwritten report, addressed to Buss, of Payne's inspection of the school on 24, 27 and 28 July 1874, Archive box, "History of School 1850–75," North London Collegiate School Archives.

13. Grey to Buss, 23 December 1871, Archive box, "FMB and family," North London Collegiate School Archives.

14. *Educational Times* XXIV, 130 (February 1872), p. 259, and 131 (March 1872), p. 277.

15. A copy of the lecture programme bound in with the report for 12 February 1872, Head Mistresses' Reports to Governors, 1871–85, North London Collegiate School Archives.

16. *Ibid.*

17. A copy of the lecture programme bound in with the report for 7 April 1873, Head Mistresses' Reports to Governors, 1871–85, North London Collegiate School Archives. See also a report of a lecture by M. A. Garvey to the teachers of the North London Collegiate Schools on the subject of the "Science and Art of teaching," *Educational Times* XXVI, 146 (June 1873), pp. 56–8.

18. Report for 1871, Head Mistresses' Reports to Governors, 1871–85, p. 9, North London Collegiate School Archives.

19. Minutes of the Governors' meeting of 9 December 1872, Governors' Minute Book, 1870–5, p. 64, North London Collegiate School Archives.

20. Quoted in Ridley, *Buss*, p. 206.

21. Quoted in Josephine Kamm, *How Different from Us: A Biography of Miss Buss and Miss Beale* (London, 1958), p. 149.

22. Ridley, *Buss*, pp. 70–1.

23. Quoted in Ridley, *Buss*, pp. 274–5.

24. Evelyn Lawrence (ed.), *Friedrich Froebel and English Education* (London, 1969), pp. 32, 45.

25. Foster Watson (ed.), *The Encyclopaedia and Dictionary of Education* (London, 4 vols., 1921–2), III, p. 1264. See, also, Ridley, *Buss*, p. 178.

26. *Transactions of the National Association for the Promotion of Social Science, 1873* (London, 1874), p. 368. Hereafter referred to as *TNAPSS*.

27. Japernoux to Payne, 13 June 1873, Author's Collection.

28. *TNAPSS, 1865*, p. 362.

29. *TNAPSS, 1871*, p. 370.

30. *TNAPSS, 1865*, p. 362.

31. *TNAPSS, 1873*, p. 368.

32. *Journal of the Women's Education Union*, I, 1 (January 1873).

33. Laurie Magnus, *The Jubilee Book of the Girls' Public Day School Trust, 1873–1923* (Cambridge, 1923), p. 17.

34. Minutes of the Council meeting of 25 November 1871, Preceptors' Council Minute Book, 1870–89, p. 68.

35. *Journal of the Women's Education Union* I, 1 (January 1873), p. 8.

36. *Ibid.*

37. *Journal of the Women's Education Union* II, 14, (February 1874), pp. 19, 50.

38. *Educational Times* XXVII, 156 (April 1874), p. 12.

39. Magnus, *Jubilee Book*, p. 53; Edward W. Ellsworth, *Liberators of the Female Mind* (Westport, 1979), p. 184.

40. Josephine Kamm, *Indicative Past: A Hundred Years of the Girls' Public Day School Trust* (London, 1971), p. 49.

41. *Ibid.*, p. 204.

42. Magnus, *Jubilee Book*, pp. 52–93.

43. *Journal of the Women's Education Union* I, 1 (January 1873), p. 40.

44. Frances Buss had presented copies of the first two pamphlets in the series to the library of the College of Preceptors. Minutes of the Council meeting of 20 April 1872, Preceptors' Council Minute Book, 1870–89, p. 87.

45. *Journal of the Women's Education Union* I, 11 (November 1873), p. 195.

46. *Journal of the Women's Education Union* III, 26 (February 1875), p. 30.

47. *Journal of the Women's Education Union* IV, 41 (May 1876), p. 70.

48. *Journal of the Women's Education Union* IV, 42 (June 1876), pp. 86–7.

49. A 3, Folder 1870–9, B 36, Folder 1880–9: Archive box, 1870–1919, Maria Grey College Archives.

50. Irene M. Lilley, *Maria Grey College, 1878–1976* (Twickenham 1981), p. 6.

51. A 2, Folder, 1870–9, Archive box, 1870–1919, Maria Grey College Archives.

52. Quoted in Ridley, *Buss*, p. 274.

53. Grey to Buss, 8 July 1876, Archive box, "FMB and family," North London Collegiate School Archives.

54. Teachers' Training and Registration Society Subscription Book, 1878–1884, Maria Grey College Archives.

55. Scholarships Awards Book, 1878–1936, Maria Grey College Archives.

56. In 1912 a particular problem arose when legal costs for transferring the Payne Memorial Prize Fund to new trustees amounted to £15. 1s. 3d, a sum reduced by the Board of Education to £8. 18s. 9d. Since, in that year, the interest was only £6. 2s. 7d, it was resolved to pay the legal fees from other College funds. Minutes of the Finance Committee meeting held on 29 January 1912, Teachers' Training and Registration Society Finance Committee Minute Book, 1900–1915, p. 195, Maria Grey College Archives.

57. Chapman, *Professional Roots*, p. 118.

58. *Paddington, Kensington and Bayswater Chronicle*, 6 May 1876.

59. *Educational Guide to English and Continental Schools*, June 1876. See also the *School Guardian*, 6 May 1876.

60. *Educational Times XXII*, 97 (May 1869), pp. 27–32.

61. *British Quarterly Review* 47 (January 1868), pp. 34–69.

62. Parliamentary Papers, 1864, XX, *Report of Her Majesty's Commissioners appointed to inquire into the Revenues and Management of certain Colleges and Schools, and the Studies pursued and Instruction given therein*.

63. *British Quarterly Review* 2 (August 1845), p. 291.

64. Evelyn to Payne, 4 March 1856, Author's Collection.

65. *British Quarterly Review* 47 (January 1868), p. 38.

66. In 1989 over a quarter of the 200 wealthiest people in Britain had attended Eton. If females and those educated abroad were to be excluded from the total the fraction of old Etonians would rise to a third.

67. *British Quarterly Review* 47 (January 1868), pp. 68–9.

68. *Ibid.*, p. 39.

69. *Ibid.*, p. 41.

70. *Ibid.*, p. 43.

71. *Ibid.*, p. 51.

72. *Ibid.*, pp. 60–1.

73. *Ibid.*, p. 68.

74. Payne, *Works*, I, p. 296.

75. Payne, *Works*, I, pp. 283–305.

76. "Why are the Results of our Primary Instruction so Unsatisfactory?" Paper presented to the annual congress of the Social Science Association in Plymouth, 1872, *TNAPPS, 1872*, p. 245.

77. *Ibid.*, p. 247.

78. *Ibid.*, pp. 247–8.

79. Payne, *Works*, I, p. 289.

80. Payne, *Works*, I, p. 290.

81. For a substantial report of the conference see the *Daily News*, 18 April 1873, although Payne subsequently complained to the editor that he had been misquoted.

82. *Fortnightly Review* (November 1873), p. 617.

83. Payne, *Works*, I, p. 298.

84. *TNAPSS, 1873*, p. 355.

85. Quoted in Payne, *Works*, I, p. 114.

86. Quoted in Lilley, *Maria Grey*, p. 5.

87. Payne, *Works*, I, p. 116.

88. Storr, *Quick*, p. 175.

89. Figures from P. H. J. H. Gosden, *The Evolution of a Profession: A Study of the Contribution of Teachers' Associations to the Development of School Teaching as a Professional Occupation* (Oxford, 1971), p. 214,

90. *TNAPSS, 1872*, p. 267.

91. *Ibid.*, p. 251.

92. *Ibid.*

93. Payne, *Works*, I, p. 139.

CHAPTER SEVEN

The Science and Art of Education

Science and Education

In his introduction to the first volume of Payne's collected works, edited by his son Joseph Frank and published in 1880, Herbert Quick wrote of "the interest in education as a science and art" which was awakened by Payne's work as lecturer and professor of the College of Preceptors. He was in Quick's words, "a pioneer in the needed science of education" and was perceived as such by many of his contemporaries. Indeed this primacy was confirmed in the very title which Joseph Frank assigned to the first volume: *Lectures on the Science and Art of Education, with other Lectures and Essays by the late Joseph Payne, the first Professor of the Science and Art of Education in the College of Preceptors.* The purpose of this chapter is to examine the dimensions of Payne's understanding and advocacy of the science (or as he would have preferred the science and art) of education.

As yet, both the origins of the movement for a science of education and Payne's pioneering work in this cause have received scant attention. Neglect of the first may be attributed in large part to the persistent hostility which has existed in Britain towards the very concept of a theory or science of education. As regards Payne himself, the neglect stems from several factors. One such factor is that his final years were not devoted to the production of a substantial and coherent statement of his educational theory. Instead Payne's views on education continued to be expressed predominantly through lectures, lectures delivered to a variety of audiences in a variety of locations. Thus, in addition to the London lectures for the College of Preceptors, he spoke at the annual conferences of the National Association for the Promotion of Social Science, as at Leeds in 1871, Plymouth in 1872, Norwich in 1873 and Glasgow in 1874, and his speeches on those occasions were published in the Society's *Transactions*. Reference has already been made to his lectures in Edinburgh, while in January 1875, at the invitation of the General Association of Ireland, Payne delivered a short course of six lectures on the "Science and Art of Education" at the Royal Dublin Society.[1]

Payne's growing fame and the sheer quality of his lectures meant that some were published in pamphlet form. Examples include *On the Importance and Necessity of improving our ordinary methods of School Instruction* (1872); *Why are the Results of our Primary Instruction so Unsatisfactory?* (1872); *The True Foundation of Science Teaching* (1873); *Froebel and the Kindergarten System of elementary education* (1874); *The Science and Art of Education* (1874); and *Pestalozzi* (1875). Other lectures and papers, however, remained unpublished during Payne's lifetime, and it was not without some difficulty, and until four years after his father's death, that Joseph Frank brought together a considerable number in what was to become the first volume of Payne's collected works.

In his preface to the first volume Joseph Frank acknowledged the "diversity of illustration and some slight variance in points of detail" which characterized the collection, but trusted "that the papers here collected have sufficient unity and completeness to give an adequate idea of Mr Payne's principles as a teacher."[2] Herbert Quick's anxieties about the book centred less upon its theoretical unity and more upon its commercial viability. He advised that its bulk and cost (some 400 pages at a price of ten shillings per copy) might be a considerable deterrent. Quick himself was no stranger to the economics of educational publishing. The print run for his own *Essays on Educational Reformers* was, on the advice of his publishers, a mere 500, and even then few were sold until he personally reduced the price from 7s. 6d. to 3s. 6d. Nevertheless a second edition of Payne's collected works appeared in 1883, and in the same year the first of many American editions was produced in Boston by

Willard Small. The second volume, also edited by Joseph Frank, which contained lectures on the history of education and the account of Payne's visit to German schools, was published in London in 1892.

A second factor in the neglect of Payne's contribution to the science of education, and particularly to its foundation in psychology, has been the preeminence accorded to Alexander Bain, Professor of Logic at the University of Aberdeen from 1860 to 1881. Bain's book, *Education as a Science*, was published in 1879, a year before the first volume of Payne's collected works. It would appear that Joseph Frank was aware of the potential rivalry between the two volumes for in 1880 he contributed a lengthy article on "educational pressure" to the July and August editions of the *Journal of Education*, an article prefaced by a notice of the forthcoming book, which was, indeed, reviewed in the *Journal*'s October edition. Joseph Frank even launched an attack on Bain's *Education as a Science*, with specific reference to its treatment of physiology and education. Both the attack and Bain's reply were also published in the *Journal of Education*, for May and June 1880.[3] This is not to deny Bain's importance. As author of *The Senses and the Intellect* (1855), *The Emotions and the Will* (1859) and as founder in 1876 and proprietor until 1892 of the journal, *Mind*, Bain was a highly significant figure in British thought of the second half of the nineteenth century. Indeed he has been hailed as the father of modern British psychology; L. S. Hearnshaw began *A Short History of British Psychology, 1840–1940*, published in 1964, with a chapter entitled "Bain and his Background."[4] But overemphasis upon Bain has led to a relative neglect of those, like Payne, who in the 1860s and 1870s were promoting the cause of a science of education. Richard Selleck's chapter on the "Scientific Educationists" in *The New Education: The English Background, 1870–1914* (1968) contains but one mention of Payne; his name is given along with those of Bain, Lake, Quick, James Ward and Sophie Bryant, as members of the Society for the Development of the Science of Education. Once again, however, Bain's work is singled out. Selleck states that "When, in 1879, Alexander Bain wrote his book *Education as a Science*, he was a voice crying in the wilderness."[5]

Before its merger with the Teachers' Guild in 1887, the Society for the Development of the Science of Education boasted a number of distinguished Presidents, among them Bain and Quick; university dons James Ward and Montagu Butler, respectively fellow and master of Trinity College, Cambridge; and distinguished headmasters—Wilson of Clifton, and Thring of Uppingham. But it was Payne who chaired the foundation meeting which took place at the College of Preceptors on 31 July 1875, and it was Payne's collaborator in the transformation of the College's examinations for Theory and Practice, the diffident but waspish Charles Lake, who was the Society's prime mover and first secretary.[6] Although Payne and Lake acted in concert to produce the reformed examination scheme for the Preceptors in June 1871, and were coworkers in the new society in 1875, by that date differences had emerged between them. Those differences, which stemmed from both intellectual and personal factors, will be referred to in the conclusion to this chapter.

A third factor has been that of misinterpretation. Selleck, in the only other two textual references to Payne in his book, follows Kolesnik and characterizes Payne as an exponent of faculty psychology.[7] Kolesnik, indeed, portrays Payne as a reactionary, both in terms of faculty training and curriculum. He cites Payne as symptomatic of the nineteenth-century British belief in the mental discipline of Classics, and concludes that "Joseph Payne again seems to speak for what might be considered the conservative point of view, taking his stand in behalf of the classics."[8]

There is no doubt that Payne had a firm belief in the value of Classics, including its value as an agent of mental discipline, but this belief should be seen in the context of his other statements on curriculum, and on the purposes and methods of schooling. Kolesnik's quotations and analysis do not encompass the publications of the 1870s, but are taken from Payne's pamphlet of 1866, entitled *The Curriculum of Modern Education, and the respective claims of Classics and Science to be represented in it considered.*[9] Even in that pamphlet, however, Payne argued that the curriculum should include both Classics and science, and declared in the preface that science teaches better, that is, more directly and soundly, than any other study, how to observe, how to arrange and classify, how to connect causes with effects, how to comprehend details under general laws, how to estimate the practical value of facts.[10]

Nevertheless, he did not, like Herbert Spencer, want to put science at the centre of all school education and to revolutionize the school curriculum at that point in time. Though science was "immensely attractive" and there was no doubt that "it will and ought to be extensively taught in schools,"[11] Payne did not believe that there would be much benefit in introducing science into schools if it were simply to be taught from textbooks—a mere accumulation of facts. In advocating "the honourable introduction of science into the curriculum,"[12] Payne argued for proper science. That meant teaching science not from textbooks but by means of experiment and observation. Science must be taught in a scientific manner—that is to say by "training the mind to scientific method, to habits of investigation, and the diligent search after truth."[13]

The curriculum scheme for a middle-class school for boys aged from eight to 16 which Payne produced to accompany his 1866 pamphlet was of a broad nature and very different from the unrelieved diet of Classics of many public schools. Pupils aged eight to ten would study reading, spelling and writing; history, both scriptural and English; geography, topical and physical; French, both speaking and reading; lessons on objects and words; arithmetic, chiefly mental. These subjects would continue for the next two years, with the addition of two sciences—botany and physics—and further arithmetic and English grammar. Scientific study, therefore, would precede Latin, which would not be introduced until age 12, although for the next two years it would receive pride of place. In a timetable of 40 hours of study per week, he proposed 20 hours for Latin (although, as with English, some of that time would be spent on such subjects as "geography, history, archaeology which may be necessary for their illustration")[14] and five apiece for French and German, Mathematics, English Language and Literature, and Physics. For pupils aged 14 to 16 Latin was reduced to 10 hours, French and German increased to 10, while Chemistry or Human Physiology also received 10. Mathematics and English Language and Literature remained at five hours each.

Payne's cautious approach in advocating the introduction of science into predominantly Classical schools was appreciated by contemporaries on both sides of the Atlantic. For example, William H. Payne, Professor of the Science and Art of Teaching in the University of Michigan, a post to which he was appointed in 1879, the first such chair in the United States,[15] was an admirer of Herbert Spencer. Indeed he considered his *Education* to be the "most thoughtful and fruitful book on education since the *Émile.*"[16] Nevertheless William Payne was keen to question some of Spencer's generalizations. In 1886, in a book entitled *Contributions to the Science of Education*, he quoted with approval from *The Curriculum of Modern Education* two of Joseph Payne's own comments upon Spencer's work.[17]

Kolesnik, indeed, quotes from William Payne (though not in respect of Herbert Spencer or Joseph Payne) but rather as an advocate of the inverse ratio between the immediate practical value of a subject and its disciplinary value.[18] He then cites Youmans as an example of a modern approach, as one who "strove to combine the practical and disciplinary values in the same curriculum through the proper choice of subject matter."[19] If, as it appears, Kolesnik is thus contrasting Joseph Payne and Youmans, such a contrast is surely open to challenge. Payne knew Edward and Eliza Youmans, who came from New York and were staunch advocates both of science in schools and of a scientific approach to education. For example on 12 October 1866 Payne chaired an evening meeting at the College of Preceptors at which Edward Youmans gave a lecture on "The Scientific Study of Human Nature," a lecture which Payne found to be of great personal interest.[20] As for Eliza Youmans, when in 1871 Payne was preparing a paper on "The Teaching of Elementary Science as a Part of the Earliest Instruction of Children" for the Leeds meeting of the Social Science Association, he was "so struck with the remarkable correspondence between the views taken by Miss Youmans and those which he had presented in his own paper,"[21] that he wrote a preface and supplement to the British edition of Eliza Youmans' *Essay on the Culture of the Observing Powers of Children especially in connection with the Study of Botany*, published in 1872.[22] Youmans went so far as to advocate Botany as a "fourth fundamental branch of study," in addition to reading, writing and arithmetic. In his supplement to the book Payne provided a further example of children's powers of observation from the elementary study of mechanics.[23]

Naturally, over a period of more than 40 years, Payne's views on education changed. But it is interesting to note that whereas in the 1830s and 1840s Payne's analysis of good teaching methods invariably referred to Classical and modern languages, by the 1870s he was drawing examples from the subject of science and seeking to generalize from the methods of teaching science to teaching as a whole. This was no sudden conversion. Indeed, it would appear that from his schoolboy days, Payne was an enthusiastic amateur in scientific matters. In a lecture on "The True Foundation of Science Teaching," delivered at the College of Preceptors on 11 December 1872,[24] he stated:

> Scientific matters have, it is true, always been intensely interesting to me from the time when, as a schoolboy, I used to stuff a volume of Joyce's *Scientific Dialogues* into my pocket to read when I ought to have been playing; but I was never trained in the method of Science, nor experienced what I have so often conceived, the intense delight of the scientific investigator.[25]

From Theory and Practice to Science and Art

In 1871 Payne's transition from the concepts and terminology of "theory and practice" to those of "science and art" received the approval of the College of Preceptors and became public in two highly visible ways. The first was the College's examination for teachers of June 1871; the second, the series of three lectures which Payne delivered at the Society of Arts in July of the same year.

The summer examination for Theory and Practice was not—as previously—a single undifferentiated collection of questions. Instead there were three separate sections: Physiology; Mental and Moral Science and Logic; Lesson-giving,

Treatment of Cases, and Criticism of Methods; and a viva voce! There can be no doubt that this new formulation occasioned considerable discussions in the College Council and initial consternation and dismay among the candidates.[26] In the long term, however, the numbers of teachers taking the examinations increased. Interestingly, the papers were printed in the *Educational Times* of August 1871 immediately after the account of Payne's lecture on "The Theory or Science of Education," delivered on 12 July.[27] This conjunction was repeated when Payne's three lectures were published by the Council of the College in 1872 as the first in the collection entitled *Lectures on Education. . . .* Further evidence of the change, moreover, was provided by the inclusion in this publication of a reading list of books on education. There can be no doubt that this list was provided by Payne. Not only did it follow the third of his lectures as printed in the collection of 1872; it was also included in the edited collection of his works published in 1880.[28]

Just as the examination of 1871 was radically different from those which had preceded it, so, too, the book list of 1871 was a considerable departure from those supplied in the later 1840s and early 1850s. It comprised a carefully structured reading list of some 85 works, with the starring of publications of particular importance. The list was divided into six sections:

> Sciences on which that of Education is based
>
> (Physical Education, Psychology and Ethics, Logic)
>
> Theory and Practice of Education
>
> (Divided into "Theory mainly" and "Practice mainly")
>
> Educational Methods
>
> Lives of Eminent Educators
>
> History of Education
>
> Miscellaneous

The year 1871 was one of transition from theory and practice to science and art: the terms were employed together in the titles of Payne's lectures. By 1872 the die was cast and Payne was appointed not simply as the College's Professor of Education, but as its "Professor of the Science and Art of Education."

Some indication of the seriousness with which the scientific dimension was now taken was provided by the Christmas examination of 1873. Under the general heading of "Theory and Practice of Education" Payne and John Ogle set three papers for "Practical teaching, Criticism of Methods etc." (for first, second and third class candidates). They also set three papers for "Mental and Moral Science and Logic" and three for "Physiology." But Joseph Frank Payne, now fully launched on his medical career, was employed to act as examiner for the separate subject of Physiology (a role which he was to fulfil for many years) for which he supplied a further two papers.[29]

The primacy of Payne's pioneering work in the science and art of education was confirmed not only by the title, but also by the arrangement of the first volume of Payne's collected works. The collection began with the three lectures on the science and art of education as previously published: the first on the theory or science of education; the second on the practice or art of education; the third on educational methods. Other examples of the centrality of this theme of the science of education, also included in the first volume of the collected works, were Payne's introductory lecture to the second year of his professorial course, delivered at the College of Preceptors on 20 January 1874, and once again entitled "The Science and Art of Education," and the paper headed "Principles of the Science of Education," which Payne had printed for students who attended the course. Although this paper was in a highly condensed form (it occupied a mere five pages in the collected works), it may be taken, to use Joseph Frank's introductory words, as "the writer's most mature conception of the educational problem."

The remainder of this chapter is devoted to an explication of Payne's basic interpretation of the science and art of education. The three following sections (on the Science, Art and Method of Education) represent a synthesis, taken mainly, though not exclusively, from the printed lectures referred to above and included in the first volume of the collected works. The argument, though simplified, appears as Joseph Payne might have presented it to his contemporaries, without quotation marks or qualifications. It is written in the present tense: its continuing relevance being beyond question.

The Science of Education

The Science (or Theory) of Education, as distinct from its Art (or Practice), embraces an enquiry into the principles on which the art or practice depends. In education, as in other areas of knowledge, practice precedes theory. But theory reacts on practice and enables the reflective practitioner to become a better teacher.

Many teachers, and others, despise educational theory and would not consider education to be a science. They believe that it is sufficient for them to know that which has to be taught. The theories and theorists of education are dismissed by them as "quackery." Yet the dictionary defines a quack as one who "practices an art with no knowledge of its principles." If medicine and engineering have principles so, too, does education. Many teachers, and others, emphasize the practical nature of teaching. Their emphasis upon the supreme importance of its practical nature, an importance which cannot be denied, leads them to see theory as being in opposition to practice. But theory and practice go hand in hand, indeed the teacher who denies the value of theory is already a theorist. Educational theory provides the means for reflection upon educational practice; the propositions of the science interpret the silent language of the art.

Some teachers, while admitting that they have educational theories, empirical theories which govern their own practice, deny the possibility of the generalization of these theories into principles, principles which would be of enhanced value to themselves or to others in the cause of education. This is a fallacy. Practical teachers who wish to see practice further improved should acknowledge that the educator has the same duty to study the principles which lie behind the practice of education as the physician does to study anatomy and therapeutics, and the civil engineer to study mechanics. Indeed, this is one reason why teachers have failed to acquire professional status. A member of a profession not only knows how to do something, but also why and when it should be done in that particular way. This is essential for real educators, for it is insufficient to teach others how to do something without also indicating why. Good practice alone is not sufficient. This is not to deny the opposite—that good theory alone is sufficient. There may well be those who, though skilled in the theories of education, are unable to apply them in practice and therefore are not fitted to be teachers. Successful personal practical experience, coupled with some knowledge of the contemporary practice of others and of the great educators of former ages, is essential.

Another objection to the Science of Education, and one which must be admitted in part, is that it is still in many ways in a rudimentary condition. Its principles remain scattered across many fields of knowledge. Although it is in the nature of any science to be in a constant state of development, in Britain the Science of Education has been hampered by its relative youth and by the generally low estimation of its value and importance. Neither teachers themselves, nor society as a whole, have generally recognized, with regard to education, that obligation so aptly stated by Thomas Arnold, that "in whatever it is our duty to act, those matters it is also our duty to study."

Accordingly some starting points, in terms of definitions and distinctions, may be suggested at this point. A science is an area of organized knowledge. The word "organized" denotes that a science is not simply a mere accumulation of facts but includes an understanding of the relationships between such facts. Knowledge may be of two kinds: that which is known by direct experience and that which is known through the experience of others. To make this second type of knowledge as secure as the first it is necessary to go through the connected chain of facts and reasonings by which the knowledge of others has been arrived at. An educator is someone who persistently, habitually and permanently draws forth and develops the powers of the person who is being educated in respect of both kinds of knowledge. An instructor is someone who places knowledge in the minds of others in an orderly way. Every educator is also an instructor, but every instructor is not necessarily an educator. The instruction which ends in itself is not complete education.

The term education may be used in two senses. In its broader sense education includes all the influences which operate upon a human being—the education of nature, the education of society, the education of circumstances. Such education, which will be referred to subsequently as natural education, is important, fundamental indeed, but it has dangers and weaknesses. For example, the young child needs to be protected from some of the lessons of nature which are extremely harsh—for instance the perils of fire and water. To touch a hot kettle may result in scalding; to walk too near the canal bank may lead to death from drowning. Another difficulty with natural education is that much of it is at the time, and remains, unconscious. It does not lead to generalization and to development.

Education, in its more specific or formal sense, builds upon this broader learning, but goes beyond it. It uses the strengths of natural education, but seeks to minimize its weaknesses. It involves the development and training of the learner's natural powers by means of instruction carried on through the conscious and persistent agency of a formal educator. Formal education is the conscious application of human power and will in the pursuit of specific goals of improvement: for example with respect to a person's bodily, mental and moral faculties. Thus physical education will make a human being more healthy and robust; intellectual education will promote thoughtfulness and reason; moral education will encourage appreciation of the good and beautiful. It is this conscious or formal sphere of education to which the Science of Education may be applied. A formal educational situation or system implies:

1. an educator;
2. a learner;
3. subject matter;
4. a method of teaching and learning;
5. an educational goal.

The first of these five elements, the educator, must take a substantial degree of responsibility for, and thus have considerable knowledge of, the succeeding four: the learner, the subject matter, the methods of teaching and learning and the end to be accomplished. The first task of the educator, therefore, is to understand the nature, capabilities and requirements of those who are to learn. This implies a knowledge both of the specific learner or learners and of learners in general. For example, the educator will need to discover the extent of the learners' existing knowledge and skills and their previous experience of various methods of learning.

Although the actual practice and methods of education will be considered at a later point in this chapter, certain broad principles may be established here. At the simplest level these will require attention to physical surroundings. For example learning of any kind—physical, mental or moral—is likely to be less, rather than more, effective if the room is too hot or too cold, if the lighting is poor and ventilation insufficient, if lessons are too long or too short. As Rousseau, in one of his many paradoxes wisely states, "The weaker the body is, the more it commands; the stronger it is, the better it obeys."

The best guide to how people learn is provided by observation of children learning from their natural surroundings. Children are naturally interested in the new, the wonderful and the beautiful. Children take delight in the simple exercise of their own powers—the pleasure of developing and growing by means of acts of observing, experimenting, discovering, inventing, performing and repeating. For the young child, mind and body are mutually interdependent, and cooperate in promoting growth. The faculties of children are developed by exercise. Exercise involves repetition which, as regards bodily movements, ends in habits of action, and, as regards impressions received by the mind, ends in clearness of perception. Therefore, just as the formal educator should base his or her actual subject matter and goals for learning upon the existing capacities, knowledge and achievements of the learners, so the methods and means of formal learning should be based upon, and be consistent with, the natural processes of learning. The basic principle which governs the relationship between learning from circumstance and formal learning is that the exercise of the learner's powers should be stimulated, but not superseded, by those of the formal educator.

One of the most fundamental principles in the Science of Education is that of teaching, and learning, by example. This applies to physical and mental education but particularly to moral education. If the purpose of moral education is to encourage virtuous inclinations, sentiments and passions, and to repress those that are evil—to cultivate habits of truthfulness, obedience, industry, temperance, prudence, and respect for the rights of others—then these must be the qualities exhibited by educators themselves. In moral education, as in physical education and the education of the intellect, the aim must be to encourage those who learn to take responsibility for their own learning and for their future actions.

In conclusion, therefore, the Science of Education is concerned with the principles which lie behind its practice. Such principles draw upon other fields of human knowledge—for example physiology, psychology, philosophy, history, ethics, logic—all of which help to explain and illustrate so many of the phenomena encountered by the educator. They cannot, however, simply be deduced from such fields, any more than they can, at the other end of the spectrum, be inferred from the prospective educator's own experiences as a learner, or from apprenticeship to a practitioner.

The Art of Education

The Art of Education involves all those means by which educators seek to stimulate learning in those whom they are charged to educate. The good teacher, the artist in education, whose art is necessarily based upon a sound understanding of the science of education, will be able to diagnose the problems of learners and call upon the appropriate remedy from a range of educational strategies. The poor teacher, on the other hand, deficient in both the science and art of education, may be able neither to diagnose the problem nor to supply the appropriate remedy.

For example, suppose a teacher to be coldly and sternly demanding the attention of a young boy to a sum in an arithmetic lesson. The problem is that the child does not know how to multiply by more than the number nine. In consequence his notions on the subject under consideration, which require him to multiply by 12, are confused. The teacher, without any attempt to interest the child, without exhibiting any real understanding of his predicament, simply issues some directions of a technical nature which enable the boy to solve the immediate problem, and then passes on, with the child still in the same basic state of confusion. Such an instance shows the teacher's ignorance both of the Science of Education (the child's preliminary lack of understanding) and of the Art of Education—the devising and application of a learning strategy to enable the boy to solve not just the immediate problem, but also how to multiply by more than nine.

Another example may be given in respect of the teaching of English. The teacher begins this initial lesson in grammar by explanations of definitions of the words "noun" and "verb." These definitions and concepts are difficult for the children to grasp, so that the teacher concludes by requiring the class to write out the definitions and to learn them by heart. The children may thus be able to parrot out the definitions on a future occasion but, like parrots, many of them have no real understanding of what they are saying. The skilled teacher will prepare for the lesson by considering certain fundamental principles of the Science of Education: for example proceeding from the known to the unknown; from the particular to the general. The art of the lesson will be to give substance to those principles, by relating that which is to be learned to objects and actions already familiar to the children. Thus the concept and word of "noun" may be introduced by asking the children to make a list of ten objects in their classroom and a further ten at home. The concept and word of "verb" may similarly be elicited by asking members of the class what actions they carry out in moving from school to home, or in preparing for bed. Thus ideas and names having been provided by the children themselves, the teacher then proceeds to generalize from these examples and provides two new ideas and names which the children may easily and effectively relate and add to their existing store of knowledge.

A third example may be taken from science. Suppose the object of the lesson to be to teach how a simple machine—say a pile driver—works. Principles drawn from the Science of

Education suggest that it is important to employ as many of the learners' senses as possible, and that there is an order of priority expressed in the following adage: to hear is to forget, to see is to understand, to do is to remember. It would be possible to centre a lesson about pile driving upon oral exposition, upon a picture, or upon a real pile driver or working model.

The teacher who produces a simple model—two strong uprights fastened into a solid base, with two cords which pass over pulleys at the top of the upright to draw up an iron weight, the fall of which drives the pile into the earth—has the perfect teaching aid. The model, placed where all can see it, attracts the children's interest. There is no need to call for attention, for their curiosity is excited. They may volunteer the purpose of the machine; if they cannot the teacher must tell them. The children, under the guidance of the teacher, do certain things. They pull on the ropes and draw the weight to its full height. They release the clutch and see the weight fall on the pile. Having established the machine's basic purpose and means of operation, they can test its effectiveness by varying the weights and substituting weights made of different substances. The heights from which the weights are released can be altered. Further experimentation can involve lifting weights without pulleys, and the introduction of an inclined plane. The final question would be to ask the children what changes they might make to improve the machine's efficiency. Experience of teaching such a lesson shows that this is a challenge to which they are eager to respond.

This lesson shows the important roles of both educator and educated, of teacher and learner. The teacher has prepared the learning situation. The teacher sets the whole process in motion and regulates it along the way. During the lesson the teacher is supplying questions, motives for action, the means of action, sympathy, encouragement, concern. But the action, both mental and physical, is that of the children.

Three conclusions may be drawn from this example. The first is that the children have enjoyed the free exercise of their own powers—seeing, handling, experimenting, discovering, investigating, even inventing—for themselves. This feeling of pleasure will accompany and stimulate their remembrance of the lesson. The second is that during the lesson the children have, to some extent, acted independently of their teacher. They, therefore, will have some sense of power over learning and knowledge. Clearly, at the end of one lesson such a sense will, and should be, very rudimentary. The whole learning situation has been created by the teacher. Nevertheless further learning of this type will properly increase the children's confidence so that they will acquire the valuable habit of independent mental self-direction. An eminent French teacher was laughed at when he said that he was continually aiming to make himself *useless* to his pupils. But it was his audience, and not he, who was mistaken. The third point to notice is that, however falteringly, the children in such a lesson have taken a few steps along the path of scientific method. Not only have they learned something about how to learn, they have also learned something about how to learn in a particular field of knowledge.

There is no single method of teaching, or of learning, no formula to be universally applied. Nevertheless it can be stated with considerable conviction that the art of the educator, who seeks to make formal education a progression and refinement of natural education, is to enable those who learn to teach themselves.

The Methods of Education

There is a distinction between a method and an art, just as there is a distinction between these and a science. A method is a particular way of administering an art, and an art is a practical display of a science.

There may be many good methods of teaching. These may vary according to such factors as buildings, equipment and subject matter, the skills and interests of the teacher, the age, numbers, abilities and aptitudes of the children. Good methods, however, will not transgress the basic principle of the Science and Art of Education. That principle is that learning is essentially self-tuition, and teaching the superintendence of that process. The purpose of education is to increase the capabilities of the pupils to know and to think. In consequence teaching methods which are characterized by manifold explanations from the teacher and mere cramming by the pupil are not true education.

Science is the newest subject in the school curriculum, but unfortunately many of its supporters do not know how to teach it. Science is often simply "got up" from books for the purpose of passing examinations. Yet observation and experiment lie at the centre of the sciences and of the scientific method. The methods of teaching science should reflect this truth so that pupils learn not merely scientific facts but also scientific methods. If children are to study botany they must handle plants and dissect them themselves. If children are studying physics they should not simply read about the powers of magnets and prisms, they must observe them themselves.

Two examples of methodology are given here. The first, which relates to a part of the pile driver lesson, concentrates upon the teacher's use of questions. By this stage in the lesson the teacher has ensured that all the children know the names of the various parts of the machine: "clutch," "pulley," etc. Each child has participated in operating the machine, the original iron weight has been detached and weighed, and other weights of equal volume made of lead and wood have been introduced. These have been weighed by the children and the effect of the different weights upon the penetration of the pile into the earth have also been recorded.

Teacher: Which weight drives the pile most, which least?
Answer: The leaden one most, the wooden one least.
T.   Why?
A.   Because the leaden one is the heavier and the wooden one the lighter.
T.   How many inches in each case?
A.   The leaden one __ inches, the wooden one __ inches.
T.   What are the weights of each?
A.   The leaden one weighs __ lbs., the wooden one __ lbs.
T.   How do you state the result?
A.   The leaden one drives the pile twice as deep as the wooden one.

T.   Measure exactly the leaden and the wooden weights; the length, height and thickness of each. What is the result?

A.   They are exactly the same size.

T.   We shall say that they are of equal volume; yet being of equal size or volume, and falling from the same height, you say that the leaden weight produces twice as great a result as the wooden one. Why?

A.   Because it is twice as heavy. We found that it weighed twice as much.

T.   Why is that so? How do you account for this?

A.   We do not know.

T.   Well, here is some wool. Divide it into two parcels of equal weight. Take one parcel and squeeze it tightly so that it becomes about half the size, or volume, of the other. What do you notice?

A.   That though the quantity of wool is the same in each, as is the weight, one occupies twice as much space as the other.

T.   Let us call the wool, as being something that we can see, touch and smell, matter, and the closeness of packing together, density. Using these two terms compare the two parcels of wool.

A.   The amount of matter in the two parcels of wool is the same but the density of one is twice the density of the other.

T.   Now, to return to the case of the leaden and wooden weights, how do you account for the fact that, though equal in volume, one weighs twice as much as the other?

A.   In the leaden one the matter is twice as closely packed, or twice as dense as in the wooden one.

T.   Now, again. What was the effect of your squeezing the parcel of wool?

A.   To bring the bits of wool closely together.

T.   Call these bits, particles. Why was it possible to bring them closer together?

A.   Because there are spaces between the particles.

> T.   Call these spaces pores, and the fact that there are such pores is called porosity. What relation has this to density?
>
> A.   It is the opposite to density. The more pores anything has the less dense it is; the more dense it is the fewer pores it has.

The teacher might then go on by the same method to introduce and develop such concepts and terms as force, momentum, friction, gravity, velocity, acceleration, cause and effect.

In this example the teacher has followed the principles of guiding the children to establish certain facts for themselves by activity and observation: for example weights and sizes. The teacher is then leading them from the known to the unknown and to generalizations. The method of so doing is that of questioning. In this extract, provided the questions are clearly framed and in the correct sequence, all children should be able to provide the answers. This is an excellent method of enabling children to extend their knowledge and to consolidate it but, as with all methods, care must be taken. For example there is no point in lengthy questioning in attempts to elicit information which the children may not have, or which may more effectively be conveyed in other ways. Nor should any method, including questioning, be used excessively so that it becomes irksome and routine.

The second example of method concerns the fundamental skill of reading. On what principles should the choice be made between two different methods of teaching reading: that of building up from letters and syllables into words on the one hand, and teaching whole words ("look and say") on the other? At first sight it might appear that the method, widely advocated, which teaches reading by building up words, via letters and syllables, is preferable. It appears to proceed from the simple to the complex, for letters and syllables are invariably shorter and less difficult to recognize than whole words. But such an interpretation may be faulty in itself, and needs to be balanced against other principles already outlined. These would include: being aware of the capacities and interests of the learner, harmonizing formal education with natural education and proceeding from the known to the unknown.

The most important basic skill and interest which is invariably brought by young children to the task of reading is that of speech. Such speech may be rudimentary in the extreme, indeed the child's first words are invariably short, in some instances merely shortened forms of proper words. They may even be substitutes for the real words—for example the noises made by animals rather than the names of the animals themselves. The essence of these first utterances, however, is that they are neither letters nor syllables. However short they may be, the essential quality of such words is that they have meaning, meaning which enables the child to communicate its wants and interests to both adults and to other children. These spoken words have both meaning and purpose. The young child says "Dada," even simply "Da" to attract the father's attention; or "cup" when thirsty.

Thus in learning to talk, which may be counted, at least in its early stages, as being part of the natural rather than of the formal sphere of education, children learn whole words rather than their constituent parts of letters and syllables. On these three grounds, therefore—awareness of children's capacities and interests, harmonization of formal with natural education and proceeding from the known to the unknown—it would seem preferable to introduce the recognition and reading of whole words at an early stage, rather than to begin solely with letters and syllables. The teaching of whole words also allows a further factor—the visual—to be brought into play. Words may be placed beneath pictures of various phenomena—animals, toys, household objects, etc.—with which the child is already familiar. There are no pictures of letters nor of syllables.

The methods of education, therefore, proceed from its science and art. Though the subject of science should not constitute the whole of the curriculum, nevertheless all teaching should be scientific in its spirit.

Science or Science and Art?

The limits of Payne's commitment to a science of education and his preference for science and art can be examined in the dispute which arose between Payne and his one-time collaborator, Charles Lake. In 1871 it would appear that Payne and Lake were in agreement upon the need to find the principles of the science of education within the principles of psychology, physiology and ethics. Subsequently differences arose between them as to how this should be achieved. These stemmed partly from differences in temperament and experience. They also stemmed from a genuine disagreement about the meaning of the word science. In truth the differences between them were not great, but they might have been exacerbated by Lake's feeling that Payne had been given the major credit for what originally had been a joint venture.

Lake's belated obituary of Payne, published some two years after his death in the *Journal of Education* for May 1878, was by no means wholly unfriendly. It stated indeed that "As an educational reformer, he deserves a pedestal in the corridor where are found the busts of Milton and Locke, Comenius and Jacotot, Pestalozzi and Froebel."[30] Nevertheless some indication of Lake's resentment is provided by the following lengthy and tortuous sentence.

> I am far from wishing to imply that to me Prof. Payne was indebted for his notion of the Science of Education; it would be equally egotistic and untrue so to do; but I do think that our interchange of ideas developed what was latent in his mind and that from 1871, when he delivered his three lectures at the College of Preceptors, about which he consulted me before their delivery, until he became Professor in 1873, this idea was consciously present to his mind, and I regard the professional [professorial?] lectures as indicating his final views with this idea assimilated as few men at the age of sixty-five could assimilate a new idea, and as the fruit of the germination of the notion that education is not the theory of this or that individual, but a science capable of exposition and demonstration.[31]

Lake's critiques of Payne's work appeared in public form during his lifetime: for example in October and November of 1872 in letters in the pages of the *Educational Times*.[32] This discussion centred upon Payne's use of the word "revolutionary," in calling for a change from didactic teaching to that which concentrated upon exercising the child's powers and intellect. A second and more substantial exchange occurred in the pages of the *Monthly Journal of Education* in the second half of 1874. This centred upon Lake's critical reviews of Payne's *Froebel and the Kindergarten System of elementary education*, and *Principles of the Science of Education*.[33] The fullest statement of Lake's own position was given on 12 November 1873 when he delivered a paper to an evening meeting at the College of Preceptors on "The Science of Education." Payne was in the chair and spoke in the ensuing discussion, but there is no record of his actual comments.[34]

Lake's basic charge against Payne was that he was insufficiently committed to a science of education. He believed that Payne's work still bore traces of his homage to Jacotot, and more generally to the role of the great educators in shaping the science of education. Lake wanted to apply scientific methods to the study of education and had the means to do so. Whereas Payne's substantial teaching experience was behind him, Lake, who became principal of Oxford House School, Chelsea, a school of some 120 boys,[35] was keen to experiment with different methods in his own school. He also encouraged other teachers to conduct demonstration lessons to show that the principles of the newly emerging science of education could be verified by practice. He regretted Payne's use of the titles, "Theory or Science," "Practice or Art," for his lectures of 1871—not as if they were alternatives, but synonyms. He implied that Payne's real interest was in the art and method rather than the science of education. Lake wanted to resolve the former and current dichotomies which he detected in Payne's writings and to make education genuinely scientific. He thus objected to Payne's distinctions, for example, between natural and formal education, and, as in his pamphlet on Froebel, between ideas and words. Lake argued rather for wholeness—that "thought and language, like mind and body, are interdependent." In contrast to Lake's assertion that "all education is based on psychology"[36] Payne replied "that education has a basis of its own, and that basis is human nature."[37]

Although to the twentieth-century observer, the similarities between Payne and Lake appear to be much greater

than their differences, Lake's criticisms of Payne's approach to
the science of education have some validity. Lake, who had
himself studied for the Preceptors' examinations and taken a
London University degree in 1867 (his particular interest was
moral science) had a burning intellectual and empirical
commitment to create a science of education, which Payne did
not entirely share. By the 1870s Payne had long ceased to be a
practising schoolteacher. He did not believe in simple solutions
or all-embracing theories. He was too sensible of the varieties
and vagaries of human nature, of the many manifestations and
locations of education, both formal and informal, to imagine that
it could be solely scientific. His approach was cautious. In a
lecture on "The Theory or Science of Education," delivered on 12
July 1871, Payne stated that he did not profess "to construct the
Science of Education—that still waits for its development."[38]

The first three objectives of the Society for the
Development of a Science of Education were:

1. To collect and classify educational facts;
2. To discuss educational problems on a definite plan, and
   to arrange and record results;
3. To give lessons and discuss the principles involved.

Although the youthful Payne of Rodney House and Denmark
Hill would no doubt have warmed to these tasks, by 1875 he
probably felt more comfortable with other parts of the Society's
agenda, for example:

5. To get acquainted with educational ideas abroad;
6. To examine and criticise the labours of eminent
   educationists.[39]

Lake, himself, did not neglect these latter objectives. Indeed in
1872, four of the first five lectures given in his course for
teachers, student teachers and others connected with the North
London Collegiate and Camden Schools were concerned with
history of education and with the ideas, principles and systems
of the "great reformers." But the first of these 30 lectures was
entitled "Education implies Science," and the empirical
dimension was emphasized throughout by the requirement that:

Each student will be expected to write out concisely in the interval from one lecture to another an account of *one* attempt in which she has endeavoured to carry out *one* idea developed in the last lecture, together with the result whether of success or failure.[40]

NOTES

1. *Journal of the Women's Education Union* III, 26 (February 1875), pp. 30–1.

2. Payne, *Works*, I, p. v.

3. See the *Journal of Education*, II, 27 (May 1880), pp. 109–112, and 28, (June 1880), pp. 128–9.

4. L. S. Hearnshaw, *A Short History of British Psychology, 1840–1940* (London, 1964).

5. R. J. W. Selleck, *The New Education: The English Background, 1870–1914* (London, 1968), p. 274.

6. For details of the Society see F. C. Turner, "The History of the Education Society," *Journal of Education* IX, 213 (April 1887), pp. 178–80, and 214 (May 1887), pp. 222–4. Between 1875 and 1878 the Society's proceedings were published in the *Monthly Journal of Education*, then until 1880 in the *Scholastic World*, and thereafter in the *Journal of Education*.

7. Selleck, *New Education*, pp. 46, 48.

8. Walter B. Kolesnik, *Mental Discipline in Modern Education* (Madison, 1962), p. 19.

9. This work was based on two lectures delivered at the College of Preceptors on 11 April and 9 May 1866.

10. Payne, *Works*, I, p. 235.

11. *Ibid.*, pp. 278–9.

12. *Ibid.*, pp. 236–7.

13. *Ibid.*, p. 236.

14. *Ibid.*, p. 282.

15. William H. Payne, *Contributions to the Science of Education* (New York, 1886), p. 337. For William Payne see George C. Poret, *The Contributions of William Harold Payne to Public Education* (Nashville, 1931).

16. William H. Payne, *Contributions*, p. x.

17. *Ibid.*, pp. 55, 75.

18. Kolesnik, *Mental Discipline*, p. 20.

19. *Ibid.*

20. *Educational Times* XIX, 68 (November 1866), pp. 167–70.

21. Payne, *Works*, I, p. 209.

22. Payne, *Works*, I, pp. 207–31. The English edition was published in London by Henry S. King and Company. Edward Youmans gave Payne a copy of his sister's book, Payne, *Works*, I, p. 209.

23. A substantial review of the book, including Payne's contribution, appeared in the *Educational Times* XXV, 137 (September 1872), p. 141.

24. Payne, *Works*, I, pp. 185–205.

25. *Ibid.*, p. 188.

26. See Lake's comments in the *Journal of Education* 29 (May 1878), p. 198.

27. *Educational Times* XXIV, 124 (August 1871), pp. 95–102.

28. *Lectures on Education delivered before the members of the College of Preceptors in the year 1871* (London, 1872) pp. 73–6; Payne, *Works*, I, pp. 89–92.

29. *Educational Times* XXVII, 156 (April 1874), pp. 8–9.

30. *Journal of Education* 29 (May 1878), p. 193.

31. *Ibid.*, pp. 197–8.

32. *Educational Times* XXV, 137 (October 1872), p. 165, and 138 (November 1872), pp. 188–9.

33. *Monthly Journal of Education* 7 (July 1874), pp. 317–9; 8 (August 1874), pp. 368–70; 9 (September 1874), pp. 393–7; 12 (December 1874), pp. 526–33; 16 (April 1875), pp. 160–3.

34. *Educational Times* XXVI, 152 (December 1873), pp. 199–205, and 153 (January 1874), pp. 223–6.

35. John Roach, *Secondary Education in England, 1870–1902: Public Activity and Private Enterprise* (London, 1991), p. 171.

36. *Monthly Journal of Education* 7 (July 1874), p. 319.

37. *Monthly Journal of Education* 8 (August 1874), p. 370.

38. Payne, *Works*, I, p. 17.

39. *Journal of Education* IX, 214 (May 1887), p. 222.

40. A copy of the lecture programme bound in with the report for 12 February 1872, Head Mistresses' Reports to Governors, 1871–85, North London Collegiate School Archives.

CHAPTER EIGHT

Historical and Comparative Dimensions

This chapter is concerned with three distinct elements in Payne's concept of the Science and Art of Education: the history of education, including the theories and practice of those to quote Payne "whose opinion and practice have so largely influenced education as it is";[1] the specific identification with Pestalozzi and Froebel, and Payne's tour of schools and kindergartens in Germany in 1874; and the example of education in the United States of America.

The History of Education

Payne's reading list for the Preceptors' teachers' examination of 1871 was divided into six sections. The first of these was "Sciences on which that of Education is based"; the third and fourth "Lives of Eminent Educators" and "History of Education." Though such distinctions might have been possible and convenient in respect of reading lists, these three categories were by no means mutually exclusive. For while such sciences as physiology and psychology might spring first to mind as being those upon which a science of education should be based, in the last quarter of the nineteenth century the claim of history to be a scientific discipline was being strongly advanced. Certainly, history of education was to be recognized as a foundation discipline of education before the end of the century and indeed to be given primacy of place in teacher training. In 1890 when day training colleges were established in England and Wales in conjunction with existing universities and university colleges, the normal master or mistress was required to "give lectures on the history and theory of education."[2] Many of the first chairs in education were held by those who achieved distinction as historians of education: Foster Watson at Aberystwyth from 1896, W. H. Woodward at Liverpool from 1899, J. W. Adamson at King's College, London, from 1903. Just as history of education was to be recognized as an essential foundation discipline, so the lives of eminent educators were to become one of the essential components of that history. Payne took a personal delight in history and believed in its importance as a source of information and inspiration. His own justification of history of education was expressed in a phrase which enjoyed some currency in Payne's own day and to which Lake made reference in his obituary of Payne: "There is another method of studying principles besides investigating them *per se*. They may be studied in the practice of those who mastered them."[3] Certainly, Payne's treatment of the "great educators" was shaped by his assessment of the extent to which such educators had themselves been successful teachers.

The second volume of the collected works, published in 1892, consisted of the lectures on history of education which comprised the third part of Payne's professorial course, together with an account of the tour of German schools which Payne made in 1874. Many of the lectures had not been prepared for publication; Joseph Frank, with some help from Quick, worked from the manuscript copies which Payne had used when actually presenting the lectures. Three lectures—those on Jacotot, Pestalozzi and Froebel—had been previously published and reflected Payne's mature judgement on these educationists. The *Visit to German Schools* was based on notes made during the autumn tour of 1874. By the spring of 1875 Joseph Payne was preparing these for publication, but the death of Eliza, his own ill-health and subsequent demise, meant that it was left to Joseph Frank, with the assistance of Hodgson, Quick and Mary Gurney to bring it to publication in September 1876. A second edition was produced in 1884.

Payne's sweep through the history of education was a veritable *tour de force*. He began with the education of ancient cultures: Chinese, Indian, Egyptian, Persian and Jewish. Greek education was the subject of his second lecture; Roman and early

Christian education of the third. The medieval period received scant treatment, but Luther, Melanchthon, Erasmus, Trotzendorf, Sturm, the Jesuits, Colet, Elyot, Ascham, Montaigne and Ratich were among educators of the period of Renaissance and Reformation. Milton and Comenius were the subjects of the sixth lecture; Locke, Rousseau and Basedow of the seventh. The next three lectures, which dealt with Jacotot, Pestalozzi (with a brief mention of Fellenberg) and Froebel, as included in the collected volume, were based on previously published pieces rather than on the lecture notes. Lecture twelve was thematic: an historical survey of the teaching of foreign languages. The final lecture considered the work of two nineteenth-century British figures: Thomas Arnold and Herbert Spencer.

Payne's lecture course on history of education was intended to serve one broad purpose: to provide information about the range of theories and methods of education which had existed in time, and in so doing to enable teachers "to rise above the grade of mere mechanics and empirics."[4] In his opening lecture he defined education in its broadest sense "as only another word for civilization,"[5] but advised his audience that to treat so large a subject within a course of a few lectures would be impossible. He therefore proposed to restrict himself "to education viewed as an art, employed by a human educator who has a definite end in view, and who adopts special means for attaining it."[6]

In preparing the course Payne researched a whole range of primary sources. Many of these sources which he had personally acquired—for example, a copy of the Latin grammar written by the sixteenth-century German religious reformer, Philip Melanchthon—Payne brought to lectures for the students to peruse themselves. Secondary references included not only those in English—for example Furnivall's articles "On Education in Early England" in two issues of the *Quarterly Journal of Education* for 1867, and Quick's, *Essays on Educational Reformers*, published in the following year—but also works in French and German. Payne appears to have drawn particularly upon the several editions of Karl von Raumer, *Geschichte der Pädagogik vom Wiederaufblühen Klassischer Studien bis auf unsere Zeit* and Karl Schmidt, *Geschichte der Pädagogik*.

Throughout the several lectures Payne sought to highlight issues to which his audience might relate. Though he frequently described events and situations without specific comment, on other occasions his judgments (not to say prejudices) clearly showed, and he sought to draw lessons. Thus the first lecture portrayed the importance in China of competitive examinations and the prevalence of cramming, the unrestricted liberty of teaching, and the operation of a system of payment for results. Discussion of education in Sparta and Athens led to a comparison (perhaps not entirely apposite) with the combatants in the recent Franco-Prussian war. The low status of schoolmasters in Rome was deplored; the doctrines of Quintilian, "a first-rate practical teacher," were commended. The experiences of Quintilian and of St. Augustine were employed to indicate the futility of corporal punishment. One thread which ran throughout Payne's treatment of the ancient and medieval worlds (and which given the composition of his audience would have been particularly appreciated) was his attention to the education of girls, and to the social position of girls and women. Another theme which ran throughout was Payne's dislike of governmental and priestly control of education. Payne divided his historical treatment of education chronologically into two: pre-Christian and Christian. One major characteristic of the earlier period to which he drew attention was the role of the state in education with particular reference to restrictions of class and gender: "Government education was designed emphatically for the *higher classes of society*, for those whom we should call gentlemen, not for the mass of the people."[7]

In his first lecture Payne gave a graphic account of Chinese examination procedures, asking his audience to imagine themselves in the capital city of a province where the triennial examination was about to be held. He commended the moral education in China, founded upon the maxims and precepts of Confucius and Mencius, but regretted the static nature of Chinese civilization which stood "at a low dead level"[8] with virtually no modern science. He also drew attention to the lack of education for women who were "generally of no account, except as servants to the men."[9] Payne interpreted education in ancient India as being "a religious monopoly managed exclusively for the Brahmins."[10] They alone received an extended education and they alone had the power of teaching the Vedas, the sacred writings. Payne acknowledged that education was more widely spread in ancient India than in China and encouraged original thought and research. Nevertheless, he emphasized that the position of women was as in China, so that "it was even a reproach to women to be able to read and write."[11]

Payne's treatment of Egyptian education was slight. He noted that a man might, on occasion, rise to a higher caste than that into which he had been born, and that, given the existence of female rulers and possibly priests, the status and education of women were doubtlessly higher than in China or India. On the particular topic of women in Egypt, he advised his audience to consult some primary evidence which was but a few hundred yards away: "Those who would know something of the domestic condition and employment of Egyptian women should pay a visit expressly to the British Museum."[12]

It seems possible that Payne's information on Persian education was drawn, in part at least, from Xenophon's *Cyropaedia*, and he outlined both the general neglect of female education and the extent to which, from the age of seven, the education of boys for the purpose of becoming soldiers became a matter of state control. Nevertheless, even from this apparently restricted source, he drew two examples which reflected his criticisms of the old public schools and his appreciation of new and more radical foundations. The Persian curriculum—"riding, shooting with the bow, hurling the javelin, and telling the truth"—Payne declared (no doubt partly with tongue in cheek) resembled "in some respects the actual, though not the ostensible, education of our own modern Eton."[13] A more interesting and telling parallel was that quarrels among Persian boys were decided by a jury chosen from among the boys themselves, a practice which Payne likened to that which existed at Bruce Castle School, Tottenham. Bruce Castle, founded by the Hill family, was one of the most interesting of nineteenth-century schools. It drew upon Utilitarian principles and the educational philosophies of Rousseau and Locke, so that its mixture of modern curriculum with pupil choice, activity methods and constitutional government won praise from such radicals as Bentham, Grote and Hume.[14] However, by the 1870s there had been some modifications in the system of pupil government, so that Bruce Castle was a more conventional private school of some 80 pupils, of the type, indeed, with which Payne had himself been associated. A footnote to Payne's lecture declared that "a plan like this has long been in use at Bruce Castle School, and seems to answer remarkably well."[15]

Payne's treatment of Jewish education centred upon the theocratic ideal. The child was the gift of God, the education of children the responsibility of parents and priests, so that "the memory was more exercised than the understanding."[16] Payne not only commented upon the neglect of female education, but also upon the fact that "daughters were often regularly sold rather than given in marriage."[17] Payne noted the considerable "native ability" of the Jewish people, but considered their learning in arts and science to have been derived principally from contact with the Egyptians and Phoenicians. His first lecture concluded with the observation: "Solomon stands almost alone in their ancient history as a representation of high education."[18]

The second lecture was devoted to Greek education, aspects of which drew forth Payne's highest praise: "the most splendid types of high intellectual culture that the world has yet known."[19] Such excellence, which Payne particularly identified with Athens, he attributed to freedom: to the absence of the controlling power "of the caste, or of the priest, or of the central government."[20] Payne contrasted this freedom for Athenian citizens with the situation in Sparta, where individuality was sacrificed to the state, and even art and music were only employed to foster the martial spirit. Only in its recognition of the importance of the education of girls and women could Spartan education be deemed to be superior to that of Athens. Payne's idealism, his belief in the power of the intellect, is well shown in the following passage:

> When we consider the influence which Athenian culture has exercised upon the history of civilization, we cannot but be struck with the thought that it is really the highest minds that educate the world. Thinking begets thinking,

and hence even when these great intellects seem chiefly engaged in pursuing the ideal, in indulging merely in speculation, they are in reality only setting other minds at work preparing for the practical. What was begotten among the clouds descends to earth and takes a tangible shape.[21]

The third lecture on Roman and early Christian education was notable for Payne's forthright expression of views about Christianity and education. He began by praising the Romans who, although a practical people and wanting originality in their own thinking, nevertheless had the wit to appreciate the originality of others, including the Greeks. He also praised the precepts and examples of home education and commended the Roman sense of duty and virtue. In what must have been a fairly radical statement to an audience composed primarily of young schoolmistresses, Payne declared that it was wrong

> to assume that there is no such thing as heathen virtue. We should be in a better position for maintaining such an assumption if we saw, what I for one do not see, that our own religious system ended as a matter of course in making our children religious, that is true followers of Christ.[22]

Payne applauded the purity of the education and way of life of the early Christians, but considered such purity to have been "somewhat sullied when the profession of Christianity became respectable, and it was seen that men by means of that profession might attain positions of eminence in the world."[23]

Payne's use of the term "men" appears to have been deliberate. His argument that females adhered more strictly than males to the original purity of Christianity was reinforced by lengthy quotations from a letter written in the fifth century by St. Jerome to a lady who wished to educate her daughter for God's service. For references to the healing roles of medieval women Payne drew upon the French romances of the thirteenth century, which indicated that women were taught (albeit in a family context) not only herbal remedies but also "surgery, and that they were generally very successful practitioners."[24]

Payne's fourth lecture, on the revival of learning, concentrated upon the work of such reformers as Luther,

Melanchthon and Sturm, but it was Erasmus who received Payne's seal of approval on several accounts: for encouraging the use of "smiles, praises, encouraging words," and for prohibiting "threats, blows, or scoldings"; for urging that knowledge alone was insufficient in a teacher, who must also possess moral worth and skill "in managing the varying dispositions of children"; for arguing that good teachers could not be too highly paid and for proclaiming that girls, even more than boys, should receive a thorough education.[25]

Though the Protestant reformers generally received Payne's approval as educators, his comments upon the Jesuits were largely hostile. He abominated "their fundamental principle of corrupting, as I think, the mind in order to gain an unrighteous dominion over it"[26]—a classic case, he believed, of instruction rather than education—but nevertheless gave grudging praise to the effectiveness of their methods in that pupils were only credited with such knowledge as they *"knew, possessed,* and *retained."*[27]

Sixteenth-century English scholars, Colet and Elyot among them, were quoted by Payne in support of the principle of learning Latin as naturally as possible, rather than through rules and grammar-grinding. His main text for this purpose, however, was *The Scholemaster*, written by Roger Ascham and published by his widow in 1570, two years after Ascham's death. Payne possessed a copy of this book and, thus armed, he expanded upon Ascham's role as tutor to the future Queen Elizabeth and to Lady Jane Grey, and upon his method of teaching Latin. Payne identified with Ascham's methods, in which "the concrete preceded the abstract; the particulars, the generalization; the examples of language, the grammatical rules."[28] He concluded that, with respect to the teaching of the Classical languages, "I cannot hesitate in expressing my opinion that Ascham's method is far superior in every way to the ordinary grammar-school method of our own days."[29] Two other "innovators" whom Payne included in this lecture were the French essayist Michel de Montaigne, born in 1533, whom he cited as an outstanding example of the natural method of learning Classical languages, for he spoke nothing but Latin until the age of six; and the German educationist Wolfgang Ratich (Ratke), born in 1571.

Payne appears to have followed von Raumer in singling out Ratich as the forerunner of that line of educational innovators which might be taken to stretch from Comenius and Locke to Jacotot and Froebel, and indeed to Payne himself. In so doing Payne identified nine educational principles put forward by Ratich:

1. Everything after the order and course of Nature;
2. One thing at a time;
3. One thing again and again repeated;
4. Everything first in the mother tongue;
5. Everything without coercion;
6. Nothing is to be learnt by rote;
7. Uniformity of plan in all things;
8. First a thing in itself, afterwards the form or fashion of the thing;
9. Everything through experimental analysis.[30]

Payne naturally sided with the "innovators" as opposed to the "ancients" like Sturm, whose main purpose was to make boys masters of Ciceronian Latin. He nevertheless pointed out that not all the advantages lay with the reformers (Ratich himself he characterized as "not very successful as a schoolmaster")[31] and drew attention to such dangers as unrealistic expectations of pupils and an excessively utilitarian approach in curriculum matters.

Payne had made a particular study of Comenius, the Czech reformer born in 1592, and acknowledged that Comenius was also "in the position of educational father of Pestalozzi and Froebel, and in a certain sense of myself."[32] This he believed was because Comenius had linked the observation of the baby and young child with the principles of the science of education. Yet Payne showed himself to be no great admirer of Comenius's two celebrated works for teaching languages: the *Janua Linguarum Reserata* and the *Orbis Sensualium Pictus*.

Another well-known book which received criticism from Payne was John Locke's *Some Thoughts Concerning Education*, first published in 1693. In this eighth lecture, which was concerned with Locke, Rousseau and Basedow, Payne chose to concentrate rather upon Rousseau and upon the *Émile*, published in 1762. Payne drew attention to what he believed to be the weaknesses in this work. He queried the particular place which Rousseau assigned to nature in education, did not share Rousseau's distrust of books and deplored his views on moral education, confessing that in some respects Rousseau's writings engendered "repulsion rather than attraction."[33] Nevertheless, though Payne was not a person given to extravagant statements, his approval of Rousseau as the exponent of the principle that to teach children wisely and efficiently we must both understand the nature of children and also work in harmony with that nature, was fulsome in the extreme.

> The *Émile* is a truly wonderful book on education, in the fullest sense of the term—a book which contains more absurdities, more paradoxes, more crudities on the subject than any other book of the kind, but at the same time more living and speaking truths regarding education, and a deeper insight into the capabilities and activities of the human mind, and of the resources of the art by which they may be developed and trained, than any book that I know.[34]

Payne's approval of Rousseauian principles led him naturally to consider Basedow (whose daughter Emilie was systematically educated from the age of nine months, learning French and Latin by the time she was five) and Pestalozzi, who attempted to make his own son into another Émile.

Payne's observations upon the teaching methods of Jacotot have been outlined at an earlier stage in this book; his connections with Pestalozzi and Froebel will be considered in the next section. Lecture twelve on the teaching of languages reiterated, with particular reference to Locke, the theme of facts before grammar, words before rules. All languages, ancient and modern, were to be treated as living tongues.

In his final lecture Payne considered Thomas Arnold, the influential headmaster of Rugby School who died in 1842, and Herbert Spencer, still at the height of his powers, who lived on until 1903. Payne did not categorize Arnold as a person with a knowledge of the science of education; he was a practical educator, an empiric. He did, however, praise Arnold for showing his "high estimate of the importance and dignity of his profession,"[35] and for his ability to convey to all at Rugby, boys and masters alike, the notion of the school as "our great self."[36] With regard to Spencer, Payne strongly recommended his *Education: intellectual, moral and physical*, published in 1861. Though querying some aspects of Spencer's educational theory, for example his possibly excessive attention to science, Payne naturally quoted with approval Spencer's emphases on making education pleasurable, on self-development and on proceeding from the empirical to the rational.

In concluding the History of Education course Payne declared that his aim had been to "revolutionize" the notions about teaching commonly held. A child was not essentially characterized by incapacity and stupidity. Instead, a child should be seen as a being who contained:

> a reservoir of forces ready to expend themselves and really expending themselves in spontaneous action, and the teacher appears as a loving and intelligent guide to their direction; in other words, the child comes before us as a self-teacher, and the educator as a superintendent of the child's own process of learning.[37]

Pestalozzi and Froebel

Pestalozzi and Froebel were the two educational theorists with whom Payne felt the closest identity.

Johann Heinrich Pestalozzi was born in Zurich in 1746 and devoted himself to the education of the children of the very poor. His early ventures in founding schools for orphans, waifs and strays foundered, but he achieved some fame with his publications, notably a social novel, *Leonard and Gertrude* (1781) and *How Gertrude Educates her Children* (1801). In 1805 Pestalozzi established a school at Yverdon, which attracted many visitors.

Substantial direct contact between British educationists and Pestalozzi had to await the ending of the French Revolutionary and Napoleonic Wars in 1815. There is no way of knowing exactly how many visitors from across the Channel were entertained at Yverdon during Pestalozzi's lifetime (he died in 1827), but they included some of the most distinguished British educationists of the day: William Allen, Andrew Bell, Henry Brougham, James Greaves, Charles Mayo and Robert Owen. Not all the visitors were complimentary in their comments, and indeed, by this date, both Pestalozzi and Yverdon were in some decline. Nevertheless, direct connections between Pestalozzi and educational establishments in Britain can be traced in the work of James Greaves and Charles Mayo, and Payne would no doubt have been familiar with Greaves' foundation, Alcott House, at Ham in Surrey, and with Cheam School established by Mayo.

Charles Mayo promoted Pestalozzianism in a variety of ways. He gave public lectures and in 1828 published *A Memoir of Pestalozzi*, a work which was later augmented by his sister Elizabeth, who taught at Cheam until 1834. Another important vehicle was the teachers' training college which was established by the Home and Colonial Society in the Gray's Inn Road in London. Elizabeth Mayo had a substantial role there as a trainer of teachers and as supervisor in the Society's schools and colleges. Her *Lessons on Objects as given to children between the ages of six and eight in a Pestalozzian School at Cheam, Surrey*, published in 1831, went through 16 editions by 1859. Pestalozzi also found a substantial place in Herbert Quick's *Essays on Educational Reformers*, first published in 1868. Indeed the 1895 edition of this work, which comprised some 550 pages and 22 chapters, devoted no fewer than 94 pages, and by far the longest chapter, to Pestalozzi.

Kate Silber, in her substantial study, *Pestalozzi: The Man and His Work* (1960),[38] argued that, although something of the spirit of Pestalozzi's ideas penetrated infant schooling and some branches of teacher training, in a specific sense, the impact of Pestalozzianism in Britain was relatively slight. Payne, in his own day, acknowledged as much, and he admitted Pestalozzi's many weaknesses: his lack of worldly wisdom; his own rudimentary educational attainments; his problems of organization; his failure to check upon the learning of his pupils; and the gaps between his educational theory and classroom practice, as in his insistence on the learning of long lists of names and other words, quite unrelated to the children's experience.

Nevertheless, having admitted Pestalozzi's problems as a teacher, in his lecture Payne concentrated upon the positive qualities and principles which he brought to the role. First among these in Payne's estimation was "that the teacher must have a heart," a heart which expressed itself in "active, practical, self-sacrificing love."[39] Second was Pestalozzi's foundation of both the moral and intellectual education of his charges upon "the near, the practical, the actual,"[40] rather than upon abstractions and generalizations. Third was his emphasis upon the senses and upon the importance of *Anschauung*, which might be translated as "observation" or "perception." Pestalozzi followed Rousseau, the only educational theorist with whose writings he was familiar, in believing in a natural order of development in children.

Payne produced his own summary of the educational principles of Pestalozzi:

1. There is a natural order in which the powers of the human being develop and unfold themselves.

2. We must study and understand this order of nature, if we would aid, and not disturb, the development.

3. We aid the development and consequently promote the growth of the faculties concerned in it, when we call them into exercise.

4. Nature exercises the faculties of children on the realities of life—on the near, the present, the actual.

5. If we would promote that exercise of the faculties which constitutes development and ends in growth, we also, as teachers, must, in the case of children, direct them to the realities of life—to the things which come in contact with them, which concern their immediate interests, feelings and thoughts.

6. Within this area of personal experience we must confine them, until, by assiduous practical exercise in it, their powers are strengthened, and they are prepared to advance to the next concentric circle, and then to the next, and so on, in unbroken succession.

7. In the order of nature, things go before words, the realities before the symbols, the substance before the shadow.[41]

This was the approach which Payne characterized as inductive or analytic—moving from individual instances to general facts and principles, as opposed to the deductive or synthetic method, which begins with definitions and general propositions and then moves to individual examples. Payne identified so strongly with Pestalozzi's approach to the education of the young that he declared that Pestalozzian principles lay at the heart of his lectures on the Science and Art of Education.

Of all the educators considered by Payne in his lecture course on History of Education Froebel was the one with whom he felt the greatest affinity. Though he frequently referred to Jacotot as his "master," Payne clearly distanced himself from some of his views: principally Jacotot's insistence on the ignorant schoolmaster and on learning by rote. Jacotot, moreover, was the inspiration of Payne's youthful years as a teacher. Froebel, if we are to believe Payne's own account of the situation, delivered in February 1874, was the confirmation of his mature theory and practice:

> The plan of my own course of lectures on the Science and Art of Education was, in fact, constructed in thought, before I had at all grasped the Froebelian idea; and was, in that sense, independent of it. But every one who hears my lectures—which are founded on the natural history of the child—must be at once aware that Froebel's notions and mine are virtually the same.[42]

Ten years later, this identity of viewpoint, particularly in respect of the importance of play to the young child, was confirmed by Emily Shirreff, the President of the Froebel Society, in *The Kindergarten at Home* (1884).[43] Payne's identification with Froebel depended in large part upon his belief in the importance of education in the early years. He frequently commended the Jesuit principle that the best teachers should be promoted to take charge of the youngest children. It was the infant teacher's job to lay the foundations, and at the earliest opportunity to enable children to associate learning with both pleasure and with power.

Friedrich Froebel, the German educationist, was born in Oberweissbach in 1782. His mother died when he was young and his father was a busy pastor, so the young Froebel grew up with little formal education but a great love of nature; indeed he worked for some time as a forester. After somewhat desultory periods of study at Jena, Gottingen and Berlin, in 1805 he began teaching at Frankfurt-am-Main. Froebel's basic aim was to help the child's mind to grow naturally and spontaneously, and to do so by providing pleasant surroundings and self-motivated activity. In 1836 he opened his first kindergarten at Blankenburg. He died in 1852. Froebel knew Pestalozzi; indeed he lived and worked for two years at Yverdon. But whereas Pestalozzi believed that the mother was the natural educator of the child until six or seven years of age, Froebel wanted children to attend kindergartens between the ages of three and seven. There they would engage with the several "gifts"—balls, spheres, cubes, cylinders—and naturally move in play to education.

Payne, as he admitted in his lecture, was not merely the expositor, but also the promoter of Froebel's principles.[44] Although he was not present at the preliminary meeting of the Kindergarten Association held on 4 November 1874 at Beata Doreck's establishment at 63, Kensington Gardens Square,[45] early in December he became a member of its Committee.[46] In the following year he joined both the General Committee and the special Examinations Committee of its successor, the Froebel Society for the Promotion of the Kindergarten System.[47] Involvement in the work of the Association and of the Society gave Payne a sound knowledge of the progress of the kindergarten movement in England. He was aware of the kindergartens in Manchester run by Miss Opple and Miss Snell, and on 27 April 1875, at the request of the Committee of the Nottingham Kindergarten, gave a lecture in Nottingham on "Froebel and the Kindergarten." This attracted an audience of some 500, "and a lively interest was excited, which was subsequently maintained by a correspondence in the *Nottingham Review*."[48]

By the 1860s the kindergarten had crossed the Atlantic, where it was being popularized in the United States through the exertions of Elizabeth Peabody in a magazine entitled the *Kindergarten Messenger*.[49] But the chief examples of the kindergarten were naturally in Germany. For the express purpose of inspecting these establishments, and of studying the relationship between the kindergarten and the early years of formal schooling, Payne undertook his tour there in the late summer of 1874. He arrived in Hamburg on 23 August and left Eisenach on 12 September, travelling home via Frankurt, Cologne and Ostend. This was not, however, his first visit either to Germany or to a German kindergarten: In the summer of 1873 he visited the kindergarten conducted by Dr Haas at Wiesbaden.[50]

The full title affixed by Joseph Frank to his father's work resulting from this trip was *A Visit to German Schools. Notes of a professional tour to inspect some of the Kindergartens, Primary Schools, Public Girls' Schools, and Schools for Technical Instruction, in Hamburg, Berlin, Dresden, Weimar, Gotha and Eisenach, in the Autumn of 1874, with Critical Discussions of the General Principles and Practice of Kindergarten and Other Schemes of Elementary Education*. The text, taken from the second edition of 1884, occupies some 70 pages in the second volume of the collected works.

It is not easy to summarize Payne's experiences and assessment of what he encountered in Germany in 1874. In the first place, he was clearly grateful to his several hosts and wary of appearing over critical. Second, his own command of the German language, though competent, was not sufficient to enable him fully to explore with the teachers concerned some of the apparent inconsistencies and gaps between Froebelian theory and practice which he witnessed. In those kindergartens he visited Payne was much impressed with the activity of the children and with their "self-active co-operation. . . . All was busy, healthy, happy life."[51] In the elementary schools (at this time schooling in Germany was generally compulsory from six to 14 years of age), Payne concluded that the education of the youngest children was generally in conformity with Froebelian and Pestalozzian principles. On the whole children worked on their own account, were interested in their tasks, and were taught reading, writing and arithmetic on "intellectual principles."[52] In words which were to be echoed a century later he stated "that the 'ideal standard' of our schools is the real standard of German elementary schools I have no doubt whatever."[53] He attributed this superiority not only to the application of a science and art of education, but also to the fact that there were no pupil teachers in German schools, and that each teacher had a separate classroom.[54]

In his several visits Payne saw no instance of punishment, except on one occasion when a teacher took away a child's pencil, and attributed "the remarkable order, attention and interest manifest in all kinds of schools. . . .to something inherent in the system of teaching."[55] "No harsh compulsion, no tears, no idleness did I observe."[56] On the other hand Payne made a number of specific criticisms. He thought the training of kindergarten teachers or governesses to be both too short (a mere year) and one which allowed insufficient expression on the part of the trainees. Though Froebel had envisaged the children not just as plants themselves, but as the cultivators of real plants, Payne saw very few gardens attached to the establishments, while those that did exist were generally in a poor state— overgrown and weed-infested. Nor were there many instances of objects—plants etc., even pictures, inside the buildings: "not a flower, twig, leaf, stone. . . . nor any models of artificial productions,"[57]—only the various "gifts"—spheres, cubes, etc.— which Froebel had enjoined. Payne, with his keen ear for tune and harmony, even found fault with much of the singing that was performed by the kindergarten children for his delight, a fault which he attributed to want of skill in the teachers.

Payne believed in a transitional use of kindergarten methods for children between the ages of three and eight. He therefore commended the Hamburg kindergarten where children of six years of age were being taught reading, writing and elementary arithmetic and did not see this as a corruption of pure Froebelianism. For Payne, the purpose of the kindergarten was to begin in play but not to end in play. Much of the play and what proceeded from it was, and should be, work. In Berlin, therefore, Payne forbore from arguing with Dr Haarbrücker, director of the Victoria-Schule of some 950 girls, who told him that kindergarten children who came to the school were so restless that it took two to three months to get them into habits of work, and that the first task with a former kindergarten child was to clear from her head the delusion of associating learning with amusement. Payne must further have swallowed hard when informed that the kindergarten destroyed all originality in children, though it was on the tip of his tongue to ask Haarbrücker what originality was possible with class sizes of 60, as in his own school.[58] Indeed, two of Payne's major criticisms of the schools (though not of the kindergartens) that he visited were the large numbers of children in a single class—as many as 70 or 80—and the lack of proper ventilation. Payne railed against the "stifling unoxygenized atmosphere of the schoolrooms,"[59] and declared himself "at a loss to understand the remarkable objection to fresh air that Germans almost universally manifest."[60]

But the overall impression from Payne's account was of the contrast between the dull rigour of the English elementary school, stultified by the effects of the Revised Code, and the excellence of the elementary teaching in such areas as Prussia and Baden which, in Payne's view, was "no doubt due to the influence of Pestalozzi's principles."[61] He concluded with the observation:

> When the different States shall add (as Saxony has done) Froebel's methods to those of Pestalozzi, the arrangements for elementary education will probably be as complete as it is possible for ordinary human ingenuity to make them.[62]

Payne had no doubts whatsoever of the value of a good kindergarten. As he acknowledged after observing the tiny tots with their building blocks in a private kindergarten in Weimar:

> If there are any of my readers who amuse themselves with the idea of a grave professor of advanced years sympathising with these innocent sports and occupations of children, and calling that education, I cannot help it. After years of both study and practice of education, I cannot frame a definition of it, which, as including development and training, does not strictly apply to the

exercises in which these little children were engaged. Their active powers, bodily and mental, were elicited by an all-sided culture, and, what is supremely important, with the continual accompaniment of satisfaction and pleasure. No harsh compulsion, no tears, no idleness did I observe in this or any of the Kindergartens of Germany. All were busy, all earnest, all interested, and this because they were at work (for the games were work) on their own account. The labour itself was a pleasure (*Labor ipse voluptas*), because it was their own labour.[63]

An American Ideal

Payne's appreciation of the Weimar kindergarten indicates that although he sought a scientific basis for his theory of education, he maintained until the end of his life his belief in education as an art and his delight in the active learning of children. He was never a cynic but always retained that positive and progressive quality which is characteristic of every good teacher. Indeed on occasion his judgments were suffused with a certain messianic quality as, when commenting on Montaigne, he spoke of the "dawn of that light which will sooner or later shine brightly over the field of education; it is long coming but it will assuredly come at last."[64] But Payne's vision of a new education was inspired not only by historical exemplars, by the educational theories of modern European reformers such as Rousseau, Jacotot, Pestalozzi and Froebel, and by the application of their theories in kindergartens and schools in such regions as Saxony, but also, and more broadly, by the new world of the United States.

Payne was a stern critic of many elements of British society. He regretted its several divisions, including those based upon social class, gender and denominational Christianity. He attacked the corruption, inefficiency and pretensions of its government and state church. He contrasted its character with that of the United States which he saw as the land of opportunity, a "remarkable country," distinguished by "political and religious liberty," as opposed to the "crowded and

stereotyped communities of Europe and Asia."[65] Payne noted
the extent to which in the United States such liberty fostered the
education of all—not to make better subjects, but better citizens.

This vision Payne compared favourably with other
theories of education. For all the high quality of education in
Ancient Greece, it was an education confined to a few. Christian
education of the early and middle ages, Payne acknowledged,
was widespread and much dependent upon the priesthood, but
the aim of such instructors "was not to make the children whom
they taught the free citizens of a free state."[66] In the
contemporary world Payne referred to the national system of
education in Prussia. This system was both universal and
efficient but, in Payne's view, the purpose of national education
in Prussia was "to secure the secondary object of making the
subjects orderly and obedient to the laws imposed on them, and
not the primary one of training citizens to become personally or
potentially makers of the laws themselves."[67] Even this,
however, was superior to the education provided in Britain: "a
merely fortuitous conglomeration of traditions and usages."[68]
Payne roundly condemned the Anglican National Society for its
appropriation of the term "National" (the Religious Census of
1851 showed that fewer than half of the population adhered to
Anglicanism) and for its use of schooling principally as a means
of social control:

> A theory of education which aims at inspiring all children
> with a profound admiration of things as they are (of
> wages at 9s. per week, of the unpaid magistracy, of game
> laws, of arbitrary arrangements respecting labourers'
> cottages, &c.), which puts reverence for the squire and the
> parson nearly on a footing with that due to God
> himself . . . such a theory, we maintain, is quite
> inconsistent with the real enlightenment of the popular
> mind.[69]

In contrast Payne interpreted the theory which underpinned
American education as being that since power proceeded from
the people, the education of all was as important as would be the
education of the royal family and aristocracy in Britain. Payne
applauded the principle, laid down in colonial New England,

that "the State's right to secure the training of its subjects overrides the parent's right, as an individual, to neglect it."[70]

Payne had no illusions about the gap between theory and practice in respect of formal schooling within the United States, and argued that in matters of sheer efficiency there was much to be learned from the operation of systems in Germany, the Netherlands and Switzerland. Payne had made a careful study of educational reports in such states as Massachusetts and New York and, while complimenting Boston, which in 1865 had 29,960 of its 32,854 children at school, with an average attendance of 24,617, contrasted this with the city of New York where, in 1866, the average attendance was only 91,984 out of a total enrollment of 222,526.[71] Other features of American education to incur Payne's criticisms were the short periods of time during which many schools were in session (in Ohio in 1865 more than half the townships had schools open for fewer than 100 days in the year), the small percentages of children who proceeded to grammar and high schools, the poverty of school buildings and equipment outside of the major cities, and the poor qualifications and remuneration of many of the teachers. Payne saw as one solution to these problems the establishment of a new department of education in Washington.

Nevertheless, in spite of the deficiencies in school provision and attendance, Payne was among those who believed that

> the men and women of the States, on the whole, display an appreciation of questions of public interest, and discuss them with an intelligence and in a style of expression, to which we can show in England nothing equal or even approximative.[72]

He also referred approvingly to the "tact, practical skill, mechanical invention and general intelligence displayed by the American workmen."[73]

How then could this phenomenon of an "intelligent, reading, knowledge-seeking, and well-informed"[74] society be explained? Payne saw the answer in a "powerful educational spirit":[75] a spirit which found expression in the appropriation of public land for educational purposes, in the expenditure of more public money on education in a single state such as New York or

Pennsylvania than in the whole of England and Wales, in private donations to education, and in the proliferation of less formal educational agencies—evening schools, Sunday schools, literary institutions, lectures, political speeches, libraries and newspapers. Three other favourable factors to which Payne drew attention were the widespread involvement of Americans in religious observance *outside* the schoolroom; the high percentage of female teachers in American schools; and the practice of coeducation of the sexes, not only in schools, but also in such colleges as Hillsdale in Michigan and Oberlin in Ohio.

Payne was a firm advocate of the educational, social and political rights of women. Though fully conscious of the difficulties which would be involved in introducing such institutions into Britain, he was particularly attracted by the idea of coeducational colleges and spelled out the potential advantages:

> Men would become more refined and women more self-reliant, while it would be more generally acknowledged that women have an especial stake in the interests of society, with an ability and a right to discuss them, which are now, to the detriment of those interests themselves, so frequently ignored or denied. . . .
>
> When the spectacle of well-informed, intelligent, sensible women, devoting their special qualifications of acute perception, ready tact, and aptness for business to the problems of society, shall become less rare than it now is, we firmly believe we shall be much nearer the solution of those problems.[76]

Though Payne commended coeducation he was also aware that all-female colleges might give greater opportunities for female professors and role models. He noted with approval that at Vassar: "The professor of astronomy is a lady (Miss Mitchell), as is also the resident physician (Miss Alida Avery). The teachers of Greek, Latin, and mathematics are ladies."[77] Payne's appreciation of education in the United States, its strengths and its weaknesses (as he perceived them), was most powerfully expressed in two substantial articles in the *British Quarterly Review* in 1868 and 1870.[78]

One of Payne's most frequent assertions was that in such countries as the United States teachers had a professional interest in their work and would buy educational books and attend lectures on education, in a way which was quite foreign to those in Britain. This belief was certainly substantiated in that Payne's own educational works (though not his textbooks) were printed and reprinted in the United States to a far greater extent than in his own country. E. Steiger of New York concentrated upon publishing Payne's lectures in pamphlet form. The first was in 1874, when Payne's lecture on *Froebel and the Kindergarten System of elementary education*, delivered at the College of Preceptors on 25 February of that year, appeared in Steiger's Kindergarten series. Two years later Steiger published *The Science and Art of Education—an introductory lecture—and Principles of the Science of Education—a paper*, and in the following year *Pestalozzi: the influence of his principles and practice on elementary education*. Another Steiger publication of 1877 was a *Cyclopaedia of Education*, edited by H. Kiddle and A. J. Schem, who claimed that this was the first such work in English. They also stated that they had been encouraged in their work by Joseph Payne, who "promptly engaged to contribute a number of important articles," but had died before he could complete them.[79]

The biggest seller by far, however, was the first volume of the collected works, *Lectures on the Science and Art of Education, with other Lectures and Essays by the late Joseph Payne. . . .* edited by Joseph Frank and first published in London in 1880 with a second edition in 1883. In 1883 the first American edition was published in Boston by Willard Small. This was undoubtedly successful, for a second edition, enlarged from 386 pages to 414 by the inclusion of the lectures on Froebel and Pestalozzi, was produced by the same publisher in the following year, together with a separate edition of *The Science and Art of Education—an introductory lecture—and Principles of the Science of Education—a paper*. In 1884 E. L. Kellogg of New York and Chicago produced a 256–page collection of Payne's writings under the title *Lectures on the Science and Art of Education, with other Lectures. By Joseph Payne*, in which he was hailed as "one of the eminent founders of the New Education." This collection was into a third edition by the following year and by 1887 had been transformed into a new

343–page edition which included Quick's introduction and Payne's obituary notice, to be reissued in yet another new edition in 1890. This last was a volume in the Practical Teacher's Library. Indeed, the widest exposure of Payne's ideas to the American reading public probably came through the adoption of the *Lectures on the Science and Art of Education* . . . as part of a series.

One feature of these popular editions was the introduction of a framework for analysis. For example the Kellogg edition of 1890 drew the reader's attention to "the analysis at the end of each lecture; also to the index at end." Similarly, when in 1885 C. W. Bardeen of Syracuse, New York, produced a Reading Club edition, he indexed each page by head lines and at the end of each lecture provided "a somewhat minute analysis, convenient not only for review, but for comparison with treatments of the same subjects in other lectures." In the same year the New England Publishing Company, based in Boston, included Payne's volume in its Teacher's Handy Library Series. At least two further editions were produced in this series—in 1889 and 1892.

Thus Payne not only drew upon American examples in his critique of British education, but also contributed, albeit in large part posthumously and through his writings rather than personally, to the development of the science and art of education in the United States. One clear instance of such contribution is that Joseph Payne's American counterpart and namesake, William H. Payne, appointed in 1879 as first Professor of the Science and Art of Teaching at the University of Michigan, was well aware of his work and referred to it in his *Contributions to the Science of Education*, published in 1886.

NOTES

1. Payne, *Works*, II, p. 2.

2. *Report of the Committee of Council on Education (England and Wales), 1889–90*, p. 205.

3. *Journal of Education* 29 (May 1878), p. 199.

4. Payne, *Works*, II, p. 2.

5. *Ibid.*, p. 1.

6. *Ibid.*, p. 2.

7. *Ibid.*, p. 3.

8. *Ibid.*, p. 6.

9. *Ibid.*

10. Payne, *Works*, II, p. 7.

11. *Ibid.*, p. 8.

12. *Ibid.*, p. 9.

13. *Ibid.*

14. Bryant, *London Experience*, pp. 177–8.

15. Payne, *Works*, II, p. 10.

16. *Ibid.*

17. Payne, *Works*, II, p. 11.

18. *Ibid.*

19. Payne, *Works*, II, p. 12.

20. *Ibid.*

21. Payne, *Works*, II, pp. 13–14.

22. *Ibid.*, p. 24.

23. *Ibid.*, p. 29.

24. *Ibid.*, p. 34.

25. *Ibid.*, pp. 41–2.

26. *Ibid.*, p. 51.

27. *Ibid.*, p. 50.

28. *Ibid.*, p. 62.

29. *Ibid.*

30. Payne, *Works*, II, pp. 67–9.

31. *Ibid.*, p. 72.

32. *Ibid.*, p. 77.

33. *Ibid.*, p. 91.

34. *Ibid.*, p. 85.

35. *Ibid.*, p. 180.

36. *Ibid.*, p. 184.

37. *Ibid.*, p. 190.

38. Kate Silber, *Pestalozzi: The Man and His Work* (London, 1960).

39. Payne, *Works*, II, p. 101.

40. *Ibid.*, p. 103.

41. *Ibid.*, p. 104.

42. *Ibid.*, p. 132.

43. Emily A. E. Shirreff, *The Kindergarten at Home* (London, 1884), p. 84.

44. See Lawrence, *Froebel*, pp. 45–7.

45. Doreck's establishment comprised three departments: a kindergarten, a preparatory school for boys and a school for girls. *Educational Times* XXVIII, 174 (October 1875), p. 157.

46. Minute Book of the Kindergarten Association, 1874–5.

47. Minute Books of the Froebel Society for the Promotion of the Kindergarten System, 1875–90. The Minute Books of the Kindergarten Association and of the Froebel Society are deposited at the National Froebel Union Office in Templeton House, Roehampton Lane in London. I am most grateful to Gillian Collins for these references.

48. Report of the Froebel Society for the Promotion of the Kindergarten System, June 1875, Stockwell Kindergarten File, British and Foreign School Society Archives, Borough Road College. I am most grateful to Bryan Seagrove for this reference. See also Lawrence, *Froebel*, p. 47, which refers to Payne's talk in December 1874 on the "greater order in Froebel's system as compared with Pestalozzi's."

49. For an introduction to the kindergarten in Germany and the United States see Anne Taylor Allen, "'Let Us Live with Our Children': Kindergarten Movements in Germany and the United States, 1840–1914," *History of Education Quarterly* 28, 1 (Spring 1988), pp. 23–48, which has one (unfortunately misleading) reference to Payne. See also, Caroline Winterer, "Avoiding a 'Hothouse System of Education': Nineteenth-Century Early Childhood Education from the Infant Schools to the Kindergartens," *History of Education Quarterly* 32, 3 (Fall 1992).

50. Payne, *Works*, II, p. 251.

51. *Ibid.*, p. 263.

52. *Ibid.*, p. 266.

53. *Ibid.*

54. *Ibid.*

55. Payne, *Works*, II, pp. 269–70.

56. *Ibid.*, p. 247.

57. *Ibid.*, p. 220.

58. *Ibid.*, p. 229.

59. *Ibid.*, p. 266.

60. *Ibid.*, p. 259.

61. *Ibid.*, p. 271.

62. *Ibid.*

63. Payne, *Works*, II, p. 247.

64. *Ibid.*, p. 67.

65. *British Quarterly Review* 48 (October 1868), p. 429.

66. *Ibid.*, p. 431.

67. *Ibid.*, p. 433.

68. *Ibid.*, a quotation from the report by Demogeot and Montucci.

69. *British Quarterly Review* 48 (October 1868), p. 434.

70. *Ibid.*, p. 436.

71. *Ibid.*, pp. 441–2.

72. *Ibid.*, pp. 451–2.

73. *Ibid.*, p. 452.

74. *Ibid.*, p. 454.

75. *Ibid.*

76. *British Quarterly Review* 52 (October 1870), pp. 433–4.

77. *Ibid.*, p. 439.

78. *British Quarterly Review*: "Education in the United States," 48 (October 1868), pp. 429–64; "The Higher Education of the United States," 52 (October 1870), pp. 420–51. Although there is no evidence that Payne was drawing upon personal experience of education in the United States, he was certainly well read in the subject. The 1868 article was headed by nine publications: *Report to the Schools Inquiry Commission on the Common School System of the United States and of the Provinces of Upper and Lower Canada*, by James Fraser, 1867; *The Educational Institutions of the United States: their character and organization.* Translated from the Swedish of P. A. Siljeström by Frederica Rowan, 1853; *Horace Mann's Reports of the Massachusetts Board of Education*, Various years; *A visit to some American Schools and Colleges*, by Sophia Jex

Blake, 1867; *Popular Education in America, illustrated by extracts drawn chiefly from the Official Reports of the United States,* by John G, Cromwell, 1868; *Thirteenth Annual Report of the Superintendent of Public Instruction of the State of New York,* 1867; *An Outline of the American School System, with remarks on the establishment of Common Schools in England,* by Jesse Collings; *Annual Report of the Visitors of the Sheffield Scientific School of Yale College,* 1866–7; *Report on the Cornell University,* 1868.

The works by Siljeström and Jex Blake appeared again at the head of the 1870 article, together with: *L'Instruction Publique aux États-Unis, Écoles Publiques, Collèges, Universités, Écoles Spéciales. Rapport adressé au Ministre de l'Instruction Publiques,* by M. C. Hippeau, 1870; *Reports of Vassar College for Young Ladies, and of Oberlin for Youth of both Sexes; The Daily Public School in the United States,* Philadelphia, 1866; and *Various Reports: Minnesota, Wisconsin, Chicago, Iowa, Illinois, and Cornell Universities; Lafayette, New York City, and Dartmouth Colleges; Norwich and other Free Academies: various Polytechnic Institutes and Industrial Universities; State Normal Schools, and Pennsylvania, Michigan, and other Agricultural Colleges,* 1867–8–9.

79. Preface. I am most grateful to Chris Stray for this reference.

CHAPTER NINE

Conclusion

Four themes are examined in this concluding chapter. The first two provide summaries of Payne's contributions to the creation of a new world of education by means of institutions and ideas; the third is concerned with interpretations of school and society in Victorian Britain; and the fourth with issues which may transcend both time and space.

Educational Institutions

Though Payne was a self-made man his creative powers were not purely self-centred. They were employed to promote the educational opportunities and progress of others, principally through the foundation and development of a wide range of educational institutions, both private and public. Thus he was the originator of a small family tutorial group and two substantial private schools to which parents of other families chose to send their children. The tutorial group was created in conjunction with Elizabeth Fletcher, the Denmark Hill Grammar School with David Fletcher, and the Mansion Grammar School with his wife, Eliza. All these creations flourished. The Denmark Hill Grammar School sprang directly from the success of the tutorial class. Both Denmark Hill and the Mansion achieved national prominence as the result of the performance of their pupils in public examinations and further recognition from the appearance of Payne, and his successor at Denmark Hill, Charles Mason, before the Taunton Commission.

In common with many other contemporary institutions of the same type the private schools with which Payne was concerned, although both continued for a while under new proprietors, did not survive the 1870s. In some places, as at Denmark Hill, much greater financial profit could be made simply by selling the land for property development. In others, as at Leatherhead, there was increased competition, from public schools, both old and new, and from the reformed grammar schools. The Education Acts of 1870 and 1902 brought local educational authorities into the worlds of elementary and secondary education. Rate-aided education of good quality further diminished the role of the private schools.

The 1870s also saw the foundation of a new range of teachers' associations, such as the National Union of Elementary Teachers (from 1889 the National Union of Teachers) and the Association of Headmistresses, the first of the "Joint Four" which came to represent the interests of headteachers and teachers in secondary grammar schools. The success of these associations, together with such twentieth-century foundations as the National Association of Schoolmasters/Union of Women Teachers and the Professional Association of Teachers, meant that although one of the new institutions of the 1840s with which Payne was connected, the College of Preceptors whose first professor he became would last to the present day, its influence would remain limited. Nor was there to be any long-term success for another new association in which Payne played a prominent part, the Scholastic Registration Association. Nevertheless, although by the 1870s Payne's educational creations of the 1830s and 1840s were being seriously challenged, his own commitment to new educational beginnings was as strong as ever. Four new associations in which he played an important role were the Women's Education Union, whose chairman he became; the Girls' Public Day School Company, of which he was a shareholder and Council member; the Froebel Society upon whose Committee he served; and the Society for the Development of the Science of Education whose foundation meeting he chaired.

In matters of schools and educational associations, therefore, Payne worked to create a new world. In his view such creation was necessitated not only by a rapidly increasing population and changing values and aspirations, but also by the inefficiency and corruption which characterized so many existing institutions. This led to his virulent attack upon what had been widely regarded over several centuries as Britain's premier school, and his charge that the "pretensions of Eton are utterly unfounded, and that her boasted education is a lamentable failure." Such comments, coupled with others in the same vein in respect of elementary education, the Anglican Church and the state, naturally did not endear Payne to certain sections of the educational, religious and political establishment of his day. As the *Dictionary of National Biography* drily observed in respect of the Eton article: "His lively attack provoked considerable attention."

There were two characteristic features of the new educational institutions with which Payne was connected. The first was their provision for groups who were excluded from traditional schools on grounds of faith or sex. Boys' public and grammar schools (like the ancient English universities) were essentially for the sons of Anglicans. The two private boys' schools founded by Payne had no such restriction and, in consequence, contained a large proportion of sons of Dissenters. Payne's support for improved access to education for girls and women was of long standing and based upon his belief that there was no essential difference between the minds of males and females. His commitment to the cause was most visible in his professorial class and in his work for the Women's Education Union and the Girls' Public Day School Company.

The second feature of the new educational institutions was their receptiveness to new educational theory and practice. It was the pamphlet of 1830, with its account of Jacotot's principles and practices and of Payne's successful application of those principles at the New Kent Road School, which led to the invitation from Elizabeth Fletcher. It was Payne's pedagogical success as a tutor in the Fletcher household that led to the foundation of the schools at Denmark Hill and Leatherhead. Payne's institutional commitment to a new and improved theory and practice of education was not simply a product of his younger years. In the 1870s it found expression in his connections with the Froebel Society and with the Society for the Development of the Science of Education.

These two features—provision for excluded groups and improved teaching and learning—were frequently present in the one institution, albeit at any particular point in time one might take precedence over the other. For example in 1846 Payne was a founder-member of the College of Preceptors. His continuing commitment, as examiner and Vice-President, stemmed from his belief that the College could, and should, improve educational theory and practice. This would be achieved by requiring its members to undertake the study of education and to submit themselves to examination. Such a process would have three substantial benefits. It would improve the quality of schools and schooling, enable consumers to distinguish between good schools and bad, and raise the status of teachers, particularly those who taught in private schools. Until the 1870s, however, the College of Preceptors did not require study and examination of its members, and very few teachers submitted themselves to the ordeal. Then the situation was transformed when the first female Council members, Buss and Doreck, were elected, and supported Payne's accession to the new roles of lecturer and professor. Not surprisingly the great majority of the members of Payne's professorial classes were women.

Educational Ideas

Payne's educational ideas may be summarized under two headings: school curricula and teaching methods; and the education of teachers.

Payne's own learning was broad, largely self-acquired and a perpetual source of delight. He was an acknowledged expert in English language and literature whose talents ranged from the authorship of bestselling school textbooks to his chairmanship of the Philological Society. He was a Classical scholar, a modern linguist, an examiner of commercial subjects and an enthusiastic, if somewhat amateur, seeker after scientific truth. He was also a practical person in the sense that he had to make his own living from an early age and was fully aware of the demands of the market economy. Accordingly, he was a stern critic of narrow curricular provision in schools, both the Classical curriculum (relieved only by games) of Eton and other public schools, and the limited "3 Rs" of elementary schools under the Revised Code of 1862. In Payne's view true education was not confined to a limited range of subjects, whether that be the dead languages of the boys' public schools, the "accomplishments" of some girls' private schools, or the "3 Rs" of the elementary schools. A broad curriculum was required and one which paid attention to the nature of particular subjects, both in respect of their intrinsic worth and of their methodologies. For example, wherever possible science should be taught and learned by the experimental method, and not simply culled from books. Payne not only wanted a broad curriculum in schools, but he also believed that formal education should be consistent with the principles of natural education: it should take account of the interests, capacities and achievements of the learner.

For it was not just the narrow curricula which limited the intellectual growth of pupils in the interest of preserving established academic and societal hierarchies that provoked Payne's anger and condemnation. It was also the unthinking routines of instruction which accompanied such curricula and which ensured the failure, both in terms of achievement and interest, of those subjected to them. Thus at Eton, traditional methods of teaching and learning, which involved large classes and the use of "cribs," were demonstrably inefficient in instilling even the rudiments of Latin and Greek into many boys. In elementary schools the Revised Code of 1862 produced mechanical routine, drill and cram, so that children often committed to memory that which they did not really understand, for the purpose of repeating the same to the inspector on the dreaded day of examination. In both cases pupils were regularly kept to such learning by the threat or use of physical punishment. For Payne, real education involved a fundamental reappraisal of the relationship between teaching and learning. The teacher was not the master or mistress, but the guide and friend of the learner. The role of the teacher was not simply to provide knowledge (a process which might be described as instruction), but also to enable the learner to use such knowledge and to extend it. True education was self-education, whether it took place in the home, the workplace or the schoolroom. Skilful teachers were those who could encourage and develop self-education in their pupils. Self-education would require no coercion.

Once Payne had identified the faults in the educational practices of his day, and the potential power of a reformed scheme of learning and teaching, the key to the achievement of a new world of education was to produce, that is to say to educate and train, skilful teachers. Two hallmarks of skilful teachers would be that they encourage interest in learning in their pupils and that they ensure that the majority of those pupils were successful in their learning.

A skilful teacher would need to study three elements: subject matter, pupils and methods of teaching and learning. The last two elements would fall under the general heading of "education." Such study should be a matter of continuing concern, and thus promote reflection upon and improvement of classroom practice. In Payne's day there was no generally accepted subject of education as such. Yet Payne believed that such a subject would be constructed in due course (indeed this was a major part of his role as Professor of the Science and Art of Education) although it would necessarily draw upon a range of other areas. For example, psychology and physiology would help teachers to understand their pupils and to produce environments conducive to good learning. Other subjects upon which education might draw included ethics and logic.

But, in Payne's view, the most important characteristic of the new subject of education, given the entrenched nature of British social and educational hierarchies and practice, should be its enquiring nature. Payne did not share the widely held, mid-Victorian faith in unrelieved progress through time, nor in the natural superiority of the institutions and practices of his own country. He, therefore, set much store by historical and comparative perspectives. For instance, he argued that the methods of teaching Latin outlined in Roger Ascham's sixteenth-century text, *The Scholemaster*, were infinitely preferable to those generally employed in the schools of his own day. In comparative terms he commended many, though not all, of the features of the German kindergartens which he visited in 1874.

In a broader sense he praised the democratic educational spirit and practices of the United States.

For Payne, the theory and practice, or science and art, of education were not in opposition to each other; a skilful teacher needed to be well-versed in both. Though in his lectures he sought to distinguish among the science, art and methods of education, his basic argument was that good teaching and good learning required that all three should be in harmony. In framing his concepts of the relationship of learning to teaching and of the skilful teacher, Payne drew upon the writings of such contemporary and near-contemporary educators as Rousseau, Jacotot, Pestalozzi and Froebel. It would be wrong, however, to say that his ideas were simply derived from such writers. For Payne drew selectively upon these works and upon his own educational thoughts and experience.

Interpretations

How then, should the life and work of Joseph Payne be interpreted? To what extent does it confirm or modify existing interpretations of school and society in Victorian Britain and in particular those outlined in the introduction to this book?

Joseph Payne was essentially a creator. In an immediate sense, as a private person, together with his wife Eliza, he created a family. But in an even more immediate sense, in common with every human being, his most important creation was himself. It was through self-education, through self-denial, through self-publicity, that Payne progressed from his humble Suffolk origins to a position of some influence in the world. In this respect he was a true child of the Enlightenment. Understandably, given his background and subsequent career, Payne put his faith in merit and good works rather than in birth or patronage. He believed in human progress and in the power of education to promote such progress. Unlike the members of the middle classes identified by Simon as descendants of the men and women of the late eighteenth-century Enlightenment, Payne's humanism and breadth of interests lasted throughout the 1850s and 1860s, and found new expression in the associations, ideas and institutions of the 1870s. Payne's career draws attention to two factors which have been largely neglected in Marxist interpretations of school and society in Victorian Britain. The first of these was gender; the second the privileged position of one group of Christians in respect of government, church, education and society. No doubt Lord Taunton and his fellow commissioners were intrigued by the appearance before them of female witnesses, Frances Buss and Emily Davies. But, notwithstanding the presence among the commissioners of Edward Baines, the statutory Nonconformist, they might also have been unfamiliar with the worlds of Congregationalist private schoolmasters such as Mason and Payne, and would probably have been perplexed (outraged even) by Payne's proposal that private schoolmasters should be appointed not only to the ranks of the government inspectorate of schools, but even to future parliamentary commissions and committees on education.

Joseph Payne was not only a creator, he was also an outsider. He was never drawn into the educational, religious or political establishment of Victorian Britain. Even were he to be the best schoolteacher and most profound educational thinker in the land, and although his pupils might carry off prizes galore, as a master of a private, as opposed to a public school, as Professor of the College of Preceptors, as opposed to occupying a chair at an ancient university, Payne would always be subject to sneers and condescension. He has also until now and largely for the same reasons been excluded from the historiography of British education. Though his campaign for a well-educated and well-trained, self-regulating teaching profession might seem logical in the extreme, and the obvious means of improving the quality of schools and of education more broadly, it fell victim to entrenched interests: in the Anglican Church, in the universities, in government and, paradoxically, in the teacher associations and unions themselves. The clearest evidence on this point comes not only from late nineteenth- and twentieth-century disputes both between teachers and with governments on the issue of teacher registration, but also from the division within the College of Preceptors in Payne's own day. School principals, founder-members of the College and others fiercely resisted proposals which would have required them to submit to the same tests which they sought to impose upon their assistants and incurred Payne's scorn as a result. In consequence, teachers did not play a full part in the rise in professional society which occurred in Britain from 1880, and they were particularly vulnerable to the attacks upon professionals and trade unionists which occurred under Conservative governments from 1979.

An outsider in an educational sense, Payne was also an outsider in matters of religion and political influence. Although Joseph and Eliza had been married in a parish church, during his lifetime many religious disabilities (including those in education) were removed, so that dissent was transformed into Nonconformity. In religious as in educational terms he remained an independent—a critic of those who used the fear of God for personal and political ends. And although John Burnell might graduate from Cambridge, teach at a public school under a future Archbishop of Canterbury and even enter the Anglican ministry himself, both he and Joseph Frank appear to have lost their Christian faith and to have ended up as members of one of the most famous groups of outsiders in Victorian Britain, the Eliot-Lewes circle. Payne's strictures were not confined to matters of education and religion. Just as he criticized ill-qualified school inspectors and heartless headmasters, bucolic bishops and devious deans, so he castigated merciless magistrates who enforced the game laws in the interests of wealthy landowners and to the detriment of the hungry poor.

While a study of Payne is useful for the light it throws on neglected areas of Victorian education and society, there is also much in his career which confirms elements of the analysis provided by Simon, Allsobrook and Wiener. Although Payne's personal commitment to educational institutions continued until his death, the demise of the schools at Denmark Hill and Leatherhead, and the general decline of the boys' private school for the sons of the emergent and aspiring commercial, industrial and professional classes, were symptomatic of the triumph of the boys' public schools, with their ethos of rural Classicism, anti-intellectualism and devotion to the games cult. Though Mason and Payne, in their evidence to the Taunton Commission, acknowledged the value of Latin, they also indicated their own support, and a strong parental demand, for a broad curriculum. This would comprise science (including laboratory work) English, mathematics, commercial subjects and the study of modern languages for business rather than for literary purposes. State intervention, however, culminating in the Balfour Education Act of 1902 and the Secondary School Regulations of 1904, severely restricted the operation of market forces in curriculum matters and ensured that grammar schools, both for boys and for girls, would continue to be cast principally in a rural Classical and humanist mould.

What of the role of the state more generally in education in Victorian Britain? This study of Payne's life and work would appear to indicate the need for caution in accepting either Andy Green's analysis that the failures of the British economy and society may be directly attributed to a lack of state-provided education, or E. G. West's preference for a voluntary system, responsive only to market forces and free from any governmental regulation. At first sight it would seem that Payne's life and work lent support to West's interpretation. Payne spent his career in boys' private schools which might, had they continued to flourish, have provided a useful challenge to the public and grammar schools of the twentieth century. As a Congregationalist he was against central control in religious matters and highly critical of the state's role and influence in education at primary, secondary and higher levels. Payne lived in a state which prevented the majority of its people from entering grammar schools and universities and ensured that positions of authority within such institutions were reserved for priests of the state church. In 1867, however, in one of those crucial moments of change or truce points identified by Smelser (although it would be difficult to disentangle financial priorities from issues of principle), the Voluntaryists accepted the need for state funds for their elementary schools. Payne's position, in common with others of his religious and political persuasion, was not simply that the state should not (or indeed should) control education. As his course on history of education showed, it all depended on the nature of the state and of its government, which in turn depended upon the nature of its society—both civil and religious. The government of Victorian Britain naturally reflected to a considerable degree the values and priorities of Victorian society, with its several hierarchies and restrictions based upon birth, sex and denominational Christianity. Payne would only support increased government power in education if that power were devoted towards the lessening rather than the confirmation of such hierarchies and restrictions. In the wrong kind of state, governmental power over education could be, indeed was being, used to bad effect: to promote social, religious and gender exclusivity in secondary and higher education, and a species of social control, which epitomized the antithesis of true education, at the elementary level. In the right kind of state—a true commonwealth which sought the good of all of its citizens (including the schooling of all children, even against the wishes of their parents)—substantial state involvement in education would be welcome. An enlightened state, however, would not seek to control all education. Nor would it prescribe the details of education (as for example under the Revised Code of 1862) but, would promote an enlightened educational structure and spirit, including a high-quality and responsible teaching profession, which would in turn produce better citizens and a better state.

A New World of Education

History is not simply to be defined as the past nor even as the study of the past but rather as the disciplined study of human events with particular reference to the dimension of time. It is therefore appropriate to conclude this book with some reference to Payne's significance in respect of school and society in the twentieth century and of the historiography of British education.

After his death Payne's writings became popular in the United States and had some influence on teachers and teaching methods there. In Britain considerable progress was made in respect of several of the causes which he had espoused. Examination, rather than patronage, became the official means of entry to many posts in the public service and professions. Girls obtained greater access both to secondary schools and to higher education. The Revised Code and payment by results were abolished and the pupil-teacher system brought to an end. Day training colleges were established in conjunction with universities, and education became a subject of academic study. In the twentieth century some of the old boundary lines of British education were redrawn. No longer would children receive all of their formal education in a single elementary or all-age school. The new primary schools, which catered to children up to the age of 11 after which they passed to a secondary school, exhibited many of the features of the relationship between learning and teaching which Payne had advocated. Training for teachers, both primary and secondary, became the norm. In the 1960s teacher training colleges were renamed colleges of education, and a new first degree, the Bachelor of Education, was introduced.

Payne no doubt would have welcomed these developments, but he might also have regretted several features of education in the last quarter of the twentieth century. Schooling in Britain never became as popular as in many other developed countries. Not until the 1990s did the majority of children continue in full-time education beyond the compulsory school attendance age. Schools for the masses and school examinations exhibited many of the characteristics of a selection system which ensured the success of the few at the expense of the failure of the many. The rich and powerful continued to purchase a separate and distinctive form of education for their sons (and daughters) and to secure the majority of undergraduate places at Oxford and Cambridge. Eton retained its pivotal role in the reproduction of the male ruling classes. Only in Scotland was a General Teaching Council established, and attempts to obtain for teachers the status, professional power and remuneration afforded to doctors and lawyers were unsuccessful. Teachers, themselves, remained divided.

For the historian of education one of the most intriguing elements in the vision of a new world put forward since 1979 by Conservative governments under Margaret Thatcher and John Major has been its justification in terms of a return to "Victorian values," the values of personal responsibility and private enterprise. There are, however, some problems with this concept. The Victorian era in Britain was characterized by a steady increase in the power and role of central government, while many of those values, such as honesty, industry and independence, which have been claimed as being typically "Victorian," were apparent in preceding and succeeding ages. The Victorians, indeed, were sharply divided about many issues, not the least are those which related to state intervention in such areas as education. Payne's values were frequently at odds with those which predominated among the leaders of state and church. Inasmuch as Margaret Thatcher and John Major were outsiders, she the first woman Prime Minister, he a self-made man who left school at 16, Payne no doubt would have applauded their personal achievements and approved of many of their stated economic, social and educational goals. Contemporary references to the need to match the educational attainments and productive power of such countries as Germany and the United States would have struck a chord with Payne, who himself had sought to draw upon the best educational features of those very two nations. But he might have questioned the means. He would certainly have deplored the arrogance of some education ministers, the ill-considered nature of their schemes for national curriculum and national testing, and their failure adequately to consult the teaching profession and parents, just as he would have objected to instances of unprofessional conduct among teachers, or lack of good parental example. He would also have regretted any regression in respect of teacher education and training, whether as the result of an absence of intellectual rigour in colleges and departments of education, or as a consequence of government denigration of a "science" or "theory" of education, and a return to school-based apprenticeship. He would have been shocked by the poverty of much of the current educational debate, particularly in respect of the crucial issues of how best to teach and learn.

This book began with Sheldon Rothblatt's comment of 1988 upon the extent to which the agenda and interpretations of the historiography of English and European education were overconcerned with present and future issues, principally those surrounding government intervention and control in education, to the exclusion of private schooling and the operation of market forces. Nevertheless, in recent years scholars such as Bryant,

Gardner, Leinster-Mackay and Roach have begun to identify several of the dimensions of private schools in nineteenth-century Britain. Furthermore, even as Rothblatt wrote, the Education Reform Act of 1988 and subsequent legislation meant that contemporary and historical attention in Britain would be drawn to many of the issues surrounding private schooling and market forces in education to which he had referred. As yet, however, there has been no major paradigm shift; historians of education have not embraced this new agenda with great enthusiasm, and some, for example Clyde Chitty and Brian Simon, have been to the fore in opposing contemporary British educational legislation and in reemphasizing the importance of state provision of mass education, though under local rather than central control.

Joseph Payne's major contribution to education, a contribution equally pertinent to state-controlled or private systems, was his unremitting emphasis upon the need for a profound understanding, both among teachers and in society more broadly, of the processes and the potential of learning and teaching. Such understanding, he believed, had a universal value which extended far beyond the confines of Victorian Britain and was as central to the work of historians of education, as it was to the endeavours of all who would shape the educational story of the present and future.

Select Bibliography

Manuscript and Other Collections

Angus Library, Regent's Park College, Oxford
  Baptist Missionary Archives
  Reeves Collection
Brotherton Library, University of Leeds
  A collection of materials pertaining to the College of
  Preceptors deposited by J. Vincent Chapman.

Cambridge University Library
   Joseph Frank Payne and Payne Family Papers
Christ Church, Leatherhead
   Church Record Book
Girls' Public Day School Trust
   Gurney Collection
Greater London Record Office
   Parish Registers
   Maps
Institute of Education, University of London
   College of Preceptors' Archives
North London Collegiate School
   Archives of the School and of Frances Mary Buss
Office of Population Censuses and Surveys, St. Catherine's House
   Registers of Births, Marriages and Deaths
Public Record Office
   Census Enumerators' Returns
Somerset House
   Wills of Joseph and Joseph Frank Payne
Southwark Local Studies Library
   Poor Law Rate Books
   Tithe Commissioners Schedules
Suffolk Record Office, Bury St. Edmunds
   Parish Registers
University of London Library
   Quick Collection
West London Institute of Higher Education (Gordon House)
   Maria Grey College Archives

Joseph Payne's Works

Separate Works

(Adapted from the list of Payne's "Chief published works,
   pamphlets and papers" which appears on pp. 11–12 of the

first volume of the Collected works. All works were published in London. Where separate copies have not been located or were not included in the Collected works the original source is given.)

A compendious exposition of the principles and practice of Professor Jacotot's System of Education, 1830.

Epitome Historiae Sacrae, adapted by a literal translation to Jacotot's method, 1830.

Select Poetry for Children: with brief explanatory notes, arranged for the use of schools and families, 1839.

Studies in English Poetry: with short biographical sketches and notes explanatory and critical, intended as a text-book for the higher classes in schools and as an introduction to the study of English literature, 1845.

Dr Arnold as an Educator, 1865.

The Curriculum of Modern Education, and the respective claims of Classics and Science to be represented in it considered, 1866.

Jacotot: his Life and System of Universal Instruction, 1867.

"Eton," 1868. (*British Quarterly Review*).

"Education in the United States," 1868. (*British Quarterly Review*).

Studies in English Prose: consisting of specimens of the language in its earliest, succeeding, and latest stages; with notes explanatory and critical. Together with a sketch of the history of the English language and a concise Anglo-Saxon grammar. Intended as a text-book for schools and colleges, 1868.

On the Past, Present and Future of the College of Preceptors, 1868.

The use of the final -e in early English and especially in Chaucer's Canterbury Tales, 1868.

Theories of Teaching with their corresponding practice, 1869.

The Training and Equipment of the Teacher for his Profession, 1869.

The Norman Element in the spoken and written English of the 12th, 13th, and 14h Centuries, and in our provincial dialects, 1869.

The Higher Education of the United States, 1870.

Three Lectures on the Science and Art of Education, delivered at the College of Preceptors in 1871, 1872.

On the Importance and Necessity of improving our ordinary methods of School Instruction, 1872.

Why are the Results of our Primary Instruction so Unsatisfactory?, 1872.

A Preface and Supplement to an Essay on the Culture of the Observing Powers of Children by Eliza Youmans, 1872.

The Importance of the training of the teacher, 1873.

The True Foundation of Science Teaching, 1873.

The Science and Art of Education: an introductory lecture, 1874.

Froebel and the Kindergarten System of elementary education, 1874.

Principles of the Science of Education as exhibited in the phenomena attendant on the unfolding of a young child's powers under the influence of natural circumstances, 1874.

Pestalozzi: the influence of his principles and practice on elementary education. A lecture delivered at the College of Preceptors, 1875.

A Visit to German Schools. Notes of a professional tour to inspect some of the Kindergartens, Primary Schools, Public Girls' Schools, and Schools for Technical Instruction, in Hamburg, Berlin, Dresden, Weimar, Gotha and Eisenach, in the Autumn of 1874, with Critical Discussions of the General Principles and Practice of Kindergarten and Other Schemes of Elementary Education, 1876.

Collected Works

(Edited by Joseph Frank Payne.)

Lectures on the Science and Art of Education, with other Lectures and Essays, by the late Joseph Payne, the first Professor of the Science and Art of Education in the College of Preceptors. London: Longmans, Green & Company, 1880. (2nd edition 1883)

Lectures on the History of Education, with A Visit to German Schools, by the late Joseph Payne, the first Professor of the Science and Art of Education in the College of Preceptors. London and New York: Longmans, Green & Company, 1892.

American Editions

(Taken from the Library of Congress National Union Catalogue Pre-1956 Imprints.)

Froebel and the Kindergarten System of elementary education. New York: E. Steiger, Steiger's Kindergarten Series, 1874.

The Science and Art of Education—an introductory lecture—and Principles of the Science of Education—a paper. New York: E. Steiger, 1876.

Pestalozzi: the influence of his principles and practice on elementary education. New York: E. Steiger, Papers on Education, First series, 1877.

Lectures on the Science and Art of Education. . . . Boston: W. Small, 1883.

Lectures on the Science and Art of Education. . . . new enlarged edition, Boston: W. Small, 1884.

The Science and Art of Education—an introductory lecture—and Principles of the Science of Education—a paper. Boston: W. Small, 1884.

Lectures on the Science and Art of Education. . . . New York: E.L. Kellogg, 1884.

Lectures on the Science and Art of Education. . . , 3rd edition. New York: E.L. Kellogg, 1885.

Lectures on the Science and Art of Education. . . . Boston: New England Publishing Company, Teacher's Handy Library Series, 1885.

Lectures on the Science and Art of Education. . . . Syracuse, NY: C.W. Bardeen, Reading Club edition. Indexed by headlines and with full analysis, 1885.

Lectures on the Science and Art of Education. . . . New York and Chicago: E.L. Kellogg, 1887.

Lectures on the Science and Art of Education. . . . Boston: Educational Publishing Company, 1889.

Lectures on the Science and Art of Education. . . . new edition. New York and Chicago: E.L. Kellogg, The Practical Teacher's Library, vol. II, no. 6, 1890.

Lectures on the Science and Art of Education. . . , new edition. Boston: Educational Publishing Company, Teacher's Handy Library Series, 1892.

Lectures on the History of Education. . . . London and New York: Longmans, Green and Company, 1892.

Contemporary Printed Works

Parliament

1839–76, *Minutes and Annual Reports of the Committee of Council on Education.*

1852–3, LXXXIX, *Census of Great Britain, 1851: Religious Worship (England and Wales).*

1852–3, XC, *Census of Great Britain, 1851: Education (England and Wales).*

1861, XXI, *Report of the Commissioners appointed to inquire into the State of Popular Education in England.*

1864, XX, *Report of Her Majesty's Commissioners appointed to inquire into the Revenues and Management of certain Colleges and Schools, and the Studies pursued and the Instruction given therein.*

1867–8, XXVIII, *Report of the Royal Commissioners on Schools not comprised within Her Majesty's two recent Commissions on Popular Education and Public Schools.*

Periodical Publications

Baptist Magazine
British Quarterly Review
Bury and Norwich Post
Congregational Year Book
Daily News
Educational Guide to English and Continental Schools
Educational News

Educational Times
Evangelical Magazine and Missionary Chronicle
Foreign Quarterly Review
Fortnightly Review
Gibbs' Educational Guide
Journal of Education
Journal of the Women's Education Union
Monthly Journal of Education
Monthly Repository and Review of Theology and General Literature
Paddington, Kensington and Bayswater Chronicle
Pall Mall Budget
Pall Mall Gazette
Quarterly Journal of Education
Scholastic Register and Educational Adviser
School Board Chronicle
School Guardian
School Newspaper
Surrey Advertiser and County Times
Sussex Agricultural Express
The Baptist
The Congregationalist
The Nonconformist
The Schoolmaster
The Times
Transactions of the National Association for the Promotion of Social Science
Wellingtonia

Works of Reference

Crockford's *Clerical Directories*
Kelly's *Directories*
Pigot's *Directories*
Post Office *Directories*

Books and Pamphlets
(All works published in London)

Allport, Douglas (1841) *Collections, illustrative of the geology, history, antiquities and associations of Camberwell and the neighbourhood.*

Blanch, William Harnett (1875) *The Parish of Camberwell.* (1976 reprint, Camberwell: Camberwell Society).

Carey, W. (1828) *Letters, official and private, from the Rev. Dr Carey relative to certain statements contained in three pamphlets lately published by the Rev. John Dyer. . . .*

Carteret-Bisson, F.S. de (1872) *Our Schools and Colleges.*

College of Preceptors (1847) *Calendar of the College. Instituted June, 1846.*

College of Preceptors (1850) *A suggestive manual on the theory and practice of education.*

College of Preceptors (1872) *Lectures on Education delivered before the members of the College of Preceptors in the year 1871.*

Cox, F.A. (1842) *History of the Baptist Missionary Society, from 1792 to 1842, 2 vols.*

Crockford's (1861) *Scholastic Directory for 1861.*

Dyer, John (1828) *A Letter to John Broadley Wilson. . . .*

Marshman, John Clark (1830) *Review of two pamphlets, by the Rev. John Dyer, and the Rev. E. Carey and W. Yates. . . .*

Marshman, Joshua (1831) *Reply to the Rev. John Dyer's Letter to John Broadley Wilson.*

Quick, R.H. (1868) *Essays on Educational Reformers.*

Steane, Edward (1841) *A Sermon occasioned by the death of The Rev. John Dyer. To which is annexed the oration at the grave, by F.A. Cox.*

Books

Addison, W. Innes (1913) *The Matriculation Albums of the University of Glasgow from 1728 to 1858*. Glasgow: James Maclehose.

Aldrich, Richard (1982) *An Introduction to the History of Education*. London: Hodder and Stoughton.

Aldrich, Richard and Gordon, Peter (1989) *Dictionary of British Educationists*. London: Woburn Press.

Allport, D.H. (1911) *Camberwell Green: The story of a hundred years, being a brief record of school work in connection with the Congregational Church at Camberwell*. Camberwell: privately printed.

Allport, D.H. (1951) *A Short History of Wilson's Grammar School*. London: Old Wilsonians' Association.

Allsobrook, David Ian (1986) *Schools for the Shires: The Reform of Middle-Class Education in Mid-Victorian England*. Manchester: Manchester University Press.

Anderson, Robert (1983) *Education and Opportunity in Victorian Scotland: Schools and Universities*. Oxford: Clarendon Press.

Archer, R.L. (1921) *Secondary Education in the Nineteenth Century*. Cambridge: Cambridge University Press. (1966 reprint, London: Frank Cass).

Armytage, W.H.G. (1967) *The American Influence on English Education*. London and Boston: Routledge & Kegan Paul.

Armytage, W.H.G. (1968) *The French Influence on English Education*. London: Routledge & Kegan Paul.

Armytage, W.H.G. (1969) *The German Influence on English Education*. London: Routledge & Kegan Paul.

Baptist Missionary Society (1892) *The Centenary Volume of the Baptist Missionary Society, 1792–1892*. London: The Baptist Missionary Society.

Baylor, Ruth M. (1965) *Elizabeth Palmer Peabody, Kindergarten Pioneer*. Philadelphia: University of Pennsylvania Press.

Benson, A.C. (1899–1900) *The Life of Edward White Benson*, 2 vols. London: Macmillan.

Benson, A.C. (1923) *The Trefoil. Wellington College, Lincoln and Truro.* London: John Murray.

Bevir, J.L. (1920) *The Making of Wellington College.* London: Edward Arnold.

Bevir, J.L., and Fox-Strangways, A. H. (eds.) (1890) *Wellington College Register, 1859–1888.* Wellington: Wellington College.

Binfield, Clyde, (1977) *So Down to Prayers: Studies in English Nonconformity, 1780–1920.* London: Dent; Totowa, NJ: Rowman and Littlefield.

Bryant, Margaret (1979) *The Unexpected Revolution: A Study in the History of the Education of Women and Girls in the Nineteenth Century.* London: Institute of Education, University of London.

Bryant, Margaret (1986) *The London Experience of Secondary Education.* London and Atlantic Highlands, NJ: Athlone Press.

Burstall, Sarah A. (1938) *Frances Mary Buss: An Educational Pioneer.* London: Society for Promoting Christian Knowledge.

Burtchaell, G.D., and Sadleir, T.U. (eds.) (1935) *Alumni Dublinenses. A register of the Students, Graduates, Professors and Provosts of Trinity College in the University of Dublin, 1593–1860.* Dublin: Alex Thom and Company.

Chadwick, Owen (1966) *The Victorian Church. Part I 1829–1859.* London: Adam and Charles Black.

Chadwick, Owen (1970) *The Victorian Church. Part II 1860–1901.* London: Adam and Charles Black.

Chandos, John (1984) *Boys Together: English Public Schools 1800–1864.* London: Hutchinson.

Chapman, J. Vincent (1985) *Professional Roots: The College of Preceptors in British Society.* Epping: Theydon Bois Publications.

Chitty, Clyde, and Simon, Brian (1993) *SOS: Save Our Schools.* London: Lawrence & Wishart.

Clarke, M.L. (1959) *Classical Education in Britain, 1500–1900.* Cambridge: Cambridge University Press.

Cleal, Edward E. (1908) *The Story of Congregationalism in Surrey.* London: James Clarke and Company.

College of Preceptors, (1896) *Fifty Years of Progress in Education. A review of the work of the College of Preceptors, from its foundation in 1846 to its Jubilee in 1896*. London: C.F. Hodgson.

Davidoff, Leonore, and Hall, Catherine (1987) *Family Fortunes: Men and Women of the English Middle Class, 1780–1850*. London: Hutchinson.

Dictionary of National Biography.

Duffy, Charles Gavan (1898) *My Life in Two Hemispheres*, 2 vols. London: T. Fisher Unwin.

Dyhouse, Carol (1981) *Girls Growing Up in Late Victorian and Edwardian England*. London: Routledge & Kegan Paul.

Dyos, H.J. (1961) *Victorian Suburb: A Study of the Growth of Camberwell*. Leicester: Leicester University Press.

Ellsworth, Edward W. (1979) *Liberators of the Female Mind: The Shirreff Sisters, Educational Reform, and the Women's Movement*. Westport, CT: Greenwood Press.

Fiske, John (1894) *Life and Letters of Edward Livingston Youmans, comprising correspondence with Spencer, Huxley, Tyndall and others*. London: Chapman and Hall.

Fletcher, Sheila (1980) *Feminists and Bureaucrats: A Study in the Development of Girls' Education in the Nineteenth Century*. Cambridge: Cambridge University Press.

Foster, Joseph (1968) *Alumni Oxonienses: The Members of the University of Oxford, 1715–1886*. Nedeln, Liechtenstein: Kraus Reprint.

Gardner, Phil (1984) *The Lost Elementary Schools of Victorian England: The People's Education*. London: Croom Helm.

Gidney, R.D., and Millar, W.P.J. (1990) *Inventing Secondary Education: The Rise of the High School in Nineteenth-Century Ontario*. Montreal and Kingston: McGill-Queen's University Press.

Goodenow, Ronald K., and Marsden, William E. (eds.) (1992) *The City and Education in Four Nations*. Cambridge and New York: Cambridge University Press.

Goodson, Ivor F. (1988) *The Making of Curriculum: Collected Essays*. London: Falmer Press.

Gordon, Peter and Szreter, Richard (eds.) (1989) *History of Education: The Making of a Discipline*. London: Woburn Press.

Gosden, P. H. J. H. (1971) *The Evolution of a Profession: A Study of the Contribution of Teachers' Associations to the Development of School Teaching as a Professional Occupation*. Oxford: Basil Blackwell.

Green, Andy (1990) *Education and State Formation: The Rise of Education Systems in England, France and the USA*. London: Macmillan; New York: St. Martin's.

Haight, Gordon S. (ed.) (1954–78) *The George Eliot Letters*, 9 vols. New Haven, CT: Yale University Press.

Hearnshaw, L.S. (1964) *A Short History of British Psychology, 1840–1940*. London: Methuen.

Heath, Linda (1986) *Of Good Report: The Story of the Leatherhead Schools*. Leatherhead: Leatherhead and District Local History Society.

Hervey, S.H.A. (1908) *Biographical List of Boys educated at King Edward VI Free Grammar School, Bury St. Edmunds from 1550 to 1900*. Bury St. Edmunds: Suffolk Green Books.

Hobsbawm, E.J. (1977) *The Age of Capital, 1848–1875*. London: Weidenfeld and Nicolson.

Hughes, Richard (1987) *St. John's Foundation School, 1851–1872; the Founding and Early History of St. John's School, Leatherhead*. Leatherhead: St. John's Foundation School.

Jones, R. Tudur (1962) *Congregationalism in England, 1662–1962*. London: Independent Press.

Kamm, Josephine (1958) *How Different from Us: A Biography of Miss Buss and Miss Beale*. London: Bodley Head.

Kamm, Josephine (1971) *Indicative Past: A Hundred Years of the Girls' Public Day School Trust*. London: Allen and Unwin.

Kolesnik, Walter B. (1962) *Mental Discipline in Modern Education*. Madison: University of Wisconsin Press.

Laqueur, Thomas Walter (1976) *Religion and Respectability: Sunday Schools and Working-Class Culture, 1780–1850*. New Haven, CT: Yale University Press.

Lawrence, Evelyn (ed.) (1969) *Friedrich Froebel and English Education*. London: Routledge & Kegan Paul.

Lawson, John and Silver, Harold (1973) *A Social History of Education in England*. London: Methuen.

Leinster-Mackay, D.P. (1984) *The Rise of the English Prep School*. London: Falmer.

Lilley, Irene M. (1981) *Maria Grey College, 1878–1976*. Twickenham: West London Institute of Higher Education.

Lomax, D.E. (ed.) (1973) *The Education of Teachers in Britain*. London: John Wiley.

Lord, F. Townley (1942) *Achievement: A Short History of the Baptist Missionary Society, 1792–1942*. London: Carey Press.

McCann, Phillip (ed.) (1977) *Popular Education and Socialization in the Nineteenth Century*. London: Methuen.

Machin, G.I.T. (1977) *Politics and the Churches in Britain, 1832 to 1868*. Oxford: Clarendon Press.

Machin, G.I.T. (1987) *Politics and the Churches in Great Britain, 1869 to 1921*. Oxford: Clarendon Press.

Mack, Edward C. (1938) *Public Schools and British Opinion, 1780–1860: An Examination of the Relationship Between Contemporary Ideas and the Evolution of an English Institution*. London: Methuen. (1973 reprint, Westport, CT: Greenwood Press.)

Mack, Edward C. (1941) *Public Schools and British Opinion Since 1860: The Relationship Between Contemporary Ideas and the Evolution of an English Institution*. New York: Columbia University Press. (1971 reprint, Westport, CT: Greenwood Press.)

Magnus, Laurie (1923) *The Jubilee Book of the Girls' Public Day School Trust, 1873–1923*. Cambridge: Cambridge University Press.

Meiklejohn, J.M.D. (ed.) (1883) *Life and letters of William Ballantyne Hodgson*. Edinburgh: D. Douglas.

Mitchell, B.R. and Deane, Phyllis (1962) *Abstract of British Historical Statistics*. Cambridge: Cambridge University Press.

Monroe, Paul (ed.) (1911–13) *A Cyclopaedia of Education*. New York: Macmillan.

Montgomery, Robert John (1965) *Examinations: An Account of Their Evolution as Administrative Devices in England*. London: Longmans.

Müller, Detlef K., Ringer, Fritz and Simon, Brian (eds.) (1987) *The Rise of the Modern Educational System: Structural Change and Social Reproduction, 1870–1920.* Cambridge: Cambridge University Press.

Murphy, James (1971) *Church, State and Schools in Britain, 1800–1970.* London: Routledge & Kegan Paul.

Newsome, David (1959) *A History of Wellington College, 1859–1959.* London: John Murray.

Norman, E.R. (1976) *Church and Society in England, 1770–1970: An Historical Study.* Oxford: Clarendon Press.

Paris, Bernard J. (1965) *Experiments in Life: George Eliot's Quest for Values.* Detroit: Wayne State University Press.

Payne, Ernest A. (1936) *The First Generation: Early Leaders of the Baptist Missionary Society in England and India.* London: Carey Press.

Payne, Ernest A. (1938) *The Great Succession: Leaders of the Baptist Missionary Society during the Nineteenth Century.* London: Carey Press.

Payne, Ernest A. (1944) *The Free Church Tradition in the Life of England.* London: SCM Press.

Payne, William H. (1886) *Contributions to the Science of Education.* New York: Harper & Bros.

Pedersen, Joyce Sanders (1987) *The Reform of Girls' Secondary and Higher Education in Victorian England: A Study of Elites and Educational Change.* New York: Garland.

Perkin, Harold (1969) *The Origins of Modern English Society, 1780–1880.* London: Routledge & Kegan Paul.

Perkin, Harold (1989) *The Rise of Professional Society: England Since 1880.* London: Routledge & Kegan Paul.

Poret, George C. (1931) *The Contributions of William Harold Payne to Public Education.* Nashville: George Peabody College for Teachers.

Rancière, Jacques (1991) *The Ignorant Schoolmaster: Five Lessons in Intellectual Emancipation* (ed. Kristin Ross). Stanford: Stanford University Press.

Ridley, Annie E. (1895) *Frances Mary Buss: and her work for education.* London: Longmans, Green & Company.

Rich, R.W. (1933) *The Training of Teachers in England and Wales during the Nineteenth Century*. Cambridge: Cambridge University Press. (1972 reprint, Bath: Cedric Chivers.)

Roach, John (1971) *Public Examinations in England, 1850–1900*. London: Cambridge University Press.

Roach, John (1978) *Social Reform in England, 1780–1880*. London: Batsford.

Roach, John (1986) *A History of Secondary Education in England, 1800–1870*. London: Longman.

Roach, John (1991) *Secondary Education in England, 1870–1902: Public Activity and Private Enterprise*. London: Routledge & Kegan Paul.

Robbins, Keith (1989) *Nineteenth-Century Britain: England, Scotland and Wales: The Making of a Nation*. Oxford: Oxford University Press.

Rothblatt, Sheldon (1968) *The Revolution of the Dons: Cambridge and Society in Victorian England*. London: Faber and Faber.

Royle, Edward (1974) *Victorian Infidels: The Origins of the British Secularist Movement, 1791–1866*. Manchester: Manchester University Press.

Selleck, R.J.W. (1968) *The New Education: The English Background, 1870–1914*. London: Pitman.

Shirreff, Emily A.E. (1884) *The Kindergarten at Home*. London: Joseph Hughes.

Silber, Kate (1960) *Pestalozzi: The Man and His Work*. London: Routledge & Kegan Paul.

Silver, Harold (1975) *English Education and the Radicals, 1780–1850*. London: Routledge & Kegan Paul.

Silver, Harold (1980) *Education and the Social Condition*. London: Methuen.

Silver, Harold (1983) *Education as History: Interpreting Nineteenth- and Twentieth-Century Education*. London: Methuen.

Simms, T.H. (1979) *Homerton College, 1695–1978: From Dissenting Academy to Approved Society in the University of Cambridge*. Cambridge: Homerton College.

Simon, Brian (1974) *The Two Nations and the Educational Structure, 1780–1870*. London: Lawrence & Wishart.

Simon, Brian (1974) *Education and the Labour Movement, 1870–1920*. London: Lawrence & Wishart.

Simon, Brian (1985) *Does Education Matter?* London: Lawrence & Wishart.

Smelser, Neil J. (1991) *Social Paralysis and Social Change: British Working-Class Education in the Nineteenth Century*. Berkeley and Los Angeles: University of California Press; New York: Russell Sage Foundation.

Smith, Duncan (1979) *A Short History of Christ Church (United Reformed) Leatherhead*. Leatherhead: Christ Church.

Stanford, Charles (1882) *A Memorial of the Rev. Edward Steane, D.D.* London: Hodder and Stoughton.

Stanley, Brian (1992) *The History of the Baptist Missionary Society, 1792–1992*. Edinburgh: T & T Clark.

Stewart, W.A.C. (1972) *Progressives and Radicals in English Education, 1750–1950*. London: Macmillan.

Storr, F. (ed.) (1899) *Life and Remains of the Rev. R. H. Quick*. Cambridge: Cambridge University Press.

Thompson, E.P. (1963) *The Making of the English Working Class*. London: Gollancz.

Underwood, A.C. (1947) *A History of the English Baptists*. London: Baptist Union Publication Department.

Vardey, Edwina (ed.) (1988) *History of Leatherhead: A Town at the Crossroads*. Leatherhead: Leatherhead and District Local History Society.

Vaughan, Michalina and Archer, Margaret Scotford (1971) *Social Conflict and Educational Change in England and France, 1789–1848*. London: Cambridge University Press.

Venn, J. A. (1940–7) *Alumni Cantabrigienses, 1752–1900*, 6 vols. Cambridge: Cambridge University Press.

Vidler, Alec R. (1962) *The Church in an Age of Revolution: 1789 to the Present Day*. London: Hodder and Stoughton.

Walker, Olive M. (1954) *A Tour of Camberwell*. London: H. H. Greaves.

Watson, Foster (ed.) (1921–2) *The Encyclopaedia and Dictionary of Education*, 4 vols. London: Pitman.

West, E.G. (1975) *Education and the Industrial Revolution*. London: Batsford.

West, W.M.S. (1983) *To Be a Pilgrim: A Memoir of Ernest A. Payne*. Guildford: Lutterworth Press.

Wiener, Martin J. (1981) *English Culture and the Decline of the Industrial Spirit, 1850–1980*. Cambridge: Cambridge University Press.

Williams, Raymond (1958) *Culture and Society, 1780–1950*. London: Chatto and Windus.

Witting, Clifford (ed.) (1952) *The Glory of the Sons. A History of Eltham College School for the Sons of Missionaries*. London: Eltham College.

Articles

Albisetti, James C., "American Women's Colleges through European Eyes," *History of Education Quarterly* 32, 4 (Winter 1992).

Allen, Anne Taylor, "'Let Us Live with Our Children': Kindergarten Movements in Germany and the United States, 1840–1914," *History of Education Quarterly* 28, 1 (Spring 1988).

Allen, Janet E., "Voluntaryism: A 'Laissez-faire' Movement in Mid-Nineteenth Century Elementary Education," *History of Education* 10, 2 (June 1981).

Arnstein, Walter, Bright, Michael, Peterson, Linda and Temperley, Nicholas, "Recent Studies in Victorian Religion," *Victorian Studies* 33, 1 (Autumn 1989).

Bayley, Susan N. and Ronish, Donna Yavorsky, "Gender, Modern Languages and the Curriculum in Victorian England," *History of Education* 21, 4 (December 1992).

Benger, F.B., "The Mansion, Leatherhead," *Proceedings of the Leatherhead and District Local History Society* I, 7 (1953).

Cohen, Sol, "Representations of History," *History of Education* 20, 2 (June 1991).

Depaepe, Marc, "Social and Personal Factors in the Inception of Experimental Research in Education (1890–1914): An

Exploratory Study," *History of Education* 16, 4 (December 1987).

Dormer, D.E., "The Quick Memorial Library and Other Books on Education in the University of London Library," *Institute of Education Bulletin* 25 (Autumn 1957).

Fitch, Miriam G., "Joseph Payne, First Professor of Education in England," *Journal of Education* 66, 774–9 (January-June 1934).

Heward, Christine, "Men and Women and the Rise of Professional Society: The Intriguing History of Teacher Educators," *History of Education* 22, 1 (March 1993).

Higginson, J.H., "Establishing a History of Education Course: The Work of Professor Michael Sadler, 1903–1911," *History of Education* 9, 3 (September 1980).

Leinster-Mackay, D.P., "*Regina v. Hopley*: Some Historical Reflections on Corporal Punishment," *Journal of Educational Administration and History* IX, 1 (January 1977).

Leinster-Mackay, D.P., "A Question of Ephemerality: Indices for the Longevity of Nineteenth-Century Private Schools," *Journal of Educational Administration and History* X, 2 (July 1978).

Leinster-Mackay, D.P., "Private or Public Schools: The Education Debate in *Laissez-Faire* England," *Journal of Educational Administration and History* XV, 2 (July 1983).

Miller, Pavla, "Historiography of Compulsory Schooling: What Is the Problem?" *History of Education* 18, 2 (June 1989).

Miller, Pavla, "Education and the State: The Uses of Marxist and Feminist Approaches in the Writing of Histories of Schooling," *Historical Studies in Education/Revue d'Histoire de l'Éducation* 1, 2 (Fall 1989).

Payne, Ernest A., "The Diaries of John Dyer," *Baptist Quarterly* XIII (1949–50).

Payne, Ernest A., "Gleanings from the Correspondence of George Eliot," *Baptist Quarterly* XVII (1957–8).

Payne, J.F., "On the Connexion of Physiology and Education," *Journal of Education* II, 130 (May 1880).

Rothblatt, Sheldon, "Supply and Demand: The 'Two Histories' of English Education," *History of Education Quarterly* 28, 4 (Winter 1988).

Simon, Brian, "The Study of Education as a University Subject in Britain," *Studies in Higher Education* 8, 1 (1983).

Thomas, J.B., "The Curriculum of a Day Training College: The Logbooks of J. W. Adamson," *Journal of Educational Administration and History* XI, 2 (July 1979).

Thompson, David M., "The 1851 Religious Census: Problems and Possibilities," *Victorian Studies* 11 (September 1967).

Turner, F.C., "The History of the Education Society," *Journal of Education* IX, 213–4 (April-May 1887).

Urban, Wayne J., "New Directions in the Historical Study of Teacher Unionism," *Historical Studies in Education/Revue d'Histoire de l'Éducation* 2, 1 (Spring 1990).

Winterer, Caroline, "Avoiding a 'Hothouse System of Education': Nineteenth-Century Early Childhood Education from the Infant Schools to the Kindergartens," *History of Education Quarterly* 32, 3 (Fall 1992).

Joseph Payne
A carte-de-visite photograph, author's collection.

Joseph Payne
A photograph in the family album of John Waite.

Joseph Payn[e]
Æt. 65.

Joseph Payne, Professor of Education, aged 65.
A portrait etched by W. Sherborn
from a photograph by Messrs Sawyer and Bird. From the
first volume of the collected works.

Eliza Payne
A photograph in the family album of John Waite.

Joseph Frank Payne
A portrait by John Singer Sargent
in the Royal College of Physicians of London.

Denmark Hill Grammar about 1870
A drawing in the Southwark Local Studies Library.

The Mansion Grammar School, Leatherhead
A photograph of the rear dated 1859, author's collection.

The Mansion Grammar School, Leatherhead

An engraving of the rear upon writing paper in the possession of G. D. Powell.

Rodney House Academy today.

Grove Hill House today.

Index